BEAT
the
BANK

3RD
EDITION

BEAT
the
BANK

*How
to Win
the Mortgage
Game in
Canada*

THE ULTIMATE GUIDE ON MORTGAGES

PAUL MEREDITH

Published by
SeaLord Publishing
640-110 Sheppard Ave E
Toronto, ON M2N 6Y8

10 9 8 7 6 5 4 3

Meredith, Paul J., 1971-, author

Beat the Bank: How to Win the Mortgage Game in Canada / Paul Meredith.

ISBN 978-0-9938551-6-0 (softcover)

Quantity sales: Special discounts are available on quantity purchases by corporations, associations, and others. For details, contact the author directly at paulm@citycan.com

Paul Meredith, Mortgage Broker, CityCan Financial Corp. Lic. 10532

pmteam@citycan.com
www.easy123mortgage.ca

CONTENTS

PREFACE TO THE THIRD EDITION

If you read the first or second editions of *Beat the Bank*, this third edition will seem like an entirely different book. I started off with a time budget of 40 hours to complete the update. However, what began as an update turned into a complete rewrite, taking roughly 300 hours to complete. Yes, my quest for perfection resulted in my not just exceeding my original time budget... but soaring past it.

I've expanded on the previous content, adding four more chapters and more than 150 pages of new information. Originally written as a comprehensive guide for the Canadian consumer, Beat the Bank has evolved into a widely recognized training resource for mortgage professionals and lenders alike. This third edition elevates its educational value, especially for those newly venturing into the mortgage industry, making it the ultimate resource guide on Canadian mortgages.

When I first decided to enter the mortgage business at the beginning of 2007, I wanted to arm myself with as much knowledge as possible. I went on Amazon with the intention of purchasing every book on Canadian mortgages that I could find. However, they didn't exist. Not even a single book. I had to rely purely on American publications, which provided little value given that the Canadian mortgage industry is radically different.

Beat the Bank can catapult the experience level of new mortgage agents, giving them a running start with additional knowledge as they enter their new careers.

I believe that the significant time and effort that I've poured into the third edition is palpably reflected in the quality and depth of the content. It is my sincere hope that this book not only enlightens but also empowers its readers to understand the intricate world of mortgages in Canada.

INTRODUCTION

I can still remember when I applied for my first mortgage. I had recently been through some serious financial turmoil after making some bad business decisions. I had accumulated a significant amount of debt, and at that point, my income was quite low. Despite my troubles, I was tired of paying rent and wanted to buy a place of my own now that I was earning a regular salary, although not a lot.

The thought of looking for a mortgage both excited and scared me. I had struggled with credit issues and business failures throughout my twenties, and I felt I was just now starting to get a handle on everything. I walked into one of the major banks to see if I could get approved for a mortgage. As I was still rebuilding my credit, I felt like the chances of me getting approved were about the same as Vin Diesel winning the Oscar for Best Actor. Likely not going to happen. But with nothing to lose, why not give it a shot? I met with Sandra, one of the mortgage advisors at the branch. She was very personable... all smiles and professional charm. I explained my situation and completed my application. I asked a few questions, but she didn't give me much information. At least, not anything useful other than her saying that she would get back to me. I interpreted that as banker-talk for "Don't call us, we'll call you". But I was okay with that as I wasn't too optimistic.

A couple of days later, she called and told me I was approved for $320,000.

I was ecstatic!

I couldn't believe they approved me. I was so happy!

But then the logical side of my brain kicked in. I realized she didn't check my credit, nor did she even ask me about my debt, which was still quite high relative to my income. In fact, it was double my annual income!

"How can they approve me for anything without even checking my credit or asking about my debt?", I thought.

Curious and somewhat skeptical, I voiced my concern to Sandra. She told me to just go shopping for a home up to the 'pre-approved' value and then come back to her once I had my offer to purchase accepted. She then added that she would conduct a thorough review of my debt and credit at that time.

What?

I knew absolutely nothing about mortgages, but it just

didn't seem right to me. I told her that I didn't want to waste my time if I wasn't going to be approved. Reluctantly, she proceeded with the credit check. Once again, she told me it would be a couple of days before I could expect an answer (as an experienced broker now, I still wonder what could have possibly taken so long).

A few days later, I followed up with Sandra, as I had not yet heard from her, or from anyone else from the bank for that matter. When I called her extension, someone else answered, so I of course asked for her.

The response I got was an ecstatic... "Did you hear the good news???" I asked if the good news was that I was approved with a big smile on my face. After finding out who I was, she said, oh... no. You have been declined, but Sandra was promoted! Isn't that great?!?!"

Seriously????

There was silence for what seemed like 30 seconds, but was probably only five. I couldn't believe what I was hearing.

Needless to say, as great as this news was, there couldn't have been anything I could have cared less about at that particular time. And why would they consider giving someone like this a promotion? It's beyond my comprehension.

I had more questions and was once again told that they would have to get back to me. Unfortunately, nobody ever did.

Every time I thought about mortgages, I would think back to that experience. It shouldn't have been that challenging to find out something as simple as whether I was approved for a mortgage or not. People should be able to find out if they qualify quickly, and they need to be treated with more respect. There is no excuse for taking days to get answers to even the simplest of questions. Ridiculous.

Since I wasn't happy with my current profession, I decided to look at a career in mortgages.

MY VENTURE INTO THE MORTGAGE WORLD

When I started in this business, I wanted to ensure that my clients had a better experience than I did. In fact, I wanted to provide a better experience than they would get anywhere else... which is the tagline on my website to this day. I believe everyone deserves to have their questions answered quickly and professionally and should never be left in the dark, wondering if anything is actually being done. Communication is crucial to their overall experience, so communication they will get!

My team is wholeheartedly committed to guiding our clients down the right path, dedicating time to clarify their options with care and precision. Our clients can expect the same level of treatment that we would give to our own family. This is one of our seven core values that shape our daily conduct and service.

Having worked as a mortgage broker since 2007, I have noticed many patterns among mortgage seekers that they may not be aware of. These negative patterns are costing them literally thousands of their hard-earned dollars, while padding the massive profits of the banks.

I wrote this book to help more people gain clarity on the mortgage industry, the roles of the various professionals involved, and to highlight points of concern within their mortgage agreements. Much of the advice contained in this book is not what you can expect to receive from your local bank. And in some cases, it's advice they don't want you to get.

Why would I share this hard-earned knowledge?

The act of helping others brings me immense joy and fulfillment. There's a profound sense of satisfaction that comes from positively impacting the lives of others. The more people I can assist, the greater my sense of happiness and purpose. This passion for service drives me, fueling my enthusiasm and dedication to my work and personal life.

Not everyone out there is as honest as they could be. It's unfortunate that some are just in the business to make a quick buck for themselves with no concern for the well-being of the client. They may advise you based on what makes them the most money, or what they're incentivized on by their employer. These unscrupulous "professionals" are out there, and they hurt the mortgage industry as a whole. This is why it is so important to ask questions before hiring a mortgage professional, regardless of whether it is a broker or a mortgage specialist at a bank. All mortgage professionals are not created equal. A mortgage is a huge financial decision that you don't want to trust to just anyone.

Banks, like any other business, are there for one reason, and that is to make a profit. There is definitely nothing wrong with that, but banks have certain policies that you may not be aware of. Policies that can end up costing you thousands of dollars. If you aren't aware of what is going on, you may fall right into their trap. These traps are not just limited to banks. There can be certain dangers with any mortgage lender. By providing clarity on what you should be looking for, you can get closer to paying off your mortgage all that much quicker. You can be the one with the last laugh by 'beating the bank' at their own game.

HOW TO USE THIS BOOK

There are exceptions to every rule and not every suggestion made in this book will be right 100% of the time. This information aims to guide you on key factors to consider when shopping for a mortgage, ensuring you receive fair treatment.

Whether you're a first-time home buyer, an experienced mortgage shopper, or even a mortgage industry professional looking to strengthen your knowledgebase, Beat the Bank has something for everyone. As it's written for such a wide variety of audiences, it does not need to be read cover to cover. Instead, I suggest skipping straight to the sections that are of most interest to you.

Not everything will be applicable in every situation. In some cases, I'll be generalizing to appeal to the majority. The information provided is a combination of facts and personal opinions based on my seventeen plus years of experience as a mortgage broker. Individual situations may vary, so I recommend seeking professional advice based on your specific needs.

In certain examples, I'll be using fictitious names to illustrate points. I've also changed the names and some of the details used in the stories to protect the identities of my clients. Anyone having these names would be purely coincidental.

Let's get started with giving you the upper hand so you can Beat the Bank at their own game!

1

YOUR FIRST MORTGAGE

"Success is neither magical nor mysterious. Success is the natural consequence of consistently applying the basic fundamentals."
~Jim Rohn

For a first-time homebuyer, there is no question that shopping for a mortgage can be somewhat overwhelming. Fixed, variable, open, closed, amortization, shorter terms, longer terms, HELOCs, high-ratio, conventional, etc., etc. The list of common terminology goes on and on. There are literally hundreds of combinations that can be enough to make your head spin if you're new to the mortgage world.

Having a clear and detailed understanding of your options is essential for making informed and confident decisions.

GENERAL MORTGAGE TERMINOLOGY

If you're new to the exciting world of mortgages (okay, maybe not that exciting), then there is some common terminology you'll need to become familiar with which will be repeated throughout this book.

Term

This is the length in which your mortgage contract with the lender is valid for. The most common term length is five years, but terms can be as short as six months, or as long as 10 years... and everything in between. At the end of your term, your contract with your mortgage lender expires and balance becomes due and payable. You then have the option of renewing the mortgage with the same lender, transferring it to a different lender, or paying the mortgage off in full.

I'll be explaining more about these options and how to maximize your savings at renewal in Chapter Ten.

Amortization

This is the amount of time it would take for you to pay your mortgage down to a zero balance assuming equal payments. The most common amortization is 25 years, however with a down payment or equity position of 20% or greater, you can go as high as 30 years. Some lenders even offer a 35-year amortization, however these options are quite rare, and you'll typically pay a rate premium, along with a fee.

Loan to Value (LTV)

Loan to value is the amount of your mortgage in relation to the value of the property expressed as a percentage. For example, if you were to purchase a home with a down payment of 5%, the LTV is 95%.

If you had a 20%, the LTV would be 80%.

If zero down was possible, it would be 100% LTV.

Fixed Rate Mortgage

As the name implies, a fixed rate mortgage is where both your rate and your payment are fixed for the mortgage term. Regardless of what the market does or where interest rates move, your rate and payment will remain the same. A fixed rate mortgage is suited to borrowers who are less tolerant to risk and feel more comfortable knowing that their rate and payment will not change for the term. Fixed rate mortgages are *almost* always higher than variable rate mortgages. Key word: *Almost*

Variable Rate Mortgage

Unlike a fixed rate, the rate on a variable rate mortgage will fluctuate with the prime rate. The prime rate is set by the Bank of Canada[1], who typically has eight scheduled rate announcements per year. Unscheduled rate announcements are possible, but quite rare. I'll be talking about variable rate mortgages in detail in Chapter Four.

Closing Date

The closing date is when the lender releases the funds for your mortgage. If you're buying a new property, it's the day you take ownership. In other words, the day you receive the

---

1 The Bank of Canada sets what's called an 'overnight rate', which is what the prime rate is based on. For simplicity, I'll just be using the term prime rate throughout this book.

keys and are free to move into your new home or condo.

In scenarios where you are refinancing your mortgage or transferring it to a different lender, the closing date is when the new transaction is completed. It's when the new mortgage becomes active, and any previous mortgages are settled and replaced by the new one.

Deposit

When purchasing a new home, you will need to provide a deposit once your offer to purchase has been accepted, typically within 24 hours. This deposit serves as a financial commitment, indicating to the seller that you, as the buyer, have a vested interest in the transaction and are serious about proceeding with the purchase of the property.

If your offer to purchase is conditional on financing, you are entitled to receive your deposit back if you're unable to secure the mortgage required. This deposit is held in trust by the real estate listing brokerage until the purchase has closed. The deposit is then released and paid to the seller, contributing towards the total purchase price along with the balance of your down payment.

There is no predetermined amount of the deposit, and it's something that should be discussed with your real estate agent. Larger deposits can carry more weight with a seller, therefore increasing your chances of having your offer accepted. For instance, a $1,000 deposit doesn't express the same level of commitment as a $100,000 deposit.

Down Payment

When purchasing a property, you'll be required to provide a sum of money prior to your closing date which is known as your down payment. The minimum down payment can be anywhere from 5% of the purchase price, up to 20% or even greater in some situations.

The deposit is part of your down payment. For example, if your total down payment is $200,000 and your deposit was $50,000, then you would owe the remaining $150,000 to complete your down payment at the time of closing on your new purchase.

Mortgage Commitment

A mortgage commitment is a document issued by a lender once your mortgage application has been approved. It details key aspects of the loan agreement such as the interest rate, closing date, mortgage balance, and payment amount, along with other specific terms of the approval. However, it's important to note that this commitment is conditional, based on the terms outlined in the document. It does not serve as an absolute guarantee that the lender will fund the mortgage on the specified closing date. Common conditions in most mortgage commitments typically include the verification of income, confirmation of the down payment, and occasionally, an appraisal to confirm the property's value.

COMMONLY MISUNDERSTOOD TERMS

HIGH RATIO VS. CONVENTIONAL MORTGAGES

Mortgages can be placed into one of two categories, high ratio or conventional, depending on the amount of the down payment. If your down payment is 20% or greater, your mortgage is classified as conventional. If it's less than 20%, it would be considered high-ratio.

A high-ratio mortgage will require mortgage default insurance, which is simply insurance protecting the lender in the event of default by the borrower. In other words, if you think it might be more fun to shoot off to Vegas for the weekend than it would be to make your mortgage payment, you would then be considered in default. Not that Vegas isn't fun!

The cost of the mortgage default insurance varies depending on the amount of your down payment. The greater your down payment, the lower your insurance premium:

Down Payment Percentage	Insurance Premium Cost
5 to 9.99%	4.00%
10 to 14.99%	3.10%
15 to 19.99%	2.80%

The premium is paid by the borrower and added to the total amount borrowed.

There are three companies offering mortgage default insurance, which are CMHC, Sagen and Canada Guaranty.

CMHC is the most widely recognized of the three. For this reason, mortgage default insurance is commonly referred to as CMHC insurance.

While the purpose of mortgage default insurance is to serve the lender, it's not as though the borrower doesn't get anything out of it. It allows people to purchase a home with as little as 5% down. Without it, 20% would be the minimum requirement, which would put homeownership out of reach for many. You will also find that there are often better rates available on high ratio mortgages vs. conventional. Why are the rates lower? I explain this in detail in Chapter Three.

OPEN VS. CLOSED

A mortgage is considered open or closed based on its terms of prepayment. An open mortgage allows you to pay off the entire mortgage at any time during the term without incurring a penalty. Very similar to the payment terms of a credit card or line of credit in this sense, however, you would not be able to re-access the funds once it's been paid. For the most part, open mortgages are not worth considering as they carry a much higher interest rate. They are meant to be short-term solutions only, which is why the maximum term offered on an open mortgage is usually six months.

Most mortgages are closed. Unless it's specifically referred to as an open mortgage, any fixed or variable rate mortgage would come with a closed term. All this means is that terms of prepayment are limited and paying the mortgage off in full will incur a penalty. I'll be talking more about penalties for returning your mortgage early in Chapter Ten.

MORTGAGE PREAPPROVAL

Probably the most frequently misunderstood term is a mortgage preapproval. A preapproval is the first step in the home buying process. It's where your financial situation is evaluated to determine the maximum mortgage amount you can expect to qualify for, as well as to lock in an interest rate. If you have already purchased a home and are asking for a preapproval, you're moving backwards. It's like finishing your dinner a restaurant and then asking to see the menu. If you're offer to purchase a property has been accepted, then you are shopping around for a new mortgage, or looking for the full approval. The preapproval should have been completed prior to reaching this stage in the process.

FIRST-TIME HOMEBUYER INCENTIVES

Purchasing your first home is one of life's major milestones which certainly brings its share of excitement! However, the process can seem overwhelming at times. Everything is new to you, and just like going through anything the first time, the excitement can be mixed with stress and anxiety. Fortunately, you're reading this book which will give you all the tools you need to become a pro!

DO YOU QUALIFY AS A FIRST-TIME HOMEBUYER?

For the most part, determining your eligibility is relatively easy. Have you ever bought a home before?

No?

Great! You're a first-time homebuyer.

This will be correct for the majority, however, there are some areas where it may not be quite as clear.

Below are the requirements that will determine if you're eligible for the first-time homebuyer programs according to the Income Tax Act:

- You must be a Canadian citizen or have received your permanent residence status at the time when funds are withdrawn from a registered account.

- You must not have lived in a home you owned at any time in the current year, or in the previous four calendar years. This includes homes that were jointly owned or were owned by your spouse or common law partner. But if you are recently separated from your spouse or common law partner and have lived apart for a minimum of 90 days, then you become eligible once again. That is, providing that you haven't moved in with a new spouse or common law partner. And if you did... I would have to say you certainly didn't waste any time!

- You must intend to live in the home as your primary residence within one year of the new purchase.

Note that these requirements can differ depending on which program you're applying for. I'll point out any differences as I explain the incentives.

THE INCENTIVES

There are three government programs to assist first time

homebuyers with getting into the game:

- First-Time Home Buyer's Plan (HBP)
- Land Transfer Tax Refund
- First Home Savings Account (FHSA)

First-Time Home Buyers Plan (HBP)

The HBP allows first-time homebuyers to withdraw up to $35,000 from their RRSPs tax free. If you are purchasing a home with another first-time homebuyer, then each of you are eligible to take advantage of the program which would give you maximum of $70,000.

You have up to 15 years to return the funds to the account. However, the payback process has to start within two years. This essentially means that you need to make the first payment after the first year, so the two-year rule can sound a bit misleading. If you haven't begun repayments by that time then you'll be taxed on the prorated portion for that year.

While the withdrawal is generally used for down payment, it can be used for any purpose you like. Technically, it doesn't even have to be used for the home purchase at all, nor does it need to be withdrawn at that time. You have up to 30 days after closing on your new home to withdraw the funds... or it can be done more than a year in advance of the new purchase. In this case, the purchase would need to close by October 1st of the year following the withdrawal. For instance, if you made the withdrawal in February, then your new home purchase would need to close by October 1st the following year... providing that you already have a written purchase agreement in place.

To be eligible, the following criteria must be met:

You must:

- Have the funds in your RRSP account for at least 90 days before they become eligible for withdrawal.
- Be a resident of Canada at the time of the withdrawal.
- Have a written agreement to purchase a property.
- Occupy the property as your primary residence within one year of closing.
- Be a first-time homebuyer.

Even if you previously owned a home, you may still be eligible. Providing that you have not owned a property in the last four years, and you did not occupy a home owned by a spouse or a common law partner, then you may still be eligible under the program. If you previously used the HBP, then you must have fully paid the previously withdrawn funds back to your RRSP to be eligible.

Land Transfer Tax Rebate

Land transfer tax is applicable in most provinces and is eligible for all residential real estate purchases. If you're purchasing a condo, then the name itself is a bit misleading given that there is technically no 'land' being purchased... yet the tax still applies.

The land transfer tax is the largest of your closing costs. Depending on the province, it can be anywhere from $0 to more than 2% of the purchase. Some provinces offer a land transfer tax rebate for first-time homebuyers, namely Ontario, BC and PEI.

Ontario

A first-time homebuyer purchasing in Ontario will be eligible for a maximum land transfer tax rebate of $4,000. If purchasing a new property for $1,000,000 the total land transfer tax charged by the Ontario government would be $12,475. With the $4,000 tax rebate, it would bring it down to $8,475.

However, if you're purchasing in the city of Toronto then you get nailed for the land transfer tax twice. $12,475 to the province and another $12,475 to the city for a total of $24,950. As a first-time homebuyer, you'll also receive a rebate of up to $4,475 on the municipal portion which would bring the total land transfer tax cost for a first-time homebuyer down to $16,475.

There is no cap on the maximum purchase price to be eligible for the rebate. You could be a first-time homebuyer inking the deal on the purchase of a $10 million home... and you'll still get the same $4,000 provincial rebate and the same $4,475 municipal rebate if buying in Toronto.

While the cost of provincial and municipal land transfer tax is equal if buying in Toronto, it's only up to a purchase price of $3,000,000. Once you climb up over this mark, the rate of the municipal portion rises.

How much would the total land transfer tax come to if you were buying a $10 million home in Toronto? $652,950.

That's $236,475 to the Ontario government, with a whopping $416,475 going to the city. But hey, if you're a first-time homebuyer pulling the trigger on this mansion, then you can knock off a cool $8,475. Just think of what you can do with the money you saved!

British Columbia

In BC, it's referred to as property transfer tax, which is a slightly different name for the same thing. There is good news and bad news about BC's rebate program. The good news is that they will provide a rebate for 100% of the property transfer tax. That's $8,000 on a $500,000 property.

Pretty sweet, eh?

That is, until I tell you the bad news.

The maximum purchase price is $500,000. That doesn't really give much hope to those buying in Vancouver. Do they really think a first-time homebuyer will have any luck finding something in that city for under $500K? Or any popular area in BC?

For the big spenders, they will give you a partial tax rebate if you're buying as high as $525,000. Yup. That's right. A partial rebate, but only for another $25,000. The rebate progressively decreases as you get closer to the $525,000 limit. If you were purchasing for $524,999, then you'll be eligible for a property transfer tax rebate of a cool 34¢.

For anything $525,000 and up, the rebate is zero.

Just for fun... I thought I would look up the average home price in BC... around $971,000 in 2023[2]. And that's all of BC.

---

2   Source: www.statista.com

Prince Edward Island

Real property transfer tax is what it's called in PEI. It's easy to calculate as it's simply 1% of the purchase price. Much like BC, PEI will also give first-time homebuyers a rebate for 100% of the cost. But in PEI, it's only up to a maximum purchase price of $200,000... with no progressively decreasing threshold above this amount.

The average home price in PEI?

$382,659[3] in 2023.

For those buying in PEI that are not first-time homebuyers, there is a way to get it waived all together. You just have to buy a home for less than $30,000 and you won't have to worry about it. Good luck!

In any of the three provinces offering land transfer tax rebates, they all require you to be a true first-time homebuyer. In other words, you cannot have previously owned property anywhere in the world. Ever.

FIRST HOME SAVINGS ACCOUNT (FHSA)

Launched in April 2023, the First Home Savings Account is a program that all first-time homebuyers should be taking advantage of. Unlike the FTHBI which sounds great until you learn that it's only available to a select few, the FHSA is open to all first-time homebuyers.

It's like having an RRSP and a TFSA rolled into one account. Much like an RRSP, contributions to the FHSA reduce your

---

3   Source: www.statista.com

taxable income. For instance, if you're in a 30% tax bracket and deposit $8,000 into the account, you would save $2,400 on your taxes for that year. It's like free money!

But unlike an RRSP, which requires funds to remain in the account for at least 90 days before they can be used for a home purchase, the FHSA has no such waiting period. The funds can be withdrawn at any time as long as you're buying a new home. Like RRSP withdrawals, the funds do not need to be used toward the home purchase itself and can be withdrawn up to 30 days after your closing date.

You can deposit up to $8,000 into the FHSA annually, up to a total of $40,000 over its 15-year maximum lifespan. If buying a home with a partner, then both of you can contribute, doubling the potential total to $80,000. Should you contribute less than $8,000 in any year, the unused difference carries forward the following year.

As the FHSA is for first time home purchase only, it would have to be closed permanently once you have utilized the program. That means there is no requirement for you to replenish the account and the tax savings are yours to keep.

And now for the best part!

Like a TFSA, any income generated within the FHSA is completely tax-free. For instance, if you invest your initial $8,000 in GICs, mutual funds or stocks, and it grows to $10,000, the entire amount can be withdrawn without paying taxes.

To access the funds, you must have signed an agreement to purchase a new home. Otherwise, the funds will be taxed as usual. Moreover, if the FHSA isn't used for buying a home within its 15-year limit, the account must be closed, and the funds will then become taxable.

The eligibility requirements for the First Home Savings Account align with those of other first-time homebuyer incentives previously discussed.

CHAPTER ONE HIGHLIGHTS

- Understand the basic terminology before shopping for a mortgage.

- A high ratio mortgage is one with less than 20% down payment and therefore requires default insurance (CMHC).

- A variable rate mortgage has an interest rate that changes with the prime rate, which moves with the Bank of Canada rate.

- The mortgage commitment is what a lender issues when they have approved your application, however, it's still conditional on the terms outlined in the document.

- Most mortgages have closed terms, which only means that there will be a penalty if you need to break the mortgage early.

- A preapproval is completed prior to shopping for your new home purchase.

- There are three government incentive programs for first time homebuyers: Home Buyers Plan, Land Transfer Tax rebate, and First Home Savings Account.

- Under the Home Buyers Plan (HBP), each applicant can withdraw up to $35,000 from the RRSPs tax free with up to 15 years to replenish the account.

- If purchasing in Toronto, you'll pay double the land transfer tax.

- Land transfer tax rebates are available in the provinces of Ontario, BC, and PEI. The purchase price must be below $525,000 if buying in BC, or below $200,000 if buying in PEI. There is no maximum purchase price in Ontario.

- All first-time homebuyers should have a First Home Savings Account (FHSA). It's like an RRSP and TFSA rolled into one account.

- Any income earned from investments held within the FHSA is tax free.

- Once the FHSA has been used, the funds never have to be repaid.

Having a decent understanding of the basics can eliminate some of the mind-clutter when talking to a professional about getting your first mortgage. This alone will help to give you a better experience with your mortgage and will make it easier for you to focus on which options are best for you.

2

MORTGAGE PREAPPROVAL

"The way to get started is to quit talking and begin doing."
~Walt Disney

Now that you have a good understanding of the basic mortgage lingo, it's time to get serious. Whether you're a first-time homebuyer, or if you're a seasoned home-buying veteran, purchasing a new home can be an exciting time. But regardless of your experience level, the first step in the process will be to reach out to a mortgage professional to get preapproved. This can be done through a mortgage broker or through a bank.

WHAT DOES IT MEAN TO BE PREAPPROVED?

A preapproval serves two main purposes:

1. To determine the size of the mortgage you will qualify for.

2. To lock in a rate.

However, the term 'preapproval' can be misleading.

From the sound of it, a preapproval means that you're approved for a mortgage prior to purchasing a new home.

But are you *really* approved?

A diligent broker or bank mortgage specialist will complete the application, pull your credit report, and gather the necessary documents to support the information provided on the application. However, preapprovals are generally not fully underwritten by mortgage lenders.

When the application is received, a lender will do a quick review of the information provided, along with a quick glance at your credit bureau. While there are some documents the underwriter may want to review at this stage, they will usually issue the prepapproval certificate based solely on the information you provide when completing your application. If they do review any of your documents, they will not be scrutinized in the same way they would if it were a live deal. A live deal meaning that your offer to purchase a property has been accepted by the seller.

While they are usually fairly accurate, they are by no means firm approvals. A mortgage lender does not have any legal obligation to stand by the preapproval. If they aren't done correctly, then they are not worth the paper they are written on. Quite often, they are not much more than a rate hold.

THE PREAPPROVAL PROCESS

Here's a detailed breakdown of what's involved with getting preapproved for your mortgage:

APPLICATION AND CREDIT CHECK

You'll be asked to complete a mortgage application which provides the lender with a snapshot of your financial health. This includes your employment information, income, assets, properties owned, current mortgages, etc. Note that applications will not always ask you for your debts. This information will be taken from the credit bureau, which will be pulled by the mortgage professional upon review of your application.

DOCUMENT COLLECTION

You'll be required to provide documentation to support the information provided on the application. This can include paystubs, letter of employment, bank statements, tax returns, etc. The exact documentation required can vary depending on your situation.

PRELIMINARY REVIEW

Your application, credit bureau, and document package will then be reviewed by the mortgage professional. Adjustments may be made to the application if there is any contradictory information between the application and supporting documents.

PRESENTATION OF OPTIONS

After review of your application and document package, your mortgage professional will then provide you with a list of your options, along with the maximum mortgage you can expect to qualify for.

SUBMISSION TO LENDER / UNDERWRITER

Once you have chosen the product you would like to proceed with, the mortgage professional will then submit your application to the lender or underwriter for review.

LENDER ISSUES PREAPPROVAL CERTIFICATE

This is a basic document that confirms your rate, term, mortgage amount and expiry date... which is generally after 120 days.

PREAPPROVAL VS. PREQUALIFICATION

You may hear of this part of the process being referred to as a preapproval or a prequalification. The precise definition of each of these terms is subject to interpretation. Some may view a preapproval as being more solid than a prequalification. However, one is not necessarily any more solid than the other. Let's first establish the difference between each of these terms.

PREAPPROVAL

A mortgage preapproval is issued directly by a lender. But just because it's coming from a lender, it doesn't make it any more meaningful than a prequalification. A preapproval letter or certificate is often issued with little to no underwriting done by the lender. It's often based solely on the information provided on the application... without verification. If proper diligence is not taken by the mortgage agent during the review process, the accuracy of the amount stated on the preapproval certificate might be not just questionable... but flat out wrong.

Mortgage preapprovals generally involve locking in a rate for up to 120 days. This means your new purchase would have to close within this period. If the closing occurs outside this window, then your rate would get reset to the going rate with that lender at the time. Providing that you close within the rate hold window, the lender will honour the rate... as long as you qualify when it comes down to underwriting your file once your offer to purchase has been accepted.

Most lenders do not offer preapprovals and would only process your application once your offer to purchase has been accepted. This means there are far more options available once you have inked your agreement to purchase... which can mean the availability of much lower rates. But don't worry, you are in no way obligated to go with the rate on the preapproval certificate, or even the same lender for that matter.

Even if you're working with a lender who offers preapprovals, the rate is usually higher than what they would give you once you have a purchase agreement in place. The difference in rate can sometimes be substantial. Depending on the current trend in mortgage rates, it may not even be worth locking one in.

Prequalification

As mortgage preapprovals are not really approvals at all, prequalification is more of an accurate term. In my opinion, this is the term the mortgage industry should be using for all preapprovals across the board. However, the term 'preapproval' is still preferred by most, despite its misleading context.

After all, you're being 'prequalified', but you are not technically being 'approved' for anything.

A prequalification doesn't get sent through to a lender's underwriting department. However, this doesn't mean it has less value than a preapproval. The maximum mortgage amount outlined in both preapprovals and prequalifications will depend on the accuracy of the application submitted... along with the level at which the documentation was reviewed. Both preapprovals and prequalifications can be issued with a full document package, or without any documents provided at all. One does not carry any more weight than the other, so it really comes down to the diligence of the mortgage agent processing the application.

HOW TO ENSURE YOUR PREAPPROVAL IS SOLID

As the accuracy of your preapproval is heavily dependent on the person reviewing your file, choosing the right mortgage professional is an important decision. It doesn't matter if you're working with a broker or with the bank directly, always take the time to ask questions about their qualifications before you put your trust in them. I'll be discussing how to choose a mortgage professional in detail in Chapter Seven.

Providing that you're working with a seasoned broker or bank mortgage specialist, you shouldn't have any issues with the accuracy of your preapproval. This can give you added peace of mind, allowing you to shop for your new home with confidence.

INCLUDE A FINANCE CONDITION

Most Realtors will expect you to have completed a preapproval before they take you out on showings. They want to ensure you'll qualify, not to mention, a preapproved client is more attractive to a seller than one who is not.

But regardless of how much work is done at the preapproval stage, I still recommend putting in an offer that is conditional on financing. This would allow you to back out of the deal if the lender were to decline your application for any reason. Most real estate purchase agreements will give you five business days to obtain financing satisfactory to you. But they can be longer or shorter, depending on the situation. This gives the mortgage professional enough time to submit your file to the lender for approval and have it fully underwritten before you firm up on your offer. This can relieve a tremendous amount of worry and anxiety during this part of the process, while waiting to hear those beautiful words:

Your mortgage application has been approved!

A finance condition protects you if we encounter an unexpected surprise during the approval process.

PUTTING IN A CONDITION-FREE OFFER

If the real estate market is particularly hot, there may be times when you need to put in an unconditional offer if you want to have a chance of it being accepted. This can also be referred to as a subject free offer in some provinces, however, the meaning is the same. If you're up against other bidders on the property, then a finance condition may make your offer less attractive to the seller. This could mean the difference between having your offer accepted or being passed over in favour of one that's condition free. Sometimes the winning bid may even be lower than yours but may be preferred by the seller given that it doesn't give the buyer the opportunity to back out of the deal.

This is where a preapproval is crucial. Before any broker or bank gives you the green light to put in an offer without a finance condition, they should verify all your documentation to ensure everything is in order. You may think your situation is solid, but the world of mortgage financing can be complex and confusing. You may think you can easily afford to make the payments on the mortgage, but that doesn't mean the lender will agree.

If we have completed your preapproval for you, then you shouldn't have anything to worry about. I'm very selective in the staff I hire, which gives me a highly talented team of mortgage professionals. However, there are always things that can pop up that we may not have been aware of:

- Appraisal value lower than the purchase price
- Property not accepted by the lender
- Your down payment source could be rejected
- Additional debt not reporting on your credit bureau
- Credit bureau surprises

I'll explain each one of these points of concern in detail.

APPRAISED VALUE LOWER THAN THE PURCHASE PRICE

An appraisal is often required by the lender to reassure them that the property you are purchasing is worth what you've agreed to pay for it. If the appraisal values the property lower than the purchase price, then this could present issues with your mortgage, regardless of how solid your qualification is on paper.

In my experience, the appraisal comes back supporting the purchase price in more than 99% of real estate purchases. However, there is that 1% of the time where the appraisal falls short. Should you find yourself in this position, then you would need to cover the difference between the purchase price and the appraised value.

While having your appraisal come in short is concerning for anyone buying a new home, the biggest risk is to buyers with 5% or 20% down payment.

Let's look at three different scenarios with varying down payments to see how a low appraisal might affect the borrower:

Scenario 1 – 20% Down Payment

Purchase price: $1,500,000
Down payment: $300,000 (20%)
Mortgage amount: $1,200,000
Appraised value: $1,450,000

In this example, the 20% down payment would be calculated on the lower appraised value of $1,450,000, which is $290,000. $10,000 lower than the $300,000 required if the home appraised for the full $1.5 million. The borrower would then be required to cover the difference between the appraised value and the purchase price, which would be an additional $50,000 for a total minimum down payment of $340,000. $40,000 higher than it would have been if the home appraised for the purchase price.

The mortgage amount would then drop to $1,160,000. It's not possible to go higher than this considering that the minimum down payment on properties with a purchase price of $1 million or greater is 20%.

Scenario 2 – 5% Down Payment

Purchase price: $500,000
Down payment: $25,000 (5%)
Mortgage amount: $475,000 (not including insurance premium)
Appraised value: $490,000

In this example, the borrower is purchasing with minimum down payment where mortgage default insurance is required. In 99% of these situations, an appraisal is not needed as the value is guaranteed for the lender by the insurer. While the insurer will support value in the vast majority of high ratio (insured) purchases, this is not always the case.

If the insurer has concerns about the value of the property, they will order an appraisal. If the appraisal were to come in low, the same rules would apply as described above. If the borrower did not have the additional funds to cover the difference between the purchase price and the appraised value, then they would not be able to complete the purchase.

In this situation, the 5% down payment will now be calculated on the lower appraised value of $490,000, which is $24,500. $500 less. But then the borrower has to come up with the additional $10,000 for a total minimum down payment of $34,500. If a buyer is putting in every last penny for their down payment and closing costs, then this would put them in a tough spot.

Scenario 3 – 35% Down Payment

Purchase price: $900,000
Down payment: $315,000
Mortgage amount: $585,000
Appraised value: $870,000

In this example, the borrower has a down payment far greater than the 20% minimum required to avoid mortgage default insurance. If the appraisal were to come in $30,000 below the purchase price, then this would not affect the borrower's qualification status. Since the down payment is already sufficient to bridge the gap, no additional funds would be required.

However, there could be another issue in this scenario.

In many situations, a down payment of 35% or greater is

required to get the lowest mortgage rate. If an appraisal values the home at $870,000, then the 35% down payment must be calculated on this number to be eligible for the lower rate.

Now, you may be thinking, "But I have $315,000 for down payment, so that's greater than 35% of $870,000".

Yes, but the lender is deducting $30,000 from your $315,000 down payment to cover the gap between the purchase price and the appraised value. In their eyes, that $30,000 is not part of your down payment. It's just bridging the gap.

This leaves us with $285,000, which is the down payment the lender will use to determine your rate.

If the purchase price was supported by the appraisal, the mortgage would be $585,000. When you divide $585,000 by the appraised value of $870,000, you get a loan to value ratio of 67.24%.

Subtracting this from 100% gives a down payment percentage of 32.76%. Since this is less than the 35% needed for the lower rate, the lender would then reprice your mortgage with the slightly higher rate.

To maintain the preferred interest rate, you would need to add $19,500 to the down payment, bringing it to a full 35% of the appraised value… $870,000 in this case.

Rate aside, the total down payment required to complete the purchase in this scenario would remain unchanged at $315,000. But if the borrower wants to hold on to the lower mortgage rate, they will need to increase it to $334,500.

Note that this only applies in some situations when the purchase price is under $1 million and the amortization does not exceed 25 years. If the purchase price was over $1 million, or if the amortization was greater than 25 years, then the lower appraisal would not have an impact on the mortgage rate, nor would the borrower be required to come up with any additional down payment. The biggest issue in this case would be that the client is overpaying for the property by $30,000, but it would not have any impact on their mortgage approval.

Reducing the Down Payment to Below 20%

When the purchase price is under $1 million, buyers intending to put down 20% may have the flexibility to decrease their down payment to make up for any shortfall between the appraised value and the purchase price. This would require the mortgage to be CMHC insured. But this move isn't without its complications. Insured mortgages are bound by a maximum amortization of 25 years, which will result in higher monthly payments. This would create qualification issues if the borrower was relying on a 30-year amortization to complete the purchase.

Those with larger down payments do not have as much risk. The larger the down payment, the lower the risk.

What Happens if the Appraised Value is Higher?

It's a common question, albeit a bit tangential. Some buyers in this situation wonder if they can use the additional equity as down payment, therefore reducing the cash they'll need to shell out to complete the purchase.

Sounds logical, right? After all, if the equity position doesn't change, then why would the lender object?

It doesn't work that way unfortunately.

Your minimum down payment is based on the lower of the purchase price or the appraised value. While it's nice to know that you scored a great deal on your purchase, it will not change the down payment requirement.

PROPERTY NOT ACCEPTED BY THE LENDER

You could be the most qualified buyer in Canada, with high income, substantial down payment, and robust financial assets. But the issue could be with the property itself, and that can lead to your application being declined by the lender.

There is a multitude of reasons that could lead to your dream home being rejected by mortgage lenders:

- Kitec plumbing
- Knob and tube or aluminum wiring
- Property is a fixer upper (tear down, not livable, not safe, structural issues, etc)
- Undisclosed stigma (former grow-op, site of previous murder)
- Low reserve fund, special assessments, lawsuits, or issues with status certificate (condos)
- Co-op or co-ownership property
- Leased land
- Construction not complete
- Asbestos / UFFI

- Evidence of mould
- Leaky basement (could mean mould or structural issue)
- Property has incomplete renovations
- Non-residential zoning (agricultural, commercial, etc)
- Non-traditional property (log home, off-the-grid, commercial component, floating home, hobby or operating farm, etc)
- Remote location, etc.

There can be a number of other reasons why a lender might decide that the property is not for them. Any of the above could lead to your mortgage being declined by the lender. These are not common scenarios, but they do pop up occasionally. The vast majority of properties do not have any issues with qualifying. Read the comments on the MLS listing, as issues will usually be disclosed. Make sure you read the purchase agreement as sellers will at times make their disclosures there. If you see anything that seems out of the ordinary, then you'll want to point this out to your mortgage professional.

If you're putting in a firm offer, we ask our clients to send us the MLS listing for us to review in advance. If there are any concerns with the property, we'll advise them accordingly.

Negotiating a Lower Purchase Price After Your Offer Was Accepted

Everyone loves snagging a bargain, and buying a home is no exception. If your offer to purchase is conditional on home inspection, you might uncover a bargaining chip that can be used to negotiate a reduction in price with the seller. It could be a minor issue, maybe one that doesn't even bother you, but it could serve as a leverage point for negotiation.

Even if you have already secured a mortgage approval, you need to proceed with caution, as you're now tipping the lender off to potential issues with the property.

If the seller agrees to the price reduction, your Realtor will create an amendment to reflect the lower amount. As the purchase price has now changed, the lender will need to see both the original agreement, as well as the amendment. This will be required regardless of whether you're staying with the same lender that has already approved you or moving to a different one.

The lender will want to know the reason for the price drop. After all, you and the seller had already agreed on the price. So why is the seller now willing to drop the price after already coming to an agreement? Is it out of the goodness of their own hearts? Quite unlikely.

The lender suspects something is wrong with the property, which is understandable. After all, there IS an issue with it, which is the reason why you're requesting the price reduction in the first place. It may be something trivial, but it's still signaling to the lender that there are potential problems, even if the price drop is just a few thousand. The lender will then ask about the reasoning for the drop in price.

Along with the explanation, the lender will generally ask to see a copy of the property inspection which they will review in detail.

If the problem is something minor, such as a dripping faucet or leaky gutters, the lender is not going to have an issue with it. Their concern is whether there could be safety, health, or structural issues with the property.

After reviewing the property inspection, the lender will do one of four things:

1. Issue a new commitment
2. Request a holdback to complete the repairs after closing
3. Request that the work be completed by the seller prior to closing
4. Decline your application

1. Issue a new commitment (approval) reflecting the lower purchase price.

This is the most favorable result you can hope for. It means the lender has reviewed all the details and has no concerns. It's an assurance that from their professional standpoint, everything checks out, and you're on solid ground to continue with your home purchase.

2. Request a holdback of funds to complete the repairs after closing.

If the property requires $10,000 in repairs, a lender will reduce the advance provided to you on closing by this amount. For example, if you're borrowing $500,000, then the lender will release $490,000 to your lawyer at closing. This means you would need to come up with the additional $10K. Once the lender has confirmed that the renovations have been completed, they will authorize your lawyer to release the funds to you.

If you don't have the additional funds, then your mortgage could be set up as a purchase plus improvements. This is where the lender will increase the loan amount by $10,000 in this case. That ensures you are not short of funds at closing. They would then release the funds to you once they have confirmed that the renovations have been completed.

3. Request that the work be completed by the seller prior to closing.

This would generally be done if the lender perceives the issue to be a major safety concern. For instance, a weak step that poses a risk of injury and is marked as needing urgent repair. This would be a red flag for the lender. They may insist on having the repair completed as a condition for proceeding with the mortgage agreement.

4. Declines your application

It doesn't matter if the lender has already issued you a mortgage commitment or not. They can still back out if they do not feel comfortable with something. If the property was found to have structural issues, or any significant health or safety concerns, then they may not want anything to do with the property at all. When reviewing the property inspection, the lender could also find something else about the property that could be concerning. It might not have anything to do with the reason why you were asking for the discount to begin with.

Always check with your mortgage professional before negotiating with the seller.

Down Payment Source Gets Rejected

Lenders will ask for a 90-day history of bank or investment statements to show the natural accumulation of down payment (if 100% of down payment is coming from the sale of a property, then this may not be required). If there are any larger, or unusual deposits, then the lender will need to see the source of those deposits. If transferred from another account, then the full 90-day history of the source account will also be required. The lender will need to see the full paper trail. There are, however, times when other deposits pop up that may not be accepted by the lender.

Here are some examples:

- Gifts from friends
- Repayment of loans from friends
- Cash deposits
- Gifts from non-immediate family members (cousins)
- Gifts from sanctioned countries

There may be solutions for some of the above, and they will not necessarily result in your mortgage being declined, however, every situation is different, and there are some that will be a hard stop for many lenders.

I discuss down payment requirements in detail in Chapter Eight.

ADDITIONAL DEBT NOT REPORTING ON YOUR CREDIT BUREAU

A bank or broker will see a complete list of your debts once they pull your credit bureau. While your credit report generally reflects all debts, there might be instances where one may not be reporting. Most mortgage lenders will use Equifax, but may also pull your TransUnion report to cross-check the data. It's rare for debt to report on one report but not the other, but it can happen on occasion. Any additional debt not reporting on your credit bureau will change your debt-to-income ratio and may adversely affect the amount you thought you qualified for.

CREDIT BUREAU SURPRISES

If you ask someone if they like surprises, most people will respond with a resounding YES with a big smile on their face. But this isn't exactly true. They like the surprises that they want! However, life is filled with unexpected surprises that we would prefer to avoid.

While you may think you have solid credit, a credit bureau can sometimes contain surprises... and I don't mean the pleasant type. There could be possible collections or delinquencies that you may not be aware of. They can be legitimate or erroneous, but either way, you'll want to ensure your credit is solid prior to shopping for your new home. The last thing you want is to get all excited about finding your dream home, only to find out that you don't qualify due to an unexpected issue with your credit.

A credit bureau can sometimes contain possible collections or delinquencies that you may not be aware of.

Putting in a firm, condition free offer is always done at your own risk. Our role in the preapproval process is to strategically minimize these risks. My team is extensively trained to conduct a thorough financial assessment. This will allow you to submit your offer with confidence, paving the way for a seamless and successful home buying experience.

DO NOT MAKE THIS MISTAKE

The mortgage qualification process can be intricate and even downright puzzling. At times, the industry will defy logic or what is seemingly common sense. What seems logical to you... or anyone for that matter, might not align with the criteria mortgage lenders use for qualification.

It doesn't matter how much your corporation earns.

It doesn't matter how good your credit is.

It doesn't matter if you have never missed a mortgage payment.

It doesn't matter how much money you have in the bank.

The income you earned last year might not be the same as what a lender will use to qualify you.

The list can go on and on.

We'll sometimes have clients tell us that they think they should qualify for a higher amount because they have great credit and have never missed a mortgage payment. However, these are just the minimum expectations for demonstrating financial responsibility, and therefore will not get you any special privileges. You either qualify on credit or you don't. Someone with a perfect 900 credit score will not qualify for any more than someone with a 700 credit score.

I see time and time again, people trying to purchase homes that are out of their qualified price range. I'll sometimes have a client tell me "but I have so much equity in my home!" That's great, but you cannot make mortgage payments with equity. And that's why it's not considered for your mortgage approval.

Some of the snags that could create issues with your approval are as follows:

- Probationary employment
- Non-permanent employment
- Change of employment before closing
- Insufficient employment history
- Self-employed status
- Newer, contract employment
- Insufficient or unacceptable down payment
- Thin credit (not enough credit)
- Past or current credit delinquencies that you may or may not be aware of
- Outstanding collections that you may or may not be aware of

- Non-permanent resident of Canada

These are just some of the reasons why you should never assume that you will qualify for a mortgage. It could be a costly mistake that could easily be avoided by speaking with a seasoned mortgage professional in advance.

Some of the above points may not affect your approval depending on the exact situation, however, you'll want to have them addressed prior to putting in an offer.

For those running into challenges with their mortgage approval, don't lose hope! There are some lenders who are more flexible, and sometimes certain exceptions can be considered. There may also be alternative options from lenders just waiting to approve you based on your situation. You may not get the absolute lowest rate out there. But the lowest rate on the market is meaningless if you don't qualify for it.

Are Your Expectations Realistic?

Many individuals have a good understanding of their financial limits and are realistic about what they can afford to purchase. However, there are some who lack this awareness. In fact, there are some who are completely oblivious, setting their sights on properties that would stretch their finances thin, not just causing hardship, but potentially leading to foreclosure.

Some time ago, I received an inquiry from Steve, who was looking to purchase a condo that was not only far above what he would qualify for, but completely unrealistic in terms of his affordability.

After discussing his financial situation with him in detail, it was determined that Steve earned a salary of $2,500 per month with no debt, and no remaining savings after factoring in his down payment and closing costs. I compassionately explained that he wouldn't qualify for the mortgage he needed. He was shocked. After all, he had solid credit and had a stable income. Why wouldn't anyone lend him the money? In his eyes, he was the perfect candidate. I made my best effort to explain:

"Steve, I completely understand how much you want this condo. Let's take a closer look at your carrying costs if you were to complete the purchase. Once we add the mortgage payment, property taxes and maintenance fees, you would be looking at roughly $2,000 per month."

I was expecting him to respond with a big... OHHHHHH... as he realizes it wouldn't be manageable for him.

Nope!

"But I CAN afford it as I make $2,500 per month!".

Oh boy.... He was one of those people who was convinced he was right and I was wrong. I attempted to bring him down to reality.

"I understand what you're saying Steve, you earn more than the carrying costs on the property. May I ask how much you're taking home after taxes?".

He thought for a moment. "$2,200!! I'll still have $200 left over each month. You see??? I CAN afford it!!".

In order to put this into perspective for him, I asked him

about his other basic living expenses. Groceries, clothing, cell phone, utilities, entertainment, etc. Despite my efforts to bring him back to earth, he kept trying to justify how he could make do on the $200 per month surplus... as if I were the one who set the rules around qualifying. It didn't matter what I told him, in his mind, he was right. Why listen to me? It's not like I'm one of the top mortgage brokers in the country or anything.

Steve was an extreme case of someone who had unrealistic expectations around their affordability. Most people in his situation would clearly understand that they wouldn't qualify. However, we encounter many who are surprised that their annual income doesn't qualify them for a higher amount.

Steve was on the far end of the spectrum when it came to having a skewed perception of his borrowing power. In his mind, he should qualify given that he had a couple hundred left over to cover his monthly living expenses. Most people with a grasp on reality would quickly recognize the mismatch between their income and their mortgage ambitions. But Steve was genuinely taken aback to discover that his income wasn't sufficient to get him into the property he had his sights on.

CHAPTER TWO HIGHLIGHTS

- Never assume that you will qualify for a mortgage.

- A preapproval serves two purposes: to lock in a rate and to determine the size of the mortgage you will qualify for.

- A preapproval is no more solid than a prequalification.

- Choose a solid mortgage professional to ensure you're dealing with someone you trust.

- Make your offer to purchase conditional on financing where possible.

- Putting in a firm, unconditional offer is always done at your own risk.

- Never assume that you will qualify for a mortgage.

- Ensure that your expectations regarding what you can afford are realistic.

The importance of getting a preapproved or prequalified before starting your hunt for the perfect new home cannot be understated. It can be easy to get caught up in the excitement of the home buying process.

Signing the purchase agreement on a new home is a great

feeling! But that great feeling can quickly sour if you hit snags with your mortgage qualification. You might feel confident in your ability to make the mortgage payments, but lenders have their own criteria for determining your eligibility. Before you start dreaming of your future home, consult with a mortgage professional to ensure that you're looking at homes within your reach.

The mortgage process can become quite perplexing at times, especially when you consider how convoluted this industry has become. It's growing in complexity, which can make it even more confusing, not just for the first-time borrower, but for seasoned mortgage shoppers as well. This has led us to a new age of mortgages, which is what we'll be discussing next.

3

THE NEW AGE OF MORTGAGES

"The secret of change is to focus all of your energy, not on fighting the old, but on building the new".
~Socrates

Before I became a mortgage broker in 2007, I worked in the United States as a National Sales Manager for a specialty paint company. While my office was based in Canada, I spent about 75% of the year in the US... all over the country. When I told my American colleagues that I would be leaving the paint industry to become a mortgage broker, they thought I had lost my mind! After all, the collapse of the US housing market was just starting to unfold. Huge mortgage lenders and brokerages were going bankrupt as millions of homeowners were forced into foreclosure. From an American's point of view, this would have been the worst time in history to even think about becoming a mortgage broker! It was this financial disaster that led to the radical overhaul of mortgage regulations in both the US and Canada.

A CHANGING MORTGAGE INDUSTRY

The mortgage industry has undergone significant changes since I entered the field in 2007. Back then, it was possible to purchase a home with no money down and amortize the mortgage over 40 years. Even a rental property could be purchased with a down payment as little as 5%. This was short lived in my career as significant changes to mortgage regulations were implemented in the latter half of 2008.

The minimum down payment for rental properties increased from 5% to 20%.

The maximum amortization dropped from 40 years to 35 years.

The Gross Debt Service Ratio (GDS)[4] dropped from 44% to 39%, however, this was only for those with credit scores over 680. For those with scores under 680, it dropped to 35% (this was the first time a tiered system was used).

The maximum loan to value on a refinance dropped from 95% to 80%.

The amount of rental income that could be considered for qualification dropped from 80% to 50%.

As there were so many changes being made, it felt as though I had to re-learn everything that I was just starting to feel comfortable with.

---

4   The GDS is your total mortgage payment including principal and interest, in addition to your property tax and heating costs (commonly written as PITH) divided by your income. See Chapter Eight for more details.

A few years later, the maximum amortization dropped from 35 years to 30 years. Borrowers seeking variable rate mortgages or terms shorter than five years now had to qualify based on the benchmark rate, which was set by the Bank of Canada at that time (now set by the Office of the Superintendent of Financial Institutions, or simply, OSFI). As the benchmark rate was significantly higher than the contract rate (the rate your payments are based on), this significantly reduced the amount one would qualify for when choosing these products. This forced many into 5-year fixed mortgages, even though their preference may have been for shorter terms or variable rate products.

Then on October 3rd, 2016, Canadian Finance Minister Bill Morneau announced yet another set of new mortgage regulations in attempt to cool a very hot housing market. Those purchasing with less than 20% down payment suddenly found it much harder to qualify for a mortgage. Quoting rates became more complicated than it had been in the past and added more complexity to an already complex industry.

These were the most radical set of changes to date. They were changes that sent our entire industry into a state of confusion. Lenders and brokers alike scrambled to figure out how to interpret them.

I remember the date well as I had literally just finished the initial version of Beat the Bank on October 1st, 2016. Fully edited and ready to be formatted for print. Then two days later on October 3rd, these new mortgage regulations were announced. I had to go back through the entire book as it contained information that was no longer relevant. I also had to add a new chapter, which is the one you're reading right now.

The new mortgage regulations led to the creation of two new categories of mortgages:

Insurable and Uninsurable.

INSURABLE MORTGAGES

As explained in Chapter One, any purchase with a down payment of less than 20% would incur mortgage default insurance, which is paid by the borrower resulting in a high-ratio (insured) mortgage. This is fairly common knowledge for anyone who has shopped for a mortgage in the past.

What is less known is that many mortgage lenders will buy bulk portfolio insurance on some of their mortgages through one of the three mortgage insurers, CMHC, Sagen, or Canada Guaranty. This is regardless of the size of your down payment. You could be putting down 70% and therefore only be requiring a mortgage of 30%... and they will still insure it. When you have 20% or greater down payment, it will be the lender flipping the bill for the insurance, not you.

Most lenders, including banks, will buy bulk portfolio insurance on some of their mortgages through one of the three mortgage insurers.

This also enables the lender to securitize the mortgage. This involves breaking illiquid mortgage loans into smaller chunks or bundling whole loans together and converting them into tradable securities. Examples of these would be Canada Mortgage Bonds (CMB) or Mortgage Backed Securities (MBS). This is a common way for lenders to raise the capital needed to fund your mortgage. This also reduces the lender's cost of acquiring the funds. They are then able to pass this savings on to you in the form of a lower rate.

This is nothing new as lenders have been doing this for decades. What is new is the additional limitations that have led to a new category of conventional mortgages called *insurable*. As insurable mortgages have lower funding costs for the lender, rates are generally lower when compared with uninsurable mortgages.

While the mortgage is still insured on a back end, there is no insurance premium paid by the borrower, nor does it have any negative impact on them. This is all part of the inner workings of mortgages.

An insurable mortgage must meet the following criteria:

- 25-year maximum amortization
- Maximum purchase price must be less than $1 million
- Purchases or transfers only (no refinances)
- Owner occupied or second homes

UNINSURABLE MORTGAGES

As the name implies, an uninsurable mortgage is one that is ineligible for bulk portfolio insurance. Anything outside the limits of an insured (less than 20% down), or an insurable mortgage would be considered uninsurable.

An uninsurable mortgage would be any of the following:

- 30-year amortization
- Purchase price over $1 million
- Refinancing
- Rental properties

The category your mortgage falls into... whether insured, insurable, or uninsurable... will play a key role in the interest rate you're offered. The difference in rates across these categories can be significant.

WHY DIFFERENT RATES APPLY FOR DIFFERENT SITUATIONS

INSURED (HIGH RATIO) RATES

In the new age, high ratio mortgages will typically receive the lowest rates. In fact, the rate could be as much as 0.30% lower, and in some cases, even lower than that!

What? So you are telling me that if I put LESS money down then I'll get a lower rate?

YES! In many cases, you will!

From the sound of it, this makes no sense at all. Logic and common sense tell us that, if anything, putting more money down would result in a lower rate. After all, you have a higher down payment, which is less risky for the lender, therefore you should be rewarded with a lower rate, right? This would only make sense. However, as I've already mentioned earlier in this book, the mortgage industry often defies logic and common sense.

The rates a lender will offer a qualified buyer do not have anything to do with their risk. You either qualify for the mortgage or you don't. It's the lender's cost in sourcing the funds that will determine the lowest rate offered.

As insured mortgages have the lowest cost of funds, they will generally have the lowest rates.

INSURABLE RATES

After high ratio, the next lowest rates are most often with insurable mortgages. As the down payment would be 20% or greater, the lender is the one forking out for the insurance premium. This is also where things start to make a bit more sense, as a higher down payment will often lead to a lower rate. Often, you'll find that the interest rate decreases incrementally with each additional 5% you put towards the down payment (or equity if switching your mortgage to a different lender at the end of your term).

For example, if you are purchasing with 25% down payment then you may get a lower rate compared to putting down only 20%. Increasing it to 30% might get you a bit lower yet. The lowest insurable rates are usually available with 35% or greater down payment. Additional down payment beyond 35% will not get you a further discount on the rate. It doesn't matter if you are putting down 50, 70 or even 90%, the rate will be the same.

The lowest insurable rates are usually available with 35% or greater down payment.

Some lenders can have as many as seven different 5-year fixed rates, depending on the down payment, transaction type, and use of the property (rental vs. owner occupied).

A lender's rate structure on 5-year fixed mortgages might look something like this:

Loan To Value	5-Year Fixed Rate
80.01% - 95%	2.84%
75.01 – 80%	3.29%
70.01 – 75%	3.19%
65.01% - 70%	3.09%
65% and under	2.99%
Rental Properties	3.59%
Uninsurable	3.49%

When you add in 1-4 year terms and variable rate mortgages, a broker could be looking at a sea of potential rate offerings.

Not every lender uses a tiered system. It's common for

major banks and credit unions to have a single rate for all conventional mortgages (20% down payment or greater). Pretty much all monoline lenders use the tiered system for determining your mortgage rate. I'll be discussing the different types of mortgage lenders in Chapter Six.

UNINSURABLE RATES

The highest rates of the three categories would be with uninsurable mortgages. Bulk portfolio insurance is no longer an option for the lender, hence the name 'uninsurable.' The unavailability of insurance eliminates their ability to securitize the mortgage, which means they must find alternate sources of funding.

The result is an increased cost of funds to the lender resulting in higher rates for the borrower. The cost of an uninsurable mortgage can be as much as 25 basis points (0.25%) higher than that of an insurable mortgage, or even higher. I've seen the difference as high as 50 basis points.

Unlike insurable mortgages, there is no tiered system used for rate classification. It doesn't matter if you have 20% for your down payment, or 50%, the rate will be the same.

While all purchases over $1 million will be uninsurable, some lenders will still charge an additional rate premium on mortgages with an amortization period greater than 25 years. This premium is often 0.10% on your rate.

CHOOSING AN INSURED MORTGAGE TO GET A LOWER RATE

As the lowest rates are generally found with insured mortgages, some will ask if they should put less money down to take advantage of them. But is this a cost-effective move? Let's take a closer look and find out.

Kamal and Priya have just purchased their first home for $900,000. They were planning on putting 20% down so they can save the CMHC insurance premium, which would give them a mortgage amount of $720,000. They were quoted a 5-year fixed rate of 3.29%, which they would amortize over 25 years. Their mortgage broker told them that they could get a much lower rate if they reduced their down payment by only one dollar as their mortgage would then be considered high ratio. In fact, their rate would drop to 2.99%. A respectable 0.30% difference.

The insurance premium in this case would be 2.80%, which is added to the amount borrowed. This will tack on an additional $20,160.03 for a total starting balance of $740,161.03.

Let's now compare both options to see if the 0.30% difference in rate is enough to offset the insurance premium.

The payment with 20% down at 3.29% would be $3,515.40 per month.

When adding in the insurance premium, the payment on the 2.99% option would be slightly less at $3,498.99.

A difference of only $16.41 per month. Not very much

considering the cost of insurance was $20,160. The payment difference over 60 months (5 years) is $984.60. However, the difference in payment is not what's used to compare the two options.

We need to look at the difference in balances at the end of the term. We also have to consider the time value of money, which is a principle stating that money in your pocket at the present time will have a higher value than the same amount at a future date. But why?

Money on its own has the capacity to earn interest. With the lower rate option, the difference in payment can be applied to other interest earning investments. Even if you choose to keep the additional money in your chequing account, the time value principle still applies. This is because the amount remains unchanged, however, inflation continues, therefore decreasing the practical value of the money over time. In other words, the money is depreciating.

To calculate the time value of money, we need to increase the payment on the lower rate option by $16.42 to match the payment on the higher rate option. This gives us a payment of $3,515.40 for both:

2.99%: $3,515.40 monthly

3.29%: $3,515.40 monthly

Now we're comparing apples to apples.

We then need to calculate the difference between the balances at the end of the term. This results in a savings far greater than the $16.42 difference in monthly payment, but is this enough to offset the insurance premium?

Let's compare the numbers on the two options side by side.

MORTGAGE DETAILS	UNINSURED	INSURED
Down Payment	20%	20% less $1.00
Purchase Price	$900,000	$900,000
Rate	3.29%	2.99%
Down Payment	$180,000	$179,999
Insurance Premium	$0	$20,160.03
Amount Mortgaged	$720,000	$740,161.03
Monthly Payment	$3,515.40	$3,515.40*
Balance at Term End	$618,808.12	$631,467.49

*Whenever comparing two options, the higher of the two payments must be used for both.

That's a difference of $12,659.37

While the lower rate looks nice and shiny on paper, it would set Kamal and Priya back $12,659.37 at the end of their term. Choosing the lower rate option would be more costly by far. While the broker thought his clients would appreciate the lower rate, the insurance premium is too much to overcome. It would have been a bad choice.

For them to break even on the two options, the rate would have to be 2.64%, which would be a ridiculous 0.65% lower than the original rate of 3.29%. You won't see that big of difference in rate, and even if you did, that's just to break even. And that's IF you made it to the end of the five-year term. To come out ahead, the high ratio rate would need to be even lower.

It never makes sense to pay an insurance premium just to get a lower rate.

DETERMINING YOUR LOWEST MORTGAGE RATE

Prior to new mortgage regulations that took effect on November 30, 2016, a lender would typically offer a single rate for each term. It made things a lot easier for everyone, but in the new age of mortgages, those days are long gone. There can be a slew of information required to determine the lowest rates you will be eligible for. And that's before we even into qualification for the mortgage.

The first thing we need to determine is the type of transaction. There are three possibilities:

- Refinancing
- New property purchase
- Mortgage switch / transfer

REFINANCING

If you're looking to take equity out of your home, or extend your amortization to lower your payments, then you would need to refinance your current mortgage. There are three things we need to know before we can determine the lowest potential rate:

- Market value
- Requested mortgage size
- Property location

Market Value

The market value of the property is used with the requested mortgage amount to determine your loan to value. As refinancing would make the mortgage uninsurable, the market value is used more to determine the maximum amount you can borrow, rather than to determine your lowest rate. While the value of the home won't influence your rate directly, it can determine the size of the mortgage, which may, in turn, affect your rate.

Requested Mortgage Size

The total amount of funds you need to borrow can have an impact on your rate. At times, it can be easier to access lower rates with larger mortgages. Many believe that risk is a factor in determining your rate. While that can be true in alternative mortgages (explained in Chapter 12), the specific risk associated with your application will not affect the rate offered to you. You either meet a lender's qualification requirements or you don't. Larger mortgages represent greater profits for the lender, which can give them more flexibility to offer lower rates. This is not the case with all lenders but is common with some of the major banks.

Property Location

There are some mortgage lenders that have geographic restrictions on where they will lend. This is commonplace for local credit unions. There are also some rate promotions that may not be available in all provinces. There are also several mortgage lenders who do not lend in the province of Quebec. If you're in one of the territories, then there are even fewer options.

New Property Purchase

When buying a new home or condo, there are four pieces of information required:

- Purchase price
- Down payment percentage
- Property location
- Closing date

Purchase Price

If the purchase price is $1 million or greater, then that tells us that your mortgage will be uninsurable.

Down Payment Percentage

If the purchase price is under $1 million, you could fall into the insurable category, proving that you qualify with a 25-year maximum amortization. That's where the down payment percentage comes into play. Once we have determined your loan to value, we then know which pricing category you'll fall into.

While the down payment percentage is generally required to determine your rate for an insurable mortgage, it can also be a factor for uninsurable. While uninsurable mortgages are not priced with tiers like their insurable counterparts, the size of the mortgage can make a difference. Some of the major banks will offer lower rates on larger mortgages. For example, if you require a mortgage of $2 million, you may get a lower rate than if you needed an uninsurable mortgage for $200,000.

Property Location

(described above)

Closing Date

While the closing date of your new home purchase has nothing to do with the pricing category of your new mortgage, it can still influence the rate you're offered. While the standard maximum rate hold period is 120 days, some mortgage products may have a maximum of 90 days, 60, or sometimes even less. If the quick close promotions offer the lowest rates available, your closing date will indicate if it aligns with the promotional period's timeframe.

MORTGAGE SWITCHES / TRANSFERS

Where the insurability of your mortgage can become more complicated is when you're transferring it to another lender at the end of the term. This is also referred to as a mortgage switch. If you have a mortgage that is approaching its renewal date, then the following information will be required to determine the lowest rates available:

- Exact maturity (renewal) date
- Expected mortgage balance at renewal
- Approximate market value of the property

- Original purchase price
- Original purchase date
- Name of current lender
- Insured status (high ratio or conventional)
- If you have refinanced at any point
- If your mortgage has a second component, such as a HELOC
- Owner occupied, second home, or rental property
- Property location
- Mortgage qualification concerns

Maturity Date

This is also known as your renewal date. The date that your current mortgage contract expires. The exact date is required as it not only lets us know if potential quick close products will be available to you, but it also confirms that you're within the rate hold window, or that there is enough time to complete the transaction.

Expected Balance at Renewal

The mortgage amount required can sometimes have an impact on the rate you're offered. The balance also helps us to calculate your loan-to-value which is required for insurable pricing.

Approximate Market Value

(described above)

Original Purchase Price

Even if your current home value is over $1 million, you may still be eligible for insurable pricing if your original purchase price was under $1 million.

Original Purchase Date

The date you closed on your property can play a major role in determining your mortgage's insurable status. If you bought your home prior to November 30th, 2016, then you may still be eligible for insurable rates, even if your original purchase price was $1 million or greater.

Name of Current Lender

Each lender has a list of other lenders that they will accept mortgage transfers from, which can limit your options at times. Some lenders will register all of their mortgages as a collateral charge, which can affect the rate offered to you, or result in additional fees. I'll be discussing this in detail in Chapter Ten.

Insured Status

If you put down less than 20% when you purchased the property, your mortgage is considered high ratio. The insured status of the mortgage can result in potentially lower rates.

Have You Ever Refinanced Your Mortgage?

A refinance is done when you replace your current mortgage with another one that involves taking out additional funds or extending your amortization. Depending on the date of the refinance, it can influence your mortgage's insurable status.

Does Your Mortgage Have a Second Component Such as a HELOC?

An example of this would be if you had your mortgage set up as half fixed, half variable, multiple term lengths, or those with a HELOC attached (Home Equity Line of Credit). These hybrid mortgages will be registered as a collateral charge, which can affect the rate offered, or add additional costs to the transfer. (Explained in Chapter Ten).

Owner Occupied, Second Home or Rental Property

The usage of the home can have a big impact on rates. Even if your property meets all insurable guidelines, if you've rented it out, the mortgage will be considered uninsurable. Not to mention, there is generally a rate premium of anywhere from 0.05% to 0.35% over the regular, uninsurable rates. This can lead some to present their home as owner occupied to get around the rate premium. It's understandable that everyone wants to maximize their savings, but misrepresenting the usage of the home is considered fraud. Always make sure you're properly disclosing how the property is being used.

Second homes would be considered insurable, providing they meet the criteria. A second home could be a vacation property, or a property owned by relatives.

Property Location

(described above)

Mortgage Qualification Concerns

The information required to determine the lowest rates applies to qualified applicants only. If you have questionable credit, new employment, minimal documented income, or anything else that you think could affect your ability to qualify, then this can have a major impact on the rates quoted. If you have any concerns about your ability to qualify, you'll want to let your mortgage professional know. I see time and time again, people shopping around for the lowest rate when they should be more concerned with finding a lender who will approve them. The lowest rate is meaningless if you don't qualify for it, so make sure you disclose all your concerns to your mortgage professional so they can advise you based on your specific situation.

Mortgage Insurability with Major Banks

The terms insurable and uninsurable generally apply only to mortgages through credit unions and monoline lenders. It's not likely that a mortgage specialist with a major bank would be familiar with these terms, or even the concept. As major banks do not generally follow the tiered structure of insurable mortgages, they may not ask these questions to determine the lowest rates available to you.

If your mortgage is deemed insurable, then chances are strong that there could be much lower rates available to you by using a non-bank lender.

Rate Classification and Qualfication

Note that this is just the information required to determine the lowest rates that you could potentially be eligible for. Additional information will be required to determine your qualification, including credit worthiness, and capacity to carry the loan. Qualification requirements will be discussed in detail in Chapter Eight.

THE STRESS TEST

At the same time insurable and uninsurable mortgages were established, the term stress test was also introduced. This requires borrowers to qualify for a mortgage based on a higher rate than the one used to calculate their scheduled mortgage payments.

The stress test (although not called that at the time) originally applied to all terms under five years, as well as variable rate mortgages. However, the term 'stress test' did not come into our vocabulary until late 2016, which is when 5-year fixed high ratio mortgages were also required to pass it. By January 1st, 2018, it was required for all mortgages.

The purpose of the stress test is to protect homeowners from rising rates. The stress test ensures that they will still be able to cover their payments in a rising rate environment.

The stress test was criticized by many as it significantly reduced the size of the mortgage that people could otherwise qualify for. However, I've always been a supporter of it as it serves a very important purpose. It was introduced as a safeguard to ensure everyone would still qualify to cover their payments if rates were higher at the time of renewal.

For example, in January 2019, the lowest 5-year fixed rate for an insured mortgage was 3.39%. On a $600,000 mortgage amortized over 25 years, the monthly payment would be $2,960.89. However, it would have had to qualify based on a rate of 5.39%, translating to a payment of $3,624.02. $663.13 higher than the actual mortgage payment. As this mortgage was a 5-year term, it would be due for renewal in January 2024. At the time, the lowest 5-year fixed for a comparable mortgage had risen to 5.09%. Coincidentally, not much different than the rate the borrower had to qualify on five years before. As they were originally qualified based on a similar rate, the borrower should still be okay to carry the higher payment.

If the stress test had not been implemented, then many renewing in 2023 or early 2024 (when this edition was released) would be facing an affordability crisis.

In 2021, 5-year fixed rates hit an all-time low of 1.39% for an insured mortgage. If the stress test didn't exist, then rapidly rising mortgage rates could lead to an affordability issue, which could result in a monumental economic disaster. As borrowers were already qualified to make the higher payments based on the stress test rate, the higher rates would still be affordable.... At least on paper. That doesn't mean that rising rates are not uncomfortable for pretty much everyone. But if the stress test was never implemented, then we would have a much bigger problem on our hands. If people are no longer able to comfortably cover their mortgage payments, then we could have been facing a major housing crisis.

How the Stress Test Works

The stress test rate used for your qualification is the higher of the benchmark rate, or 2.00% above your contract rate (the rate your payments are based on). The benchmark rate is set by the Office of the Superintendent of Financial Institutions (OSFI), which was 5.25% at the time of writing.

If the rate you're offered is 4.99% (term not important) and you added two percent, you would have a total of 6.99%. As this rate is higher than the benchmark rate of 5.25%, the stress test would then be based on 6.99% since it's the higher of the two.

On the other hand, if you were offered a rate of 2.99%, then adding two percent brings you to 4.99%. In this case, the benchmark rate of 5.25% is used for your qualification as it's the higher of the two rates.

Is There a Way Around the Stress Test?

If you have a down payment of 20% or greater, then some local credit unions have products that will qualify you based on the contract rate... that is, the rate your payments are based on. However, the rate can be quite a bit higher.

There are also some lenders with more flexible debt servicing guidelines which may be enough to get you qualified for a higher amount, providing that your application is strong. There may even be options to boost your maximum qualified amount substantially through an alternative lender. Rates are generally higher, plus you can expect to pay a 1% lender fee. Despite the higher costs involved, this could be the deciding factor that enables you to move into the home of your dreams rather than compromising on one that falls short of what will truly make you happy.

Should your down payment fall below the 20% threshold, you will be unequivocally subject to the stringent requirements of the stress test. When the mortgage insurers are involved, there is no way around it.

The Biggest Flaw to the Stress Test

The stress test was a great idea for the reasons mentioned above. But there is one major exception.

Mortgage transfers.

Whether you're in the middle of your term or your mortgage is coming up for renewal, there are often lower rate promotions available that could potentially save you thousands by switching to a different lender.

But you're still required to pass the stress test.

WHY????

You're not borrowing more money.

You're not accumulating more debt.

If a borrower doesn't pass the stress test, then they would have no choice but to renew their mortgage with their current lender at the higher rate.

Things are already tight for these people, and rising rates aren't making it any easier. So why on earth would our government tie their hands like this? There is zero logic involved here. They are forcing people who are already stretched thin to pay a higher rate... for no reason at all.

There are two exceptions:

1. You purchased your home prior to November 30, 2016

2. Your mortgage is high ratio

If you purchased your home prior to November 30th, 2016 and have not refinanced your original mortgage then it's possible to bypass the stress test with many lenders. The date is important as it's when the new age of mortgages began. If you purchased prior to this date, then some lenders will grandfather in old mortgage rules, which would allow you to qualify based on the contract rate to get your mortgage transfer approved. Note that this would apply to 5-year fixed rates only. A version of the stress test has been in place on shorter term and variable rate mortgages since 2011.

The second exception is if your mortgage is high ratio, meaning you put down less than 20% when you purchased the property. Providing that you have not refinanced after the purchase, you would not be required to pass the stress test. Just as if you purchased your property prior to November 30, 2016, this would only be possible if choosing a 5-year fixed mortgage for the new term.

Requiring people to pass the stress test when they are simply switching their mortgage to a different lender is not just defying common sense... It's flat out ridiculous.

CHAPTER THREE HIGHLIGHTS

- Mortgages can be placed into three categories. Insured, insurable and uninsurable.

- An insured or insurable mortgage has a maximum 25-year amortization and the purchase price cannot exceed million.

- Any mortgage that does not fit within the insurable criteria listed above would be classified as uninsurable.

- Lowest rates are usually found with insured mortgages, followed by insurable, then uninsurable.

- It never makes sense to pay an insurance premium just to get a lower rate.

- Since January 1st 2018, all mortgages need to pass a stress test. This means that you will have to qualify based on the higher of the benchmark rate set by the Bank of Canada, or 2% above the contract rate (the rate your payments are based on).

- Lowest rates are usually found with insured mortgages, followed by insurable, and then uninsurable.

- As credit unions are provincially regulated, some have products that don't require you to pass the stress test.

- There are lenders with more flexible lending guidelines that may enable to you qualify for a higher mortgage amount.

When these changes were implemented in late 2016, it created a lot of confusion in our industry, not to mention, confusion among consumers. Everyone was looking for answers. The dust has settled, and the new age of mortgages is now our reality.

Now that you have a clearer understanding of how mortgages are categorized, it's time to focus on the task at hand... selecting the best mortgage. We'll be discussing that next.

4

CHOOSING THE RIGHT MORTGAGE

"It's choice – not chance that determines your destiny."
~Jean Didetch, founder of Weight Watchers

With so many choices available to you, mortgage shopping can be somewhat overwhelming, even for an experienced mortgage shopper. I have potential clients contacting me regularly saying that they would like to go with a variable rate or a mortgage with a specific term. I'll then ask them for their reasoning as to why they want that specific product. One of the most common answers I get is that it's what they have always done, and it's worked out well for them in the past. In some cases, it was the first mortgage product that was sold to them when they bought their first home and have stuck with it ever since.

But is it really what's best for them every time their mortgage comes up for renewal?

UNDERSTANDING YOUR NEEDS

Just as you want to find the perfect place to live, you want to find the perfect mortgage. Before you start looking into your options, you'll first want to form a clear understanding of your needs. Not all mortgages are the same and choosing the wrong one can be an expensive mistake. Whether you're purchasing a new home, refinancing your current mortgage, or have a mortgage approaching its renewal date, it's important to take the time to analyze your personal situation before making any decisions.

Here are some reflective questions to help you to align your mortgage choice with your life plans:

1. FIVE-YEAR VISION

What are your personal and professional aspirations for the next five years?

2. HOUSING SUITABILITY

How long will the property meet your evolving needs?

3. RELATIONSHIP GOALS

Are you single and on the prowl for your future Mr. or Mrs. Right?

4. FAMILY PLANNING

Are you thinking about having kids or expanding your family?

5. Home Improvements

Do you have any plans for renovations or significant changes to your home?

6. Job Security

How stable is your current employment?

7. Geographical Flexibility

Is there a possibility that you might relocate to another province or even abroad?

8. Entrepreneurial Aspirations

Are you considering starting your own business?

Answering these questions can give you a clearer picture of what you need in a mortgage. By understanding your needs and researching different options, you can make an informed decision about which type of mortgage best suits your lifestyle and goals. Keep your answers to the above questions in mind as you read though the rest of this chapter.

SELECTING THE RIGHT TERM

When you walk into a bank looking for a mortgage, the first rate they'll often quote you is a 5-year fixed or a 5-year variable. With the odd exception, variable rate mortgages only come with 5-year terms. While there are some 3-year variable rate products available, they are not offered most lenders.

5-year terms have become standard, but who was it that all of a sudden decided that the 5-year mortgage is the best choice for everyone?

Many mortgage agents will often do the same thing. They quote their clients a five-year rate without ever taking the time to even consider that this might not be the best option for them.

For example, Bill and Jane, a vibrant couple in their late 20's, were excited about their purchase of their first property. It was a 550 square foot, one bedroom condo in downtown Toronto, set to close right before their wedding. They spoke with a mortgage specialist who presented them with a 5-year fixed and a 5-year variable rate. After some discussion, they decided that they would proceed with the 5-year fixed.

However, our beloved newlyweds had their first child exactly nine months after their wedding day. A little over a year later, they welcomed their second bundle of joy into the world. Now they're a family of four, living in a small, one bedroom apartment. Needless to say, it no longer suits their needs, and they are now on the hunt for a new home with just under three years remaining on their mortgage.

It turns out that Bill and Jane were planning to start the family all along. A 5-year fixed rate was clearly not the right product for them, but this is what all their friends were getting, they thought they would do the same. Not to mention, it was the only term length presented to them.

The chances of them making it to the end of the five-year term were slim. It was clear from the beginning that it wouldn't be long before they would need to upgrade to support their growing family. Sure, they could end up porting their mortgage, which I will discuss later, but this isn't always the best option. The mortgage specialist should have also presented them with shorter term options, explaining why these products may align better with their plans.

Any situation where your future is uncertain would make you an ideal candidate for a mortgage with a shorter term. After all, who's to say you aren't going to meet your dream man or woman the day after closing and get married a year later? (Assuming you're single of course!)

There are many circumstances that could prevent you from making it to the end of your term.

Then why do people feel so comfortable with the 5-year fixed?

We have been conditioned by the banks to think the 5-year fixed is what we need, so we sign the mortgage documents without giving it a second thought.

After all, the mortgage specialist has your best interests in mind, right?

In some cases, they very well may, but you definitely can't count on it. You need to protect yourself by having a good understanding of your own situation rather than just relying on the mortgage specialist's advice.

In many cases, both banks and mortgage brokers alike will make more money selling five-year terms over the shorter options, so often this is what they try to sell you. Don't get me wrong here, there are many situations where a 5-year fixed IS the right mortgage for someone. 5-year fixed mortgages will generally have lower rates than shorter terms, which is resulting in even more people flocking to them. Prior to the new age of mortgages, it was the exact opposite. The shorter the term, the lower the rate. Things have since changed, and the 5-year fixed has been the king of the low-rate fixed mortgage products since the end of 2016.

However, it's not always about rate, and the lowest rate doesn't always make it the best choice. 5-year mortgage products are not one-size-fits-all solutions, and there are times when shorter terms can end up saving you more money long term... despite the higher rates.

In addition to the lower rate, many people feel comfortable knowing that their rate and payment is locked for the next five years, which is one of the reasons why 5-year fixed terms are so popular. However, many people still end up breaking their mortgage before the end of five years. In many cases, the term of the mortgage may not have even be discussed at the time of application, with only five-year terms being presented. This is doing the customer a disservice as who's to say the five-year mortgage was right for them in the first place? After all, if a five-year term was right for everyone, then why are so many homeowners breaking it early? Hmmmm.

That being said, the 5-year fixed rate has established itself as the 'standard' in the industry. However, late 2022 to early 2024 (when this edition was released) was an exception as 3-year fixed products took the popularity crown by a landslide. This was because rates had reached their highest level since 2007 and were widely expected to fall substantially in coming years. At that time, I would expect the 5-year fixed to reclaim its popularity title.

....
A five-year mortgage term is not right for everyone.
....

Take the time to research your options and have a clear understanding of your needs and goals. This will help to ensure you are being offered a mortgage that is right for you rather than just relying on the advice of the mortgage specialist.

Prior to 2018, 5-year fixed terms made it possible to qualify for a larger mortgage compared with shorter term and variable rate products. This left many with no other choice. This is because 5-year fixed mortgages didn't have to pass the stress test. That is, until January 1st, 2018. (The stress test was discussed in detail in Chapter Three).

THE 10-YEAR FIXED MORTGAGE TERM

Back in 2013, the 10-year fixed term grew in popularity as it gave homeowners an opportunity to lock in a rate for a longer period. This is a product that many banks and mortgage agents alike were suggesting for their clients. The logic being that large increases to rates are coming and that locking in will protect you. It needs to be mentioned that both mortgage agents and banks make more money on 10-year mortgages than they do on shorter terms, so they have a vested interest in pushing them. You need to be cautious here.

Ten years is a long time to lock in considering that many borrowers don't even make it to the end of their five-year term, let alone make it to the end of a 10 year.

Ask yourself this:

Have you ever lived in one home for longer than 10 years?

While some have, most move around far more frequently than that.

Does that mean that 10-year fixed terms should be avoided?

I couldn't in good conscience come out and say yes without knowing more about you. What I can say is you need to ask yourself some serious questions and fully understand what you are getting into before making that decision. I do, however, think that 10-year fixed terms are not the right choice for most people.

Why?

It's because nobody expects to break their mortgage mid-term, but it happens all the time, and sometimes we are forced to. You never know when life will throw you a curveball. I have seen multiple clients with perfect credit and financial stability, come back to me a couple of years later with their credit and financial situation in shambles. Sometimes bad things happen to good people and life doesn't always go as planned.

Here are some reasons why some people may end up breaking their mortgage contract before the end of ten years, many of which are less than pleasant:

- Loss of job
- Transfer of job
- Personal injury or disability

- Illness requiring expensive medication
- Divorce
- Death of spouse
- Relocating out of province or country
- Finances get out of control
- Raise cash to start a business, education, renovations, etc.
- You're self-employed and business takes a turn for the worse

A 10-year fixed mortgage typically carries a rate of around one percent higher than the 5-year fixed. You would need to make it right to the end of the 10-year term for it to even have a chance at working out for you.

Let me take a moment to break the numbers down so you can see for yourself how everything looks on paper.

Let's say we have two options:

A 5-year fixed at 4.00% and a 10-year fixed at 5.00%

Your mortgage amount is $300,000 and you are amortizing over 25 years with monthly payments.

At the end of five years, your ending balance on the 10-year term will be $265,522.87 compared with only $250,115.61 on the five-year term. This means that at the five-year mark, you'll be ahead by $15,407.26[5] with a 5-year fixed over the

---

5   Savings is always calculated by using the payment from the higher rate for both options and then calculating the difference between the ending balance for each

10-year alternative. If you were to break your mortgage at this point, this is what it would have cost you if you chose the 10-year term... and that doesn't even include the penalty to break your mortgage, which would add thousands more.[6]

That covers the first five years. Now we have to consider the rate at renewal if you went with the five-year term. This is of course an unknown variable and all we can do is speculate.

Using the information we have available to us now, we can calculate the break-even rate, which in this case would be 6.50%.

This means that the rate for the remaining five years (to round out the 10 years) would have to be higher than 6.50% for the 10-year mortgage to have made sense. Providing of course that you even make it to the end of the 10-year term. If the five-year rate turns out to be lower than 6.50%, then you would have been better off with the five-year term from the get-go.

One thing that we can all agree on is that 10 years is a long time. Think about where you were 10 years ago. Here are some questions you can ask yourself to help put it into perspective:

What movies were out at that time?

What was the number one hit song?

Where were you living?

---

6   If breaking a longer-term mortgage after 5 years, the penalty is always three months' interest.

Where were you working?

What was your relationship status?

How old were your kids?

I've had clients come to me wanting to break their 10-year fixed mortgage as early as one year into the term. When they originally signed for it, they too thought they would be in it for the long haul. Using the above example, taking a 10-year fixed term is commensurate with betting $15,407 that mortgage rates will be higher than 6.50% in five years' time.

Is that a bet you are willing to take?

THE AGE-OLD QUESTION – FIXED OR VARIABLE?

There are mortgage professionals who have a specific stance when advising their clients on the choice between fixed and variable rate mortgages. There are some who always recommend variable, while others might always recommend a fixed rate. This is often due to their own feelings, beliefs, and risk tolerance, which is what forms the advice given to their clients. In their mind, they're giving their clients the best advice, as it's what they would do themselves, and therefore, it's what they believe their clients should be doing as well. However, everyone is a little different, and what's right for one person, may not be right for the next.

Mortgage advice should be tailored to the specific person, based on their own unique feelings, outlook, and tolerance for risk. There is no one size fits all mortgage advice. I may advise for one client to choose a fixed rate mortgage, while advising another to go variable ten minutes later. It really depends on their specific situation.

There are five key components that need to be considered when deciding on a fixed or variable rate mortgage:

- Risk tolerance
- Penalty
- Goals and plans
- Spread
- Market outlook

RISK TOLERANCE

One of the biggest considerations is your tolerance for risk. There is a certain degree of uncertainty that comes with a variable rate mortgage. Your rate is not guaranteed for the term, and often, neither is your payment. If the Bank of Canada increases their rate, then your rate will increase as well. If they drop, then your rate will of course drop. There are many people with a low tolerance for risk and the mere thought of a potential rate increase can cause them to become fraught with anxiety. If you start to get heart palpitations the moment you get word of a 'potential' rate increase, then you're likely more suited to a fixed rate mortgage.

As you'll hear me say multiple times... the best choice is not always the one that saves you the most money. It's the one that allows you to sleep soundly at night.

PENALTY

Even if you have a low tolerance for risk, there are still times when a variable rate might be a better option. Again, everyone's situation can be a bit different. One of the biggest benefits to a variable rate mortgage is that your penalty is guaranteed to be only three months' interest. Note that there can be some exceptions to this, so always best to ask. While the future of your rate and often your payment is not certain, how your penalty gets calculated IS. This provides some certainty to an otherwise uncertain mortgage option.

With a fixed rate mortgage, the penalty is generally the higher of three months' interest or the interest rate differential (IRD), which can lead to a significantly higher penalty. Your exact penalty is unknown, which creates some uncertainty around fixed rates. The biggest reason why people choose fixed is for the certainty, so it's important to keep this in mind before making your choice. The penalty to break a variable rate mortgage is predictable. However, a fixed rate penalty is not. The further mortgage rates fall below your current rate, the larger your penalty will become. Even 'fair penalty lenders' can carry large penalties if the current rates fall far enough. If you're looking for a guaranteed penalty, then your only option would be a variable rate mortgage.

Should mortgage rates fall, the lower variable rate penalty can also make it easier to switch to a lower rate mid-term. For example, if you're currently in a variable rate mortgage at prime -0.60% and you're now eligible for a rate of prime -1.25%, then switching your mortgage is almost a no brainer. I say 'almost' as there is no one-size-fits-all advice, and it can be situationally dependent. As long as you don't have any immediate plans to move, then you'll almost certainly want to switch your mortgage if you're in this situation. Easy to do with a variable rate mortgage, but the penalty to break a fixed rate mortgage can make switching mid-term cost prohibitive.

I'll be talking about penalties in depth in Chapter Ten.

GOALS AND PLANS

The majority of mortgage borrowers are convinced that their new mortgage will suit their needs for at least five years. Penalties are not important, since they don't have plans to move, nor do they have plans to break their mortgage. That is, until their circumstances or plans change... which is all too common.

Five years can be a long time. Sometimes things can change for the better, but they can also change for the worse. Divorce, death, disability, etc., are all very real, and we can never predict where life is going to take us. Life occasionally presents unexpected challenges, and accurately predicting our life situation over the next few years can be a challenging task.

There may be other times when you're clear on your plan moving forward, and you know upfront that the current mortgage won't suit your needs for the full five-year term. One common situation is if you have a mortgage coming up for renewal and you plan on buying a new home. One option might be to choose a shorter-term fixed rate, however, this isn't always the best choice. One or two-year term mortgages can carry much higher rates than the variable rate options and may carry an uncertain penalty as well. The guaranteed three months' interest penalty on a variable rate can end up being a better choice and can likely end up saving you more money overall... penalty included. Sure, you could always port a fixed rate mortgage over your new property with no penalty at all, however, porting your mortgage is not always the best option as I'll explain in Chapter Ten.

Again, every situation can be a bit different, and my advice will vary accordingly.

SPREAD BETWEEN FIXED AND VARIABLE RATES

Another major consideration is the spread between your fixed and variable rate options. In other words, the difference between the two rates. The larger the spread, the more protection you have against rising mortgage rates, and the more attractive variable rate mortgages become. When the Bank of Canada changes their overnight rate (which is what the prime rate is based on), it generally moves in increments of 0.25%. If your variable rate is 0.75% lower than your lowest fixed rate option, then it would take three standard sized increases from the Bank of Canada before your variable rate catches up. The larger spread gives you added protection against rising rates.

Even if your variable rate catches up to, or even passes the original fixed rate alternative, it doesn't mean that you should have chosen the fixed rate. It just means that it will start to eat into your savings.

While 0.25% is the standard increment, larger movements are possible, albeit, rare. A major exception was in 2022 when we saw six oversized rate increases with the largest being a whopping 1.00%. In 2020, we saw three oversized rate cuts at 0.50% a piece.

Market Outlook

Economic forecasting and predictions from the Bank of Canada can also play a key role. The state of our economy and its trend will provide indicators as to what we can expect moving forward. The Bank of Canada, as well as other leading economists, will make periodic forecasts which should also be taken into consideration. You don't necessarily want to bank on these forecasts, as they can be flat out wrong. However, it's not uncommon for them to be right. Just as with any forecast, things can change as they can only be based on the information available at the time. Who could have predicted a pandemic that would send the prime rate plummeting by an unprecedented 1.50% within just a few short weeks as we saw in 2020? Prior to the unexpected large drop, variable rates were higher than fixed, so variable didn't make a lot of sense at that time given the information available before the news broke.

In early 2022, leading economists were forecasting that the Bank of Canada would increase their rate by 4-5 times by the end of the year, all at the standard 0.25%. This would have meant that the prime rate would have increased by 1.00% to 1.25%. Instead, we saw a total of seven increases, six of which being oversized, for a total hike of 4.00% by the end of the year.

By the end of 2022, economists weren't expecting any further hikes in 2023. We got three of them.

There are some things that cannot be predicted, and what's expected to happen does not always become reality. However, it's all we have to go on.

If the spread between fixed and variable rate is minimal, and the Bank of Canada is anticipating multiple rate increases over the coming years, then you may want to gravitate towards a fixed rate. Just as if they are anticipating multiple drops, then you may want to consider the variable option. These situations are situationally dependent, so it's best to reach out to a seasoned mortgage professional to discuss your options.

The best option isn't always the one that saves you the most money. It's the one that allows you to sleep comfortably at night.

VARIABLE RATE VS. ADJUSTABLE-RATE MORTGAGES

You'll often hear floating rate mortgages referred to as either a variable or Adjustable Rate Mortgage (ARM). The terms ARM and Variable Rate Mortgage (VRM), or simply 'variable', are often used interchangeably by both consumers and industry professionals alike. There are even some lenders who refer to their adjustable rate mortgages as variable rates. However, there is a difference between the two if you want to go by strict definition.

With both types, the interest rate changes with the prime rate. If the prime rate moves up or down by 0.25%, then so does your interest rate. The key difference is how a rate change affects your payment. With a true variable, when your rate changes, your payment remains the same. If the rate drops, a larger portion of your payment is allocated to the principal balance, which in turn, reduces the amortization. Since the principal portion of the payment is larger, the loan gets paid off ahead of schedule.

If the rate increases, a larger slice of the payment is applied to interest and less to principal, therefore increasing your amortization. As the principal portion paid would no longer be enough to pay the mortgage down to zero within the original amortization period, it would take more payments to kill the loan. This is why the amortization rises.

With adjustable-rate mortgages, the payment fluctuates with the prime rate. If it rises or falls, the amount you pay each month will adjust accordingly. This means that with ARMs, borrowers need to be prepared for their payments to increase if interest rates go up.

A lender will either offer an adjustable-rate mortgage or a true variable rate, but never both.

As 'variable rate' is the popular term for all floating rate mortgages, I will be using it to describe these types of mortgages throughout the book. This ensures consistency and aligns with the terminology that readers are most likely to be familiar with.

IS VARIABLE RIGHT FOR YOU?

When choosing between fixed and variable, one borrower may not feel comfortable with any sort of risk at all, while another may have a very high tolerance for it. Your choice really comes down to where on the spectrum you fall, and your mortgage professional should take the time to discuss this with you. Just because a specific mortgage is right for one person doesn't mean it's right for another. If you aren't comfortable with the fact that your rate could increase at any time, then a variable rate mortgage probably isn't for you, regardless of how big the spread is. If the thought of an increasing rate and payment creates any anxiety for you at all, then a fixed rate mortgage might be a better choice.

HYBRID MORTGAGES

Still can't decide between a fixed and a variable rate mortgage? Some lenders offer multi-component mortgages, enabling you to divide your loan into varied segments. For example, you may choose to allocate one part to a fixed rate and another to a variable rate, giving you a tailored blend that suits your financial strategy. The portion size of each component is up to you. It could be 50/50, 90/10, or whichever ratio you prefer. You can also throw in a HELOC for a triple play.

You can even add additional components if really wanted to get adventurous. For example, part 5-year fixed, part 3-year, part variable, etc. With some banks, you can have as many as ninety-nine different components, however, this would be a nightmare for anyone to follow!

A big problem with these hybrid mortgages containing components with varying terms is that it locks you into that bank. If you have a two-year term and a five-year term as part of the same mortgage, you can't move the two-year component to another bank offering a lower rate at renewal. There are still three years remaining on the other portion. As both terms were registered together as a single charge (mortgage), the only option for transferring it to another lender is to break the mortgage and pay the penalty on the term that has not yet reached maturity.

Most lenders do not offer hybrid mortgages, so you'll be limited to the big banks, credit unions, and possibly one or two monoline (non-bank) lenders. As options are limited, you may end up with a higher mortgage rate than what might otherwise be attainable.

HOME EQUITY LINE OF CREDIT

A HELOC, or **H**ome **E**quity **L**ine **o**f **C**redit, is a simply a line of credit that is secured against your home. It can also be referred to as a SLOC (Secured Line of Credit). It allows you to draw equity out of your home when you need it.

A HELOC functions similarly to a standard line of credit, giving you the flexibility to pay down the balance as aggressively as you wish or to simply make interest-only payments each month. Unlike a traditional amortized mortgage, a HELOC allows you to re-borrow the repaid amount at any time, providing convenient access to funds up to your limit.

Sounds great, right?

Why doesn't everyone have a HELOC then?

They likely would if it wasn't for the 35% minimum down payment and higher interest rate.

Although the rate on a HELOC is generally lower than that

of a typical open mortgage, it is still significantly higher than the rates offered by closed variable rate mortgages. As of the time of writing, the interest rate on a HELOC is about 1.25% higher than the prevailing variable rates, or roughly 2.00% higher than fixed mortgage rates.

HELOCs are primarily offered through major banks and credit unions, with the odd exception. This means that you'll be more limited in options, which may result in a higher rate on the amortized mortgage portion than what you could find if you were to forgo the HELOC.

When adding the HELOC at the time of purchase, it would generally be registered together with the mortgage as part of the same charge. Simply put, a charge is another way of saying registration. It's what secures the loan to your home. This means that you have only one mortgage registered towards your home, but with two components. The term portion (amortized) and the revolving portion (HELOC).

A free standing HELOC cannot exceed 65% of the property's value (referred to as 65% Loan-to-Value or LTV). But when adding it to a traditional amortized mortgage, the two together can go up to a maximum of 80% LTV.

READVANCEABLE MORTGAGES

In scenarios where you make a down payment of at least 20%, you can qualify for what's known as a readvanceable mortgage. With this type of mortgage, the HELOC portion typically starts with a negligible limit... either zero or $1, depending on the lender... and increases automatically as you pay down the mortgage principal. This feature allows you to access the equity in your property incrementally as your mortgage balance decreases.

In the past, every dollar paid down on the mortgage principal, would result in an equal increase to the available credit limit on the HELOC. For instance, if a mortgage payment reduced your principal by $1,000, the available credit limit on your HELOC would also increase by $1,000, giving you immediate access to that equity.

But this changed on November 1st, 2023.

The limit will still increase, but not equally. For instance, if you were to pay the principal down by $1,000, the HELOC limit may only increase by $800. The exact ratio can vary from one lender to the next. This would continue with each payment until your global limit (amortized mortgage and HELOC combined) is reduced to 65% LTV. The limit will not grow any further at that point as this is the maximum limit available on all HELOCs across the country.

ADDING A HELOC SEPARATELY

If a lender offers a lower interest rate on an amortized mortgage but doesn't offer HELOCs, it's often possible to accept the lower rate and add the HELOC from another lender after closing. This option is only available when you have a down payment greater than 20% as the HELOC limit cannot exceed 80% of the home's value. The only exception is if you are closing on a new build purchase where the value has increased beyond the purchase price at the time of closing.

Adding a separate HELOC will mean that you will have two separate mortgages on the property. The first being the amortized loan. The second being the HELOC.

There are five notable drawbacks to this:

1. *Non-Increasing Limit*

   Unlike some combined mortgage and HELOC products, the limit on a standalone HELOC does not automatically increase as you pay down the amortized mortgage.

2. *Separate Application Process*

   You'll need to go through the application process a second time, which is similar to applying for a traditional mortgage.

3. *Double Discharge Fees*

   Upon selling the home, you'll face discharge fees for both the amortized mortgage and the HELOC. These fees vary by province. Usually between $300-$400 in Ontario or $75 in BC... per charge. There are generally no discharge fees in the provinces of Alberta and Quebec.

4. *Additional Registration Costs*

   As a second mortgage must be registered, there is an additional cost which can top $1,000. However, there are generally options to bring this cost down substantially.

5. *Limited Lender Options*

   There are limited options as most lenders will not

issue a HELOC behind another lender's mortgage, if they offer them at all.

A HELOC is a Mortgage

Some people will tell me that they are mortgage free, but then later tell me that they have a HELOC with $500,000 owing on it. But a HELOC is still a type of mortgage. If there is money owing against your home, then you are not mortgage free.

A mortgage can be defined as a loan secured by real estate. That's it. And that's exactly what a HELOC is. A loan secured by real estate.

The difference is that one is amortized, while the other is not.

An amortized mortgage has payments that are split between principal and interest over a specific period, usually 25 or 30 years. As the mortgage is paid down, you build equity in the home. However, you cannot re-access that equity without either refinancing, or adding a HELOC.

On the other hand, a HELOC is a revolving account, which means that you can re-access the funds at any time. There is no set amortization period as the minimum payment covers interest only.

However, they are both mortgages... just different types.

CHAPTER FOUR HIGHLIGHTS

- Consider your goals and your situation before choosing a mortgage term.

- Five-year terms are not right for everyone.

- 10-year fixed mortgages can be an expensive gamble betting on the fact that rates will be skyrocketing. You would generally need to hold the mortgage for the entire 10 years to even have a slight chance of it working out in your favour.

- The choice between fixed and variable depends on your tolerance for risk, the market outlook, and the spread between the two options.

- Always be mindful of the spread between fixed and variable before making your choice. A thinner spread means elevated risk.

- Before choosing a variable rate, consider what the experts are predicting for future rates. Just be aware that they can be wrong.

- Your goals and plans should always be considered when choosing a mortgage product.

- Just because variable has worked out for you in the past, it may not be the best choice in the future.

- A true variable rate has a fixed payment for the term. An adjustable rate mortgage will move with the prime rate. However, the term 'variable rate' is often used interchangeable by both consumers and many mortgage industry professionals.

- A HELOC can be combined with an amortized mortgage or can often be added separately after closing.

- As a HELOC is secured against your home, it's also referred to as a mortgage... just a different type.

Choosing the wrong product can cost you thousands of dollars unnecessarily. Either by paying a higher interest rate, or by paying a penalty to return the mortgage early if too long of a term was selected. Ask your mortgage professional for advice but be mindful of whose best interest he or she has in mind. Think carefully about your situation before making a final decision.

Now that you have a detailed understand of the different mortgage options available, the next step is to choose your amortization period. Many won't give amortization a second thought, but there is a reason why I have dedicated an entire chapter to it. It begins with understanding the mechanics of amortization.

5

THE MECHANICS OF AMORTIZATION

"Building wealth is a marathon, not a sprint".
~ Dave Ramsey, Author and radio personality

Think of amortization as the countdown timer to paying off your mortgage completely. It's all about how long it'll take you to whittle your mortgage balance down to zero, given you're making equal payments throughout. The longer your amortization period, the lower the payments, and the larger the mortgage you can expect to qualify for.

On a conventional mortgage (20% or more down payment), the longest you can stretch this countdown is 30 years.

On a high-ratio mortgage (less than 20% down payment), the maximum is 25 years.

HOW AMORTIZATION AFFECTS YOUR PAYMENTS

Each payment you make is split into two parts: one part chips away at the principal (the amount you borrowed), and the other part is allocated to interest. The longer the amortization period and the higher the interest rate, the more of your payment goes towards interest, leaving a smaller portion to chip away at the principal.

Let's paint a picture with numbers comparing two different scenarios:

Scenario 1 (25-year Amortization)

Imagine you have a $600,000 mortgage at a 5.99% interest rate. Your monthly payment will be $3,835.27. For the very first payment, $2,958.29 is gobbled up by interest, leaving just $876.98 to decrease your principal.

Monthly Payment	Payment #	Principal	Interest	Balance (after pmt)
$3,835.27	1	$876.98	$2,958.29	$599,123.02

As you can see, the balance is reduced by the amount of the principal payment:

$600,000 - $876.98 = $599,123.02

You can also see that the initial payment is quite interest heavy, however, this will change as you progress through the life of the mortgage. I'll illustrate this shortly.

Scenario 2 (30-year Amortization)

Now let's stretch that same mortgage over 30 years. Your monthly payment shrinks by $270.08 to $3,565.19. In this setup, you're still paying $2,958.29 in interest, but only $606.90 goes towards the principal.

Why this change?

It's simple. Spreading the mortgage over a longer period lowers your total monthly payment. The interest portion remains the same because the 5.99% interest is calculated on the full $600,000, regardless of whether you pay it off in 15, 20, 30 years, etc. However, since you're taking an extra 5 years to pay off the entire mortgage, the principal portion of your payment is reduced accordingly.

Monthly Payment	Payment #	Principal	Interest	Balance (after pmt)
$3,565.19	1	$606.90	$2,958.29	$599,393.10

In essence, longer amortization periods can make your monthly mortgage payments more manageable, but they also mean you're chipping away at the principal at a slower pace.

HOW RATE INFLUENCES THE PRINCIPAL / INTEREST PAYMENT SPLIT

The impact of the interest rate on your mortgage is substantial, particularly in how it affects the division between principal and interest in your payments. Consider a lower rate, say 2.99% instead of 5.99%, on the same $600,000 mortgage.

At this lower rate, with a 25-year amortization, your monthly payment decreases significantly to $2,836.40 from $3,835.27, saving you nearly a thousand dollars a month. This is a clear example of how a lower rate can greatly reduce your financial burden.

Here's where it gets even more interesting: The interest part of your payment is almost halved, dropping from $2,958.29 to $1,485.77. It's a direct result of the lower rate, which in this case is about half of the original 5.99%. Meanwhile, the principal part of your payment jumps from $876.98 to $1,350.63, an increase of $473.65 per month.

You might think that a higher principal portion means you'll pay off the mortgage faster, right? Not exactly. Despite this increase, the amortization period remains the same at 25 years. The mortgage will still take a quarter of a century to pay off if you stick to the regular payment schedule. I'll explain the reasoning in the next section.

Mortgage Paydown Through Scheduled Payments

Initially, your payments are dominated by interest. But with every mortgage payment made, the principal portion gradually increases, while the interest portion correspondingly decreases. This happens because each payment reduces your outstanding balance, meaning there's less principal to charge interest on. You can clearly see this outlined on the amortization schedules below covering the first six months.

25 Year - 5.99% - First Six Months

Monthly Payment	PMT #	Principal	+	Interest	-	Balance
$3,835.27	1	$876.98	/	$2,958.29	/	$599,123.02
$3,835.27	2	881.30	$4.32	2,953.97	$4.32	598,241.72
$3,835.27	3	885.64	4.34	2,949.63	4.34	597,356.08
$3,835.27	4	890.01	4.37	2,945.26	4.37	596,466.07
$3,835.27	5	894.40	4.39	2,940.87	4.39	595,571.67
$3,835.27	6	898.81	4.41	2,936.46	4.41	594,672.86

The evolution of your mortgage payments is a gradual but consistent process. Starting with a principal portion of $876.98, you'll notice a modest increase of $4.32 in the second payment. From there on, each subsequent payment sees the principal portion grow by just a few pennies over the previous month's increase. This gradual increase in the principal is mirrored by an equal decrease in the interest portion of your payment. This is illustrated in the +/- columns in the above chart, showcasing the inverse relationship between the principal and interest components over time.

Let's now see how much progress we've made when we reach the last six months of the five-year term:

25 Year - 5.99% - Last Six Months of Term

Monthly Payment	PMT #	Principal	+	Interest	-	Balance
$3,835.27	55	$1,143.75	$5.61	$2,691.52	$5.61	$544,748.31
$3,835.27	56	1,149.39	5.64	$2,685.88	5.64	543,598.92
$3,835.27	57	1,155.06	5.67	2,680.21	5.67	542,443.86
$3,835.27	58	1,160.76	5.70	2,674.51	5.70	541,283.10
$3,835.27	59	1,166.48	5.72	2,668.79	5.72	540,116.62
$3,835.27	60	1,172.23	5.75	2,663.04	5.75	538,944.39

The incremental increases in the principal portion have compounded over time. While the monthly payment remains the same, the distribution between principal and interest has shifted.

By the end of the first five-year term, the principal part of the payment will have increased by $295.25 over the first payment. The interest portion will have decreased by an equivalent amount. At this stage in the game, your payments are still predominantly directed towards interest.

Now let's teleport into the future and see how this would look in your final six months leading up to what I affectionately call "Champagne Day". The day you become mortgage free! For simplicity, we'll keep the interest rate constant over the life of the mortgage, but in reality, the rate will change with each new term.

In these last six months, you'll notice that the division of principal and interest has substantially shifted. The lion's share of each payment is now being applied to the principal, with just a token amount allocated to interest.

25 Year - 5.99% - Final Six Months of Amortization Period

Payment	PMT #	Principal	+	Interest	-	Balance
$3,835.27	295	$3,723.73	$18.27	$111.54	$18.27	$14,075.12
$3,835.27	296	3,742.09	18.36	93.18	18.36	11,273.57
$3,835.27	297	3,760.54	18.45	74.73	18.45	8,465.09
$3,835.27	298	3,779.08	18.54	56.19	18.54	5,649.65
$3,835.27	299	3,797.72	18.64	37.55	18.64	2,827.24
$3,835.27	300	3,819.08	21.36	18.83	18.72	0.00

The transformation in your mortgage payments from start to finish is quite remarkable. On your very first payment, the principal portion was $876.98, but by the time you reach your final payment, this amount has soared to $3,819.08. Conversely, the interest portion, which initially was $2,958.21, has plummeted to a mere $18.83 in the final payment.

This dramatic shift is a testament to the power of consistent mortgage payments over time, gradually shifting the balance from paying mostly interest to predominantly reducing the principal.

Congratulations on reaching this significant milestone – It's now time to pop that cork as you are now mortgage free!

Over the 25-year amortization, you'll have paid a total of $550,583.64 in interest while paying the initial $600,000 principal amount down to zero.

If we consider the same scenario but with a 30-year amortization, the total interest paid increases to $683,469.19. This represents an extra $132,885.54 in interest compared to the 25-year plan. Spread out over the life of the mortgage, this works out to an average of approximately $5,315.42 more per year.

Yes, opting for a longer amortization period will mean paying more in interest. However, it also translates to more manageable mortgage payments throughout the term, offering greater financial flexibility on a month-to-month basis. This is an important consideration for many homeowners, weighing the difference between total interest paid and monthly affordability.

CHOOSING THE RIGHT AMORTIZATION PERIOD

When you have a down payment of 20% or greater, you have the option to choose an amortization as long as 30 years. If you're looking to maximize your qualifying eligibility, then a 30-year amortization will do just that. It lowers your mortgage payments, effectively reducing your debt-to-income ratios, therefore, qualifying you for a larger mortgage.

Let's say a couple has a solid income of $250,000, good credit, and minimal debt. They have a choice between a 3-year fixed at 5.29% with a 25-year amortization, and a slightly higher rate of 5.39% amortized over 30 years.

Opting for the 25-year amortization caps their maximum mortgage at approximately $1,000,000. However, choosing the 30 option increases their borrowing capacity by an additional $100,000, allowing them to qualify for a mortgage of up to $1,100,000. If they had a down payment of $400,000, they could potentially purchase a home valued up to $1,500,000.

But what if they need more?

There are scenarios where they could secure a mortgage as high as $1.4 million, boosting their potential purchase price to $1.8 million or even higher... and they would still be eligible for competitive rates.

Still not enough?

It may be possible to qualify for them for even higher amounts through alternative options, which I'll be discussing in detail in Chapter Twelve.

IS A 25-YEAR AMORTIZATION A BETTER CHOICE?

Many people lean towards a 25-year amortization because it's considered standard, without much other thought. Advice from friends and family may also play a role, steering them towards the 25-year option. They may associate a 30-year amortization period with paying more interest and taking an additional five years to become mortgage free.

What I suggest for my clients really depends on their individual situation, goals, etc. If we are barely squeaking out an approval because the debt-to-income ratios are so tight at 25 years, then it might be worth considering bumping it to 30 if the option exists. The lower payments will give you a bit more breathing room, relieving some financial strain. If you feel comfortable with higher payments, you can increase them after closing to see how you manage. If it turns out to be too much of a squeeze, then you can revert to your original, lower payments, or anything in between. A longer amortization will provide that additional flexibility.

Choosing a 25-year amortization will often get you a lower mortgage rate, which can definitely add to its appeal. It will also result in paying less interest given the shorter payoff window as mentioned earlier in this chapter. But this doesn't necessarily mean it will be your best choice. You'll first want to determine what is most important to you:

Having lower monthly payments.

Or having a lower rate and paying less interest.

Having a lower rate and paying less interest is definitely appealing, however, there are many who will be okay with a marginally higher rate if means they are shelling out less money each month.

There can be a number of reasons why some prefer the lower payment over the lower rate:

- Tight personal finances
- Future employment/income uncertainty
- Investments
- Future purchase of an investment property

Tighter Personal Finances

Some people may be living paycheque to paycheque. With their financial situation being so tight, having those extra dollars in their pocket at the end of the month can make a world of difference.

Employment/Income Uncertainty

If you're concerned about your job stability, or are considering starting a new business, then lowering your payments to build your cash reserves can be a big help.

Investments

While many have the goal of paying their mortgage off as soon as possible, there are also many who prefer to have the increased cash flow to feed their investments. Even when rates are higher, a mortgage is still the cheapest method of borrowing money. Many savvy investors will use this as an opportunity to build wealth by reinvesting the cash flow difference at a higher return.

Future Purchase of an Investment Property

This can be a big one. When purchasing a rental property, mortgage lenders will generally use only 50% of the projected rental income when qualifying you for the new mortgage. This can make the acquisition of a rental property more challenging for many. By lowering your mortgage payment on your primary residence, you will be able to qualify for a larger mortgage on the new purchase.

AMORTIZATION COMPARISON

We've already established that a 25-year amortized mortgage will result in paying less interest due to the shorter payoff window. The potentially lower rate adds to the savings even further. But how much of a difference will it actually make? Let's do a side-by-side comparison, putting each option to the test.

In this example, we'll use a $750,000 mortgage. The borrowers have the choice between a 25-year amortization at 4.49% or a 30-year amortization for 0.10% higher at 4.59%.

Let's see how the two compare over the 5-year term:

Amortization	25 Years	30 Years	Difference
Rate	4.49%	4.59%	+0.10%
Monthly payment	$4,146.88	$3,820.99	-$325.89
Total payments	$248,812.80	$229,259.40	-$19,553.40
Interest	$157,176.58	$163,426.03	+$6,249.45
Principal paid	$91,636.22	$65,833.37	-$25,802.85
Balance at end of term	$658,363.78	$684,166.63	+$25,802.85

If you were to choose the 30-year option, your outstanding mortgage balance will be $25,802.85 higher and you'll have paid an additional $6,249.45 in interest.

While the rate is a bit higher on the 30-year amortization, you're increasing your monthly cash flow by $325.89, amounting to a total of $19,553.40 over the five-year term.

But the difference in rate isn't always 0.10%. Sometimes there may be no difference at all, while other times it can be as much as 0.50%, depending on the situation.

Let's now see how the numbers change with a larger rate difference:

Amortization	25 Years	30 Years	Difference
Rate	4.49%	4.99%	+0.50%
Monthly payment	$4,146.88	$3,998.20	-$148.68
Total payments	$248,812.80	$239,892.00	-$8,920.80
Interest over	$157,176.58	$178,008.74	+$20,832.16
Principal paid	$91,636.22	$61,883.26	-$29,752.96
Balance at end of term	$658,363.78	$688,116.74	+$29,752.96

The additional 0.50% rate premium over the previous 30-year example results in owing an additional $3,950.11, while paying an additional $14,582.71 in interest by the end of the five-year term. As the rate premium is hefty, so is the additional interest paid.

When compared with the 25-year option, you'll have paid an additional $20,832.16 in interest and will owe an additional $29,752.96 by the end of the term.

But even with the higher rate, your monthly cash flow still increased by $148.68, totaling $8,920.80 by the end of the term. Really not that impressive when comparing it with the additional cost. However, if cash flow is particularly tight, some may still want to keep those additional funds in their pocket to improve their cash flow. While the difference in payment is manageable for many, it can make a big difference to a financially struggling family.

Everyone's situation can be a bit different.

YOUR INITIAL AMORTIZATION IS IRRELEVANT

A common goal that many people have is to pay their mortgage off as quickly as possible. For this reason, they are inclined to request a shorter amortization. The shorter the amortization, the sooner they'll reach mortgage freedom, right?

Not necessarily.

From this standpoint, the original amortization only serves two purposes:

1. To set your minimum scheduled payment
2. To determine your maximum borrowing limit

Sure, you could say that it's an indication of how long it will take to pay off the mortgage in full. But that only applies if you stick with the original payment schedule. If your goal is to pay your mortgage down faster, then you'll be straying from the original payment plan.

Every extra payment towards your mortgage instantly reduces your effective amortization period. As a result, the original amortization is no longer indicative of the actual time it will take to clear your mortgage.

Beginning with a shorter amortization eliminates your ability to reduce your payment in the middle of your term. Some people are comfortable with the shorter amortization as they have no plans to reduce their payment. However, life is full of unexpected events, such as job loss, financial downturns, health issues, etc. While you may not anticipate the need to lower your mortgage payments, it's also challenging to prepare for every unforeseen twist and turn that life might throw your way.

As long as there is no change to rate, choosing a longer amortization is like having free insurance. Maintaining your ability to lower your payments is like having a financial safety net, without getting in the way of your mortgage payoff goals. The original amortization could be 100 years and it wouldn't matter. If you were to set your payments to match a 10-year amortization schedule, then you'll be mortgage free in 10 years. The original amortization would have no relevance to your mortgage payoff timeline.

Before adopting this strategy there are two key points that I want to bring to your attention:

1. You need to have the discipline.

2. Lender prepayment privileges can vary.

Discipline

Since you can't set up an increased payment plan before your new mortgage begins, self-discipline is key to successfully implementing a prepayment strategy. Whether you opt for higher scheduled payments or choose to make several lump sum payments, action is required post-closing. Some prefer a 'set it and forget it' approach, avoiding any further mortgage changes until the end of the term. It's important to know your personal habits and preferences. If you're determined to pay off your mortgage sooner, a longer amortization might be the most suitable strategy. However, if you feel you might not consistently follow through with additional steps after closing, starting with a shorter amortization could be more beneficial for you.

Prepayment Privileges

If you plan on paying off your mortgage faster, then you'll want to ensure you're choosing a lender with prepayment privileges suitable for achieving your goals. If your goal is to pay your mortgage off in 5 years and are considering starting with a 30-year amortization, then some lenders may not be flexible enough for you to reach your objective without incurring a penalty. Everyone's situation can be a bit different. A seasoned mortgage professional can discuss your requirements and devise a mortgage payoff strategy tailored to your goals.

I'll be discussing prepayment privileges in detail in Chapter Eleven.

25 and 30-Year Amortization With Equal Rates

As mentioned earlier in this section, there are times when a 30-year amortization might be available with no rate difference at all. In these situations, I'll generally suggest going with the 30 year option as it can be done without paying any additional interest at all. Let me explain.

Using a similar strategy to what I've outlined above, you can use your prepayment privileges to match the payments of the 25-year option. If you do this right from the beginning and maintain the higher payments throughout the 5-year term, then it will be 100% equal to having a 25-year amortization. Zero difference. Remember, amortization is the amount of time it takes to pay a mortgage down to zero assuming equal payments. If we change the payments, we change the amortization.

Let's say you need a $575,000 mortgage and are offered a rate of 4.39% on both a 25 and 30-year amortization.

Amortization	25 Years	30 Years	Difference
Rate	4.39%	4.39%	0.00%
Monthly payment	$3,147.40	$3,147.40	$0.00
Total payments	$188,844.00	$188,844.00	$0.00
Interest over	$117,749.64	$117,749.64	$0.00
Principal paid	$71,749.64	$71,749.64	$0.00
Balance at end of term	$503,905.64	$503,905.64	$0.00
Remaining amortization	20 Years	20 Years	0

As soon as you match the payments, they are 100% identical.

Then why not just choose the 25-year amortization from the beginning?

The benefit is that you can revert to the lower payment at any time during the term. This can be helpful if you find yourself in a financial crunch, or if you need to increase your cash flow for any reason. Just remember, anytime you make a change to your payment, your effective amortization also changes. If you increase your payment, it drops. Conversely, if you go back to your original payment, or anything in between, it will increase. Even if you move the payment back in the middle of the term, the previous payment increases will have still knocked your amortization down from the original 30 years.

This works one way, but not the other. If you start with 25 years, then the only way to reduce your payment would be to refinance to bring your amortization up to 30 years. You would then be forced to pay the penalty to return the mortgage, not to mention incur additional costs for refinancing.

....
If you select a 30-year amortization but set your payments to match 25 years, then your effective amortization automatically becomes 25 years.
....

CHAPTER FIVE HIGHLIGHTS

- A high ratio or insurable mortgage will have a maximum amortization of 25 years.

- A conventional mortgage has a maximum amortization of 30 years.

- With each payment made, the portion allocated to principal will increase, while the interest portion correspondingly decreases.

- Decide what's most important to you: paying less

interest or having lower payments.

- If unsure whether to go with a 25 or 30-year amortization, consider the 30 and then set your payments based on the 25. You can always revert to the lower payment if needed.

- Your original amortization period is not relevant if your goal is to pay down your mortgage faster. As soon as you make an additional payment, your effective amortization drops.

- A longer amortization can increase your borrowing capacity if purchasing a rental property in the future.

Amortization often doesn't receive much consideration from most people, who typically view it simply as the timeframe to pay off their mortgage. However, it becomes much less of a factor once you understand how to effectively use prepayment privileges to manipulate it.

Now that we understand the mechanics of amortization, the next choice will be to choose the right lender, which is what we will be talking about next.

6

CHOOSING THE RIGHT LENDER

*"While your past can inform you and your future can inspire you,
the moment of choice exists in the here and now."*
~Debbie Ford, Author

Gone are the days when securing a mortgage meant walking into your local bank. While this still happens today, it's an old school approach which has dramatically evolved for the better. With the introduction of mortgage brokers in the 1970's, the once bank-dominated scene has transformed into a competitive battleground. There are now more choices and opportunities for borrowers than ever before.

It's not uncommon for some new clients to tell us that they are only interested in having their mortgage through one of the big banks. The first question I'll ask is simply... Why?

This simple question opens the door to understanding their motivations and perceptions about mortgage lending.

Each person has their own reasoning, but many will stumble when presented with that question, struggling to come up with a viable reason. It may be something they were told by their parents, their friends, or commonly... by their bank. The latter is my personal favourite. It's only natural for a bank to sell against their competition. Regardless of the source of this advice, it's often based on inaccuracies, as those offering it may not have a comprehensive understanding themselves. Their only experience may have been dealing with the banks. As this is what they are familiar with, this is what they suggest.

But how can this advice be reliable if they are not well-versed in the alternative options?

I remember the first time I heard about Uber. I failed to see the point in it. Why wouldn't someone just take a cab? Why would I trust some random weirdo to pick me up in his own car? If someone asked me for my opinion on using Uber or a cab, I would have undoubtedly recommended a cab. This is because cabs were my only frame of reference, so I would have advised on what was known to me.

But now that I'm familiar with Uber, it's all I use. I was originally concerned about the safety. Then I learned that driving for Uber is not as simple as downloading the app and hitting the road. Uber has a thorough screening process, including background checks, medical examinations, and identity verification. Uber will also track your location throughout your trip. Should that driver attempt to take you anywhere other than your desired destination, there is a record of where you went and who was driving. It couldn't be safer.

Asking a big bank about other options is like asking a taxi company to share their thoughts on Uber. You can't expect to hear anything positive.

In order to make an informed decision, we need to learn about the pros and cons of having your mortgage with one lender type vs. another.

'A' LENDERS VS. 'B' LENDERS

When we present possible options to our clients, some will ask if the mortgage will be with an 'A' lender or a 'B' lender. However, few are aware of the difference. The big banks typically label themselves as 'A' lenders, subtly implying superiority, while casting all others as 'B' lenders. However, this classification has nothing to do with the quality of the lender. It's more about the specific market segment they serve.

An 'A' lender is characterized by their focus on prime borrowers, referring to those with solid credit and provable, qualifying income.

'B' lenders specialize in assisting borrowers who fall outside the lending criteria of an 'A' lender. For example, those with less than perfect credit, non-qualifying income, or other potential challenges. Essentially, 'B' lenders provide alternatives for those who don't meet the stringent requirements of traditional prime lending institutions. AKA... banks.

Examples of 'A' lenders:

- First National
- MCAP
- Merix / Lendwise
- CMLS Financial
- RFA Mortgages
- MCAN Home Mortgage
- Strive Capital
- B2B Bank
- The big six banks
- Most credit unions

Examples of 'B' lenders:

- Home Trust
- EQ Bank
- Community Trust
- Haventree Bank
- Effort Trust
- Bridgewater Bank

The 'A' and 'B' classifications refer more to the profile of the borrowers they lend to, rather than the institution themselves. To throw in another degree of complexity, some 'A' lenders also have 'B' divisions, which allow them to cater to both sides of the market. This is the case with most of the monoline lenders. It can also work the other way around. For example, EQ Bank is primarily known as a 'B' lender, but they also have an 'A' side.

In this chapter, I'll be focusing on 'A' lenders and will be talking about 'B' lenders in depth in Chapter Twelve.

There are three main types of 'A' lenders:

- Major banks
- Credit unions
- Monoline lenders

Let's now explore the key differences between each type of lender.

MAJOR BANKS

If you're like many, you probably asked your parents for advice when you were considering buying your first home. They likely suggested for you to head down to the bank and talk to them about it. For many people, getting a mortgage through a big bank seems like the logical option. After all, banks have familiar brand names, with their logos a common sight on city streets... and pretty much everywhere else you look.

The big banks are often referred to as 'The Big Six':

- Scotiabank
- TD
- RBC
- CIBC
- BMO
- National Bank

You may sometimes hear them referred to as The Big Five, which would leave National Bank out of the mix. While National Bank has branches across the country, their primary market is Quebec and New Brunswick. Despite their earnings are being notably lower than the top five banks, National Bank still ranks as the sixth largest in the country. As a result, they are considered one of the 'big banks' by many.

It's the familiarity of the brand name that will lead some people towards choosing a big bank. While there are many situations where a big bank may not be the best choice, there are also many where they are.

ADVANTAGES TO BANKS

- Brand name recognition
- Branches with convenient access
- All accounts in one place
- Wide range of financial products
- Additional flexibility
- Larger mortgages
- Lower rates

Brand Name Recognition

Big bank marketing is ubiquitous – from captivating TV commercials to eye-catching billboards, from ads on city buses to pages in our favorite magazines, and even across the internet. It's a rare day when you're not touched by their advertising in some way. This isn't by chance, as major banks invest millions into their marketing campaigns each year. Their branding is not just familiar, but almost a part of our daily lives.

Branches with Convenient Access

Major banks have an extensive network of branches throughout the country. This makes arranging a face-to-face meeting both simple and convenient, no matter where you are located. If you're someone who values discussing mortgage options in person, then choosing a lender with a widespread presence of physical branches can be a plus.

All Accounts in One Place

Opting for a mortgage from the bank that holds your other accounts offers the convenience of a unified online banking experience. This allows you to view all your financial products – mortgage, chequing, savings, RRSP, and more – in one place. Surprisingly, the simplicity and ease of monitoring all these accounts on a single page is a comfort that many are willing to pay a premium for, even if it means spending thousands more.

Wide Range of Financial Products

Banks are more than just mortgage providers, as they offer a comprehensive suite of financial products. This means when you have a mortgage with a bank, you also gain access to a variety of other services, including credit cards, lines of credit, personal loans, RRSPs, TFSAs, and various investment options.

Additional Flexibility

Major banks often have a distinct advantage in terms of flexibility compared to many non-bank lenders, primarily because they don't depend on third-party funding sources. This independence allows them to retain mortgages on their own books... in other words, they're lending their own money. This self-reliance grants them greater freedom in decision-making, enabling them to potentially make exceptions or offer accommodations that might not be feasible with other lenders. This additional leeway can be a significant benefit for borrowers seeking more flexible mortgage solutions.

Larger Mortgages

One area where the big banks truly excel is in their ability to fund on larger mortgages. For example, if you need to borrow north of $2.5 million, then a major bank may not only be your best choice... it may be your only choice.

Lower Rates

Some of the major banks can be highly aggressive with their pricing on uninsurable mortgages (explained in Chapter Three). The larger the mortgage, the more aggressive they can get on rate. This gives them a competitive edge in this space.

DISADVANTAGES TO BANKS

- Higher rates
- Limited product availability

- Higher penalties
- Requirement for branch visit
- Cross selling
- Limited branch hours

Higher Rates

Yes, you read that correctly. I've just highlighted how big banks can offer lower rates, and now I'm pointing out that they also tend to have higher rates. So, which is it?

The difference is with the type of mortgage. As mentioned above, big banks are often more competitive on uninsurable mortgages, particularly on larger loans. However, there are often lower rates available on insurable and insured mortgages if you look outside of the major banks. Sometimes much lower. While there are exceptions, it's typically not a major bank leading the industry with the lowest rates on many insured and insurable transactions. I covered these terms in detail back in Chapter Three.

Higher Penalties

Major banks will apply a more stringent formula for calculating the penalties to return (break) fixed-rate mortgages compared to most monoline lenders. Despite the similarity in wording on their mortgage agreements, it's a common misconception that the formulas for early termination penalties are also alike. In reality, there can be a significant difference in the penalties charged by major banks versus those by most monoline lenders. This can lead to higher costs for borrowers who return their mortgage early with a major bank. This is unique to fixed-rate mortgages only. Penalties to return variable rate mortgages do not differ among lender types.

Requirement for Branch Visit

It's common for major banks to require in-branch visits for mortgage discussions, sometimes even for seemingly minor matters. Many times, it's something that could be easily handled over the phone, yet they suggest an in-person meeting. In an age where technology advancements have streamlined many processes, this requirement to physically visit a branch for mortgage-related discussions can seem outdated. However, if you're dealing with one of the bank's mobile mortgage specialists, then they operate more like brokers, and much of the dealings can be done remotely.

Cross Selling

Since big banks provide a wide range of financial services, they have an extensive array of products to offer. This includes credit cards, insurance, RRSPs, mutual funds, and credit lines, among others. One thing that banks are particularly good at is maximizing their revenue. If they see an opportunity to boost their bottom line, they'll take it. If you hold a mortgage with a major bank, be prepared for them to reach out to you with various product offerings, as cross-selling is a common practice.

Limited Branch Hours

If you're looking to consult with a mortgage specialist at a bank, you are limited by the branch's operating hours. There was a time when banks opened at 10 am and shut their doors at 4 pm, operating only from Monday to Friday. However, banking hours have evolved considerably. Nowadays, banks stay open later and may even operate on weekends, with some branches offering limited services on Sundays.

To better compete with the flexibility offered by mortgage brokers, many banks have introduced mobile mortgage specialists. Despite this advancement, if you choose to visit a branch for a mortgage consultation, you'll be limited to the branch's specific hours of operation.

CREDIT UNIONS

Credit unions share similarities with banks in that they provide a local, branch-based service model and offer a full line of financial products. This includes chequing accounts, RRSPs, credit cards, business loans, and, notably... mortgages. Just like banks, they cater to a range of financial needs under one roof.

Credit unions are non-profit organizations that are frequently located in smaller cities. However, some have expanded significantly, evolving into large chains with branches in major cities too. In terms of sheer numbers, there are more credit unions than banks and monoline lenders combined.

A key distinction with credit unions is their membership-based structure. To access their services, you need to be a member, which often involves a nominal fee – sometimes as little as $1, depending on the credit union.

Credit unions have a local focus and operate exclusively within their home province. There are many who only have a single location and may operate within a specific radius of their branch. They don't extend their services beyond these geographical boundaries.

Some examples of larger and more recognized credit unions are as follows:

- Vancity (BC)
- Coast Capital (BC)
- Servus (Alberta)
- Affinity (Saskatchewan)
- Meridian (Ontario)
- DUCA (Ontario)
- Alterna Savings (Ontario)
- Steinbach (Manitoba)

Advantages to Credit Unions

- Provincially regulated
- Membership
- Additional flexibility
- Branch access

Provincially Regulated

Unlike national financial institutions like banks and monoline lenders, which are federally regulated, credit unions fall under provincial regulation. This means they're not bound by the same set of rules as their federally regulated counterparts, though they often choose to follow similar guidelines.

A notable example is that credit unions are not required to have a borrower pass the stress test for mortgage qualification. This means that you could potentially qualify for a higher loan amount through a credit union. While larger credit unions may still adhere to federal guidelines, smaller ones may have a bit more flexibility in their lending criteria.

Membership

As you are a member, you're given shares, which means you own a small piece of the company. You may also be offered profit sharing or get paid dividends. Don't get too excited about this though. The $10 you paid for membership won't exactly generate enough investment income to send you into early retirement anytime soon.

Membership also gives you a voice, which can involve voting rights on their board of directors, and the right to participate in their annual general meeting. Every credit union can be a little different, so it's best to check with them directly to find out what benefits their membership will offer you.

Additional Flexibility

One area where credit unions excel is in their flexibility when it comes to funding on specialty property. Farms, vacant land, commercial property, off-the-grid properties, or anything that might present a challenge in obtaining financing through banks or monoline lenders. Local credit unions can be king in these situations.

Branch Access

Just as with banks, credit unions have local branches. While they may not be on every street corner as they are with the big banks, they are available, and you can stop in anytime to meet with someone face to face.

DISADVANTAGES TO CREDIT UNIONS

- Geographically restricted
- Membership requirement
- Limited technology
- Limited switch options

Geographically Restricted

Credit unions are more restricted on where they will lend. Often, it's limited to a certain radius around the location of a branch. Even larger credit unions may not lend in every city or town within the province. If you were to move outside a credit union's lending area, then you may not be able to port your mortgage over to the new property and your only option would be to return the mortgage and pay the penalty. If you are moving out of province, then you will definitely have to return it, regardless of which credit union you are dealing with.

Membership Requirement

Yes, I have this listed as an advantage and a disadvantage. It's just one extra step you need to go through for what I see as limited benefits that most people won't take advantage of. I know I wouldn't. For some, it might really mean something to be a member, however, these will be the minority.

Limited Technology

The technological capabilities can vary significantly among credit unions, especially when compared to big banks and well-established monoline lenders. Smaller credit unions might not offer the same level of tech-savvy features. However, this is less likely to be an issue with the larger credit unions, who are often committed to competing directly with major banks.

Having access to an online portal for checking and managing your account can be a convenient feature, but its availability largely depends on the specific credit union you're dealing with. While larger credit unions may provide these digital services, smaller ones might not yet have such facilities in place.

Limited Switch Options

Typically, transferring your mortgage to another lender at the end of your term can be done with minimal or no cost. This is also true for mortgages held with credit unions. However, it's important to note that some lenders may not accept mortgage transfers from them. This means your options could be more limited when it's time to shop around for a better rate at the end of your term.

The good news is that there are lenders known for their competitive mortgage rates and appealing products who are open to accepting such transfers. So, while your choices might be narrower, there still may be excellent opportunities available at the end of your term to find a lender that meets your needs. However, it's possible that you may not be eligible for the absolute lowest rate out there.

MONOLINE LENDERS

Monoline lenders are financial institutions that focus exclusively on mortgages. Hence the name, 'monoline.' While the strict definition adheres to this single-product focus, the term has evolved to broadly encompass any mortgage lender that isn't a bank or credit union.

Once your mortgage is closed, they won't be pitching you an array of additional services. Unlike banks and credit unions, they don't deal in RRSPs, investments, bank accounts, personal loans, or any form of financing outside of real estate. Their expertise is concentrated entirely on providing mortgage products.

Here's a list of some of the more common monoline lenders:

- RFA Mortgages
- First National
- Merix / Lendwise
- MCAP
- MCAN Home Mortgage
- RMG Mortgages
- CMLS Financial
- Radius Financial

It's possible that you might not be familiar with monoline lenders since they typically invest little in advertising. Instead, they largely depend on mortgage brokers to promote their services. This reliance on brokers for visibility means they have lower overhead costs, which often allows them to offer more competitive rates compared to big banks.

Despite their smaller size relative to major banking institutions, monoline lenders are subject to stringent regulation. This ensures that dealing with them carries no additional risk compared to larger banks.

ADVANTAGES TO MONOLINE LENDERS

- Lower rates
- Lower penalties
- Specialists in mortgages only
- Flexible terms and conditions
- No post-closing sales pitches

Lower Rates

In many cases, monoline lenders have lower rates than big banks, specifically on insured and insurable mortgages. Without the need to maintain physical branches and with minimal spending on advertising, monoline lenders operate with significantly lower overhead costs. These savings enable them to pass on the benefits to you in the form of more competitive mortgage rates.

Lower Penalties

If you find yourself in a position where you need to return (break) a fixed rate mortgage early, the penalty with a monoline lender can be considerably less than what can be expected from a big bank. I'll be discussing return penalties in detail in Chapter Ten.

Specialists in Mortgages Only

As already established, monoline lenders specialize exclusively in mortgages, without offering other financial products. This focus allows them to become experts in the mortgage field.

No Post-Closing Sales Pitches

If you've previously held a mortgage with a major bank, you're likely familiar with receiving periodic solicitation calls for additional services like insurance or investments. As monoline lenders solely focus on mortgages, you won't receive these sales calls as they have nothing else to sell you.

DISADVANTAGES TO MONOLINE LENDERS

- No branches
- Lack of familiarity
- Limited product offering
- Strict qualification requirements
- Porting cap

No Branches

Unlike the chartered banks, monoline lenders do not have local branches, so direct face-to-face contact with the lender is not possible.

Lack of Familiarity

I hear it all the time. "Oh, the lender is 'such and such'? Never heard of them." You've never heard of them because, unlike banks, they don't spend millions of dollars on advertising. Someone has to pay for their huge advertising budget... why should it be you? Monoline lenders rely primarily on the mortgage broker network for promotion, as this is where close to 100% of their business comes from.

Strict Qualification Requirements

As monoline lenders insure most of their mortgages on the back end, they are bound by the same constraints associated with insured mortgages. Even if your debt-to-income ratio was paltry 0.001% above the maximum allowable limits, they don't have the power to grant the exception. The ratios would need to be brought in line before the lender can issue the mortgage approval.

Even on uninsurable mortgages, monoline lenders generally rely on sourcing funds from 3rd parties. This means that they need to adhere to guidelines set by their investors, which are equivalent to insurable lending criteria (explained in Chapter Three).

Porting Cap

When porting your mortgage to another property, some monoline lenders will require the purchase price on the new home to be under $1 million. This restriction is due to a change in the insurability of the mortgage. As it falls into a different pricing category, they may be unable to port your mortgage. In that situation, your only option would be to return the mortgage and apply for an entirely new one. I explain porting in detail in Chapter Ten.

Myths About Monoline Lenders

Misinformation can indeed be pervasive, affecting not only mortgages but many facets of modern life. People have a confirmation bias towards information that reinforces their existing beliefs. For instance, a compulsive smoker might overlook a multitude of studies on the dangers of smoking, yet cling to a single story of a daily smoker who lived to be 100. That's the information that confirms what she wants to believe, so that's the information that she's biased towards.

If someone has a strong preference for a major bank, they might exhibit the same cognitive dissonance, readily dismissing anything that challenges their preconceived notion that banks are superior. There are some people that want to deal with a major bank no matter what the cost. I've seen people consciously spend more than $10,000 over a 5-year term, just to have the privilege of giving their business to their bank. Is it any wonder why banks have the largest buildings in every city.

I have seen this time and time again. It's usually due to the belief of a myth, or other misconceptions about non-bank lenders. They imagine a shadowy institution, laden with hidden fees, lingering in the bushes, waiting to snatch their home at the first sign of a missed payment. Or mysteriously disappearing overnight, leaving them with a costly mess.

Nothing could be further from the truth.

Hidden fees?

There are no extra or hidden fees when dealing with a monoline lender over a big bank. There are no additional costs whatsoever.

If you miss a payment?

If you happen to miss a payment, you'll be subject to a late payment charge, which is no different when missing a payment to a bank. They aren't going to take your house. Regardless of the lender, they have no interest in this, nor are they legally eligible to do so even if they wanted to. If you're struggling to make your payments, just communicate this with them and they'll try to work out an arrangement with you.

If the lender goes out of business?

If the monoline lender closes shop, then their mortgage portfolio would get taken over by another lender. Your rate, payment, and terms and conditions will all remain intact. The only noticeable change would be the logo appearing on your mortgage statement.

For example, ING Bank's transformation into Tangerine after Scotiabank stepped in back in August, 2012. For their clients, it was business as usual... just wrapped in Tangerine's vibrant new branding.

More recently, Industrial Alliance announced the shutdown of their mortgage division in late 2019. Their mortgage portfolio was split between MCAP and National Bank. Their clients didn't miss a beat.

Additional restrictions?

Just as with big banks, some monoline lenders may have additional restrictions on certain mortgage products. This is a common aspect of the mortgage industry, not unique to any one type of lender. Whether you choose a monoline, major bank, or credit union, you might encounter specific limitations or conditions depending on the mortgage product you select.

If a lender goes out of business, their mortgage portfolio gets absorbed by another lender. All the same terms and conditions remain intact.

ARE NON-BANK LENDERS SAFE?

Given that the big banks continually bombard us with advertising, they have become familiar fixtures, almost like financial beacons of safety in our minds. As touched upon earlier in this chapter, people have a natural tendency to gravitate towards what's familiar, which explains why so many are drawn to the big banks.

One of the biggest reasons why some people hesitate to consider non-bank lenders is the concern over financial security. This is largely due to a lack of familiarity compared to the well-advertised banking giants. I've already dispelled some myths about monoline lenders, which should help to address some of the concerns held by many. However, some will still have doubts about the safety of placing their mortgage with a non-bank lender.

Some people feel more secure knowing their mortgage is held with a brand name institution. The truth is, their mortgage isn't any more secure with a major bank than it would be with any of the monoline lenders, big or small. As long as you're dealing with a NHA / CMHC approved lender, then you can feel rest assured that they are just as safe as dealing with one of the major banks.

Mortgage Lenders are Heavily Regulated

Institutional mortgage lenders, including major banks, credit unions and monoline lenders are heavily regulated by government agencies. Federally regulated lenders are overseen by The Office of the Superintendent of Financial Institutions (OSFI). Each province has its own regulatory body for credit unions. For example, the Financial Services Regulatory Authority of Ontario (FSRA) or the BC Financial Services Authority (BCFSA).

Still not convinced?

Ask yourself this... what do you think will happen if you go with a lender outside of the major banks? I've tried to address as many of these worries as I can in this book, and I'll do anything I can to give you the reassurance you need. I'm not saying going with a bank is the wrong decision. It's the best decision in many cases, which is why I do a significant amount of business with the big banks. However, there are also many situations were a monoline lender or a credit union might be the better choice.

Small Lenders

The big banks are large, globally recognized institutions. RBC is the largest bank in Canada and the 23rd largest in the world as of 2023. TD is in 2nd place, and right behind

RBC on the global stage at number 24[7]. They are enormous institutions. By comparison, anything else is small.

Many will refer to a non-bank lender as small. While some of them are smaller in size, they are all under the same degree of scrutiny from the regulatory bodies. Also, some of these 'small' lenders are also quite large:

MCAP is Canada's largest independent mortgage finance company with over $150 billion in assets under management.

First National is the second largest monoline with over $133 billion. First National also does the underwriting for TD Mortgage Services and BMO BrokerEdge. If TD and BMO are comfortable using them... maybe you can be too?

NON-BANK LENDER RISK

Spending thousands of dollars more to go with a major bank doesn't make a lot of sense financially. There are ZERO added risks to going with a non-bank lender.

ZERO. Zilch, nada, nothing.

The only real benefit to you is that you can have all your accounts with the same institution and can view them all on the screen together. Not much more.... other than recognizing the logo on your mortgage statement. Sure, you can walk into a branch to discuss your mortgage with someone face to face, but how often do you really do so?

---

7   Source: https://www.spglobal.com/marketintelligence/en/news-insights/research/the-world-s-100-largest-banks-2023

CHAPTER SIX HIGHLIGHTS

- An 'A' lender is any lender who caters to applicants with qualifying income and credit.

- A 'B' lender deals with applicants who would not qualify through an A lender.

- Three main types of 'A' lenders are banks, monoline lenders and credit unions.

- Common myths about non-bank lenders are that they have hidden fees and additional restrictions. Nothing could be further from the truth.

- There is zero risk associated with getting your mortgage through a non-bank lender.

- Some of the smaller lenders are quite large and have billions of dollars in assets under administration.

- More important than your choice of lender is the person you choose to arrange your mortgage for you.

There is certainly nothing wrong with going with a bank and certainly nothing wrong with going with a non-bank lender. Banks have their place and serve their purpose, as do non-bank lenders.

Sometimes it makes more sense to go with a bank, while other times, a non-bank lender would be the better course of action. One thing is for sure, if it were not for these non-bank lenders, the big banks would have a monopoly and free reign to set the rates wherever they choose. Fortunately, there are options.

Now that we have a clear idea on the type of lending institutions out there, it's time to take a closer look at who is going to handle your mortgage for you.

7

CHOOSING A MORTGAGE PROFESSIONAL

Look for your choices, pick the best one, then go with it"
~Pat Riley, president of the Miami Heat NBA franchise.

Your choice of mortgage professional is one of the most important decisions you'll need to make. You can have a great experience dealing with your mortgage or you can have an absolute nightmare. This can largely depend on the capabilities, competence, and service level of the professional you choose to manage the process.

I've detailed the pros and cons of dealing with different types of institutions in the last chapter, so here I'll be focusing more on the individual you choose to arrange your mortgage.

When it comes to securing a mortgage, you have two options. One is to work directly with your bank, while the other is to work with a mortgage broker.

WHAT IS A MORTGAGE BROKER?

The definition of a broker is one who brings the borrower and lender together. It's a common misconception that anyone dealing with mortgages is a mortgage broker. Nothing could be further from the truth. There is a big difference between a mortgage broker and a mortgage specialist working for a bank. A broker doesn't represent any one specific financial institution. Instead, he represents many. As the specialist at the bank works for a lender, she is not a broker as she isn't able to offer you mortgage products from any other institution other than her own. When shopping with a broker, you're shopping many different institutions at one time, and there lies the difference.

Pros to Dealing with a Broker

- More options
- Lower rates
- Unbiased advice
- Convenience
- Free service
- Ease of access
- Licensed

More Options

With access to a multitude of mortgage lenders, brokers are well-equipped to offer their clients a wider range of options. This enables them to provide solutions catering to a diverse range of financial circumstances. This can mean lower rates, more flexible products, or even the difference between your application being approved or declined. It also gives you the ability to shop multiple lenders with just a single application and credit check, which can save you a considerable amount of time and effort. Brokers will often have options you'd never even think of, for all different types of financial situations.

Lower Rates

As mortgage brokers deal with a broad range of mortgage lenders, they are well-informed about where to find the best deals. If you ask your bank for their lowest rate, they can only inform you on what they have available. But a broker? They can compare rates from Scotia, TD, BMO, First National, MCAP, National Bank, and many others... all in one shot. If a specific lender has a lower rate, a mortgage broker will generally know about it. This makes them a convenient, one stop solution for anyone looking to secure the lowest mortgage rates, without the hassle of shopping around individually with each lender. It can be a huge time saver for those leading busy lifestyles.

If you're looking for the lowest mortgage rate and you haven't reached out to a broker, then there is a very good chance that there are lower rates available. Potentially, much lower. While the lowest mortgage rates are not always through brokers, often they are.

Unbiased Advice

When you work directly with a bank, their focus is solely on their own products and services. They aren't in a position to inform you about potentially better-suited options available through other lenders. In contrast, mortgage brokers have the advantage of working with major banks, monoline lenders, and credit unions. This broad exposure allows them to provide detailed insights into each lender, helping you understand the unique benefits of one over another. For the most part, it doesn't matter to the broker which lender they put you with.

It's important to note that while brokers can speak to you about the differences between a variety of different lenders, it doesn't guarantee that you're getting the right advice. As I've previously mentioned, there are both good and bad professionals in any field, and the mortgage industry is no exception. Some mortgage products can offer higher commissions, potentially influencing certain brokers to recommend them over others that might be more suitable for you. This can happen with bank representatives as well, as they may be incentivized to promote specific products that are more profitable for the bank.

Always evaluate the reasoning for why the broker may be suggesting a specific product over another and then make your own decision from there. If you notice that a broker is strongly pushing a particular option, then they might have an incentive for doing so. A quality broker will present your options, outline the differences, and then let you decide which option you think would be best suited to you. Sure, they can provide their opinion, or they may even reiterate certain points to ensure you fully understand the differences. But pushiness can be an indication that the broker may not be acting in your best interest.

Convenience

The process can be managed over the phone and/or by email, allowing you to get your mortgage arranged without ever needing to step out of your home. Perfect for anyone with a busy lifestyle or work schedule. If you still prefer a face-to-face meeting, this can often be done in the broker's office or sometimes even within the comfort of your own home.

Free Service

For qualified borrowers, using a mortgage broker doesn't cost any more than it would to get a mortgage directly through your bank. In other words, it's free. Brokers get paid a finder's fee from the lender, so it's a cost that you don't need to cover.

In situations where you don't qualify for financing through traditional sources, a broker may have to look at alternative options to get you approved. If the broker can find a solution acceptable to you, then there may be additional fees involved, particularly if you are dealing with private mortgages. I'll be talking more about alternative financing and fees in Chapter Twelve.

Ease of Access

Mortgage brokers are not tied to any set schedule and have no set hours. It's commonplace for them to be working evenings, weekends, and even holidays. It's not uncommon for me to be returning emails on Christmas or New Year's Day.

Banks have now introduced mobile sales forces as well, so in some cases, this ease of access may also be available through them.

Licensed

Unlike mortgage specialists working for banks, mortgage brokers have licensing requirements that need to be met. In the province of Ontario for example, there are two types of licenses: Mortgage agent and mortgage broker. Both of which have to re-license every two years. The mortgage agent works directly for the mortgage broker. If someone wants to become a broker, they have to become a mortgage agent first.

They must hold their agent license for a minimum of two years before they can become a broker, which requires twice as much training.

Does that mean you should only look at brokers because they have more training?

Definitely not!

There are some fantastic mortgage agents out there. I'll be talking more about how to select the right person later in this chapter.

The designations mentioned apply to Ontario only, and other provinces may have similar designations. BC for example has the mortgage broker and then the sub-broker (mortgage agent). While the designations are different, the concept is similar.

Cons to Dealing with a Broker

- No access to certain lenders
- Limited to no product availability other than mortgages
- No other point of contact
- Inconvenient location

No Access to Certain Lenders

While mortgage brokers deal with a wide range of lenders, there are some lenders who are not accessible to them. For example, CIBC and RBC are two lenders who do not deal directly with mortgage brokers. They have not implemented channels to accept the large amount of business that the mortgage broker industry can bring to them. To access these lenders, you would need to contact them directly.

Limited to No Product Availability Other Than Mortgages

If you already have a mortgage and are looking to add a HELOC, for example, a broker has very limited, if any options. In this case, you may need to deal with the lender directly. Other products that can't be obtained through brokers would be any type of personal or business loan, personal line of credit, auto financing, etc.

No Other Point of Contact

In many cases, if the broker doesn't get back to you right away, or stops returning your calls for any reason, you may have difficulty getting someone else on the phone. Always make sure you know which brokerage they are working for and that you have their contact information as well. Many brokers work out of their homes and only give out their personal contact info. While each broker legally has to belong to a brokerage, it may be hard to find someone else who has access to your file. Personally, I would never leave a client of mine without another point of contact while going on vacation. Not to mention, I'm always accessible if there is an issue. Most quality mortgage brokers would be. I'm also fortunate to have a talented team of mortgage professionals on my staff.

Always make sure to ask if there is another point of contact, should your broker become unavailable for any reason.

Inconvenient Location

Your broker may not be located as close to you as the bank, or they may not have a brick-and-mortar office at all. Many, if not most mortgage transactions can be done completely by phone, email, and through online portals, so the need to meet in person is becoming less of an issue for many.

THE BANK MORTGAGE SPECIALIST

A bank mortgage specialist is not a broker as they work specifically for one lender. On the other hand, a broker works independently from the lender and is not tied to any specific institution, as already discussed.

There is also a difference between dealing with your bank and dealing with a mortgage specialist at the bank. A mortgage specialist is exactly as the name implies. A specialist in mortgages. However, it's not uncommon for banks to have other staff selling mortgages as well.

Someone recently told me they were dealing with the branch manager on their mortgage, simply because she was their point of contact at that branch for years. A branch manager isn't necessarily a mortgage specialist. In fact, they may not be a mortgage expert at all. While they may be knowledgeable about various banking services, their proficiency with the nuances of mortgage products could be limited when compared to a dedicated mortgage specialist.

The best way to ensure you're getting expert advice is by actively asking questions. This helps confirm that the person you're dealing with truly understands the intricacies of mortgages. Inquiring about their experience, the range of products they handle, and specific scenarios can give you a clearer picture of their expertise. There are some highly skilled mortgage specialists out there. Just make sure you're dealing with one as it will give you the confidence that your mortgage will be handled proficiently, and your questions will be accurately addressed.

There are many advising on mortgages who act more as order takers, rather than as knowledgeable advisors. They may have a basic understanding of mortgage products but lack the depth of expertise required to provide comprehensive, tailored advice. Some may assume that they are getting quality advice from a bank representative, simply because they're associated with the bank.

I'll be talking more about the questions you should be asking later in this chapter.

Pros to Dealing with a Bank Mortgage Specialist

- Face to face contact
- Convenience
- Access to additional staff
- Access to niche products

Face-to-Face Contact

While this can be done with your broker as well, it's more common when dealing directly with your bank. This could also be looked at as a con if they require you to set up a meeting to go over documents. With a broker or mobile mortgage specialist, everything can be done by phone, email, or through an online portal.

Convenience

If you prefer to meet face-to-face, there's likely a branch near your home or workplace. With branches across Canada, you have the advantage of meeting with someone to discuss your mortgage needs, regardless of where you are in the country.

Access to Additional Staff

If you have a complaint about the bank agent, there is always a manager you can speak with. If your contact suddenly goes on vacation while your mortgage is in progress, there may be others who can take over your file. But never make this assumption and always ask. I've seen bank mortgage specialists go on vacation, leaving their client hanging high and dry until their return. Always ask about alternative contacts who can assist in their absence, if needed. Any quality mortgage professional serious about their career would ensure their files are covered while on vacation. But as the majority of mortgage brokers work independently, it may be easier to find someone else to review your file when dealing with a bank.

Access to Niche Products

While four out of the big six banks have channels for servicing business originated by mortgage brokers, they may not offer their full product line outside of their branches. They may have certain specialized, or niche products tailored for specific circumstances that may only be accessible when dealing with the bank directly. While these situations are relatively rare, they do emerge at times. In these situations, a quality mortgage broker would acknowledge this and direct you to work with the branch directly if they feel it would be your most suitable option.

CONS TO DEALING WITH A BANK MORTGAGE SPECIALIST

- Limited availability
- Limited products
- Unlicensed
- Limited alternatives

Limited Availability

When engaging with a mortgage specialist at a bank, their availability is confined to the branch's operating hours and, more specifically, to their own working schedule within those hours. This can be limiting, especially if you have urgent questions or concerns about your mortgage. In such cases, you might find yourself having to wait until the specialist is back at work before you can get the answers or assistance you need.

To address this limitation, as previously mentioned, some banks have introduced mobile mortgage specialists who work on a 100% commission basis. These specialists are comparable to brokers in terms of flexibility. They often make themselves available after standard business hours and during weekends. Their commission-based structure incentivizes them to be more accommodating to your schedule, ensuring they are accessible when you need them the most.

Limited Products

A mortgage specialist employed by a bank is limited to offering products from their specific institution only. If a more suitable option is available from another lender, such as a lower interest rate or a product with more favorable terms and conditions, they wouldn't be able to offer it. Even if they're aware of better alternatives, I wouldn't expect them to tell you considering that it wouldn't align with the interests of their employer, the bank. Their primary role is to promote and sell products offered by the bank they represent, not to direct you to their competitors.

Unlicensed

Unlike mortgage brokers, bank mortgage specialists are not subject to specific licensing requirements. Consequently, there's no standardized way to gauge the extent or nature of their training. If you happen to work with a competent specialist, then their lack of a formal license wouldn't be reason for concern. But given that they may not have any formal mortgage training at all, it's important to ask thorough questions to assess their expertise and suitability for your needs.

It's important to note that holding a license is not an automatic indicator of competence. Just as with bank specialists, it's equally important to engage in a thorough questioning process with brokers. The license confirms a foundational level of knowledge and compliance with regulatory requirements, but is not an indication of the agent's expertise, experience, or moral standards.

Limited Alternatives

If you face challenges in qualifying for a mortgage due to factors like credit history, income level, or other influential criteria, a bank typically has limited alternatives to offer... if any at all. They generally don't have the flexibility to explore or offer solutions from other lenders that might better suit your unique financial situation. If you're in this position, they may not even point you in the right direction. It's common for banks to have policies prohibiting their mortgage specialists from referring you to an external mortgage professional who may be able to help you. The underlying implication of these policies is essentially... if they can't help you, then that's your problem, not theirs.

CHOOSING THE RIGHT MORTGAGE PROFESSIONAL

Now that you understand the pros and cons of dealing with each type of mortgage professional, the next step is to decide who you want to work with. It's a good idea to explore both avenues: visit a bank and consult with a mortgage broker. This will give you a firsthand sense of what each can offer you.

Regardless of whether you choose to work directly with your bank or with a broker, the most important factor is that you're comfortable with them. Base your decision on your trust and confidence in their ability, rather than simply opting for a familiar brand or logo on a business card.

Don't necessarily use the first person you speak with. Talk to multiple banks and brokers to feel them out. Remember, your mortgage is a substantial financial undertaking. The professional you choose should instill a sense of security and ensure that you're well-informed throughout the process. They should be not only knowledgeable, but also take the time to understand your needs. They should be willing to thoroughly discuss your situation, and tailor your options based on your specific financial goals.

When choosing a mortgage professional, assess their responsiveness and dependability. If you're struggling to have your calls or emails returned, or if you find it challenging to get answers to simple questions, you might need to reconsider if they are the best fit for managing your mortgage. Additionally, be wary of professionals who promise a certain rate, pending management approval, only to come back with a higher rate after an unreasonably long wait. With major banks, your file must pass through a pricing department before the specialist can confirm your rate. This process generally takes one to two days, however, it can take up to a week during excessively busy times. But if you're waiting weeks to get confirmation of rate, then you may want to raise an eyebrow as to why it's taking so long. This is a potential red flag and happens all too often.

Jim and Mary, thrilled about buying their first home, reach out to a broker after spotting an exceptionally low rate online. As this was the lowest rate they found, they decide to apply. They follow up with the broker to find out the status of their application, but their calls are not returned. A week later, they finally manage to speak with someone and are informed that their application was just submitted to the lender that morning and they are awaiting a response.

As days pass, their follow-up emails are largely ignored, and the few responses they receive are unclear and noncommittal. Another week elapses before they receive the mortgage commitment, which is dated three days earlier than when they received it. Despite the approval being granted, Jim and Mary were left uninformed. They were eventually told that the only requirements were a job letter and paystub. However, after another two weeks, the broker requested bank statements, which they promptly provided.

The closing date is now just two weeks away. Jim and Mary struggle to reach anyone for another week. Just three days before the scheduled closing, the broker finally contacts them, explaining her absence due to a vacation, and informs them that additional documents are still needed to finalize the deal.

Don't you think you deserve better treatment than this?

Never assume you're in good hands just because you're dealing with your bank.

The same thing can also be said about dealing with a licensed broker.

On either side, the role of mortgage professional unfortunately has a relatively low entry barrier of entry. For this reason, it's not uncommon to come across individuals who may lack the necessary competence yet label themselves as 'mortgage specialists.' They may be more focused on their own financial gain rather than prioritizing your needs. They may be guiding you towards products that benefit them, rather than what's most suitable for you. It's a scenario that's prevalent among both banks and brokers, outlining the importance of carefully selecting a mortgage professional. One who not only has the knowledge and skills... but who genuinely has your best interests in mind.

Make sure you are dealing with a professional who is competent and can get your mortgage closed with as little stress as possible.

Several years ago, I had a client cancel their application with me in favour of their bank, despite the rate being higher. They were told by their bank's mortgage specialist that the documentation I was requesting wasn't necessary.

I tried to explain that the requirement for these documents was standard industry practice and that the bank would eventually request them. But the clients didn't listen to me and continued to work with their bank, who was telling them what they wanted to hear. That they didn't need them.

A few weeks later, I received a call from their Realtor who had referred them to me. Just as I had advised, their bank eventually asked them for all the same documents... the day before closing. This last-minute scramble not only caused significant stress and aggravation for the clients, but their home purchase ended up closing late.

I cannot stress enough the importance of choosing the right person to handle your mortgage for you. There is a lot of incompetence in this industry, which applies to both the bank and the broker side. I can't put enough emphasis on the importance of dealing with an experienced professional. You may be inclined to put the mortgage rate first, and in many cases, you'll be fine, but there are also many who will regret the decision. Some may not realize the importance of choosing the right person until they are put into a challenging situation. Many mortgage specialists are not much more than order takers. Their experience should extend beyond just collecting applications and mechanically advancing them through the system. Unfortunately, some operate almost robotically, without the requisite experience or training to advise clients adequately and accurately.

Your mortgage is a huge financial decision and there is a lot of money riding on it. The importance of choosing the right person to handle your mortgage cannot be overstated.

Incompetence is common in this industry and can be experienced equally on both the bank and broker side.

By choosing the wrong person to handle your mortgage for you, you could be putting your deposit at risk. Not to mention your emotional sanity! It doesn't matter if you're dealing with a licensed mortgage agent or with someone who has a nice big shiny bank logo on their business card. Before entrusting someone with your mortgage needs, it's essential to thoroughly vet their expertise and experience. Don't hesitate to ask questions or conduct your own research on the individual. For all you know, they might be new to the mortgage industry. Platforms like LinkedIn can be invaluable in assessing their professional background and time in the field.

So how do you determine you are in good hands?

Simple. Make sure you ask a lot of questions to ensure you feel comfortable with the individual before choosing them to arrange your mortgage for you.

11 QUESTIONS TO ASK WHEN SELECTING A MORTGAGE PROFESSIONAL

1. HOW MUCH EXPERIENCE DO YOU HAVE?

Understanding how long someone has worked in the mortgage industry is indeed valuable, but it shouldn't be the sole measure of their expertise. For instance, I've seen mortgage agents with only six months of experience demonstrate high proficiency and competence. Conversely, I have encountered individuals with 20 years in the field who lack a fundamental understanding of key aspects of their job. This variation emphasizes the importance of not just considering the length of time someone has been in the industry, but also assessing their actual knowledge, efficiency and overall competence.

While asking about their industry tenure is important, you'll also want to ask how many mortgages they've closed, particularly in the past year. This helps ensure their experience is both current and relevant, as someone might have years of experience but limited recent activity.

If someone is newer in the industry, ask if they have a mentor or team that they work closely with. It's crucial to ensure they have access to a knowledgeable and experienced go-to person for situations that may be beyond their current expertise. Additionally, gauge their responsiveness: if they encounter a question they can't immediately answer, find out how they plan to obtain the necessary information and how long it might take for them to get back to you with a response. This approach will give you a clearer picture of their resourcefulness and commitment to providing thorough, reliable service.

2. DO YOU DO THIS FULL OR PART TIME?

I recommend avoiding part-time mortgage agents or those who divide their attention between mortgages and unrelated fields. Look for a dedicated specialist who is fully committed to managing your mortgage. You need someone whose focus is entirely on your needs, not distracted by other income sources. It's unlikely that a part-timer would have that much experience, and their divided attention can lead to difficulties in communication. Especially if they are preoccupied with their full-time job.

3. Do you have any references or testimonials?

It's reassuring to know that they have a proven track record of satisfied clients. Positive feedback from past clients can be a strong indicator of their capability and reliability. If they've consistently delivered excellent service in the past, then there is a better chance that they will do a great job for you as well.

4. What kind of education or licensing do you have?

Some professionals will have more education or training than others. As mentioned previously, brokers are licensed and bank specialists are typically not. Not being licensed isn't what I would call a deal breaker, but you definitely want to get a feel for what kind of training that person has been provided with. Chances are if they have been specializing in mortgages for years, then they should have a pretty good grasp on things. Just never make that assumption without feeling them out first.

5. How easy are you to get a hold of? How quickly do you return calls or emails?

There are going to be times when you have pressing questions or concerns, and you'll want them answered quickly. I've had people tell me on multiple occasions that they've been leaving messages for their mortgage broker or bank mortgage specialist for days or even weeks without a response. Not exactly what I would call professional or courteous service. I can't imagine how any 'professional' can even go three hours without responding to a question, let alone days.

6. What hours are you available?

It can be helpful to know that the person you are dealing with can be flexible and is willing to work with YOUR schedule, not theirs. If you're typically not available or hard to reach during the day, then you might want to consider using someone who is available at times convenient to you. Having questions answered promptly will give you a significantly better experience. It's not fun when you have a concern and your mortgage professional is unreachable.

7. How do you get most of your business?

Asking a mortgage professional about the source of their business can be revealing. Ideally, a significant portion of their clientele should come from referrals and repeat customers. This indicates that their past clients were satisfied enough with the service provided to recommend them to friends and family. A lack of referrals might suggest that the professional's service quality isn't meeting clients' expectations. Knowing that a professional's business thrives on the strength of their reputation can give you confidence in their ability to deliver quality service.

8. HOW ARE FIXED MORTGAGE RATES DETERMINED?

This is simply a question to gauge their competence level and is something that any quality mortgage professional will know right away. If they can't answer this, or if they have to 'get back to you', then they may not have the experience you are looking for. The answer is bond yields (another acceptable answer is swap rates).

9. DO YOU DO ANYTHING ELSE FOR THE BRANCH OTHER THAN MORTGAGES?

This question is for bank branch staff only and does not apply to mortgage brokers. The goal here is to determine whether you are dealing with a dedicated mortgage specialist. If they tell you that they also sell investments, then they aren't exclusively focused on mortgages. Make sure you are dealing with someone who specializes in mortgages and mortgages only.

10. WHAT HAVE YOU DONE WITH YOUR OWN MORTGAGE, AND WHY?

This can say a lot about the person you are dealing with as it can provide insight into their personal preferences and strategies for mortgage management. For example, if they're recommending a 10-year fixed rate mortgage, but have gone with a 2 year, or variable rate mortgage for themselves, then you may question why they are recommending a different approach for you. While they may have valid personal reasons for their choice, asking this question might catch them off guard. This could lead you to valuable insight about their recommendations for you and their underlying rationale. It can help you to gauge their honesty and suitability of their advice in your specific context.

11. How many different lenders do you deal with?

This question is for brokers only. It's common for brokers to advertise that they have access to over 50 different lenders. While their brokerage may have access to numerous lenders, it's nearly impossible for an individual broker to actively engage with so many. Anything over 10 would be tough to maintain as it can be a challenge to keep track of that many lenders and their products. Seven or eight is a more realistic number. While someone telling you they have access to over 50 lenders shouldn't necessarily eliminate them as an option, a better question to ask would be this:

How many lenders have you dealt with in the past year?

This is a very important question. There are some brokers who may channel all their business through only one lender. I refer to these individuals as 'non-brokers.' Even though they hold a broker's license and operate within the broker sector, they aren't doing the job of a mortgage broker considering that they are only dealing with one lender.

One of the primary advantages of working with a broker is they have access to multiple lenders, offering a range of mortgage products to suit different needs. By limiting their offerings to a single lender, these 'non-brokers' effectively eliminate this key benefit, depriving clients of the diverse choices that a broker should be offering.

Why would a broker choose to deal with only one lender?

There can be a number of reasons, but it's often related to incentives. Some lenders may offer points or additional commission to brokers once they reach a certain volume of business. This arrangement can motivate brokers to funnel all their clients through that one lender. However, such a practice is a red flag; it suggests that the broker may not be exploring the full range of options available in the market to find the best fit for their clients. Instead, their focus might be more on maximizing their own benefits rather than prioritizing the client's needs and interests. When a broker's recommendations are heavily skewed towards a single lender, it raises questions about whether they are truly acting in the best interests of their clients.

While it may be true that a broker may have access to 50 different lenders, it doesn't mean that they are doing business with all of them. To press a bit further, you can ask which lender they usually deal with and what percentage of their business is directed to them. If you find that a substantial portion of their business is concentrated with one lender, then you may want to ask why. There may be valid reasons. For example, some lenders might be exceptionally competitive in a specific mortgage category. If the bulk of the broker's business is within that category, then it would naturally lead to a higher volume of business being directed to that lender.

THE WRONG CHOICE CAN BE COSTLY

Having been in the mortgage business since 2007, I've dealt with many clients who have not only received horrible service, but horrible advice as well.

I once took a call from someone who had purchased a new home for $1.2 million. As the real estate market was hot, he had to put in a firm, condition free offer if he was to even have a chance of it being accepted. His credit and income were solid. His mortgage agent advised him that he easily qualified for the new purchase and that it was safe for him to put in a firm offer.

But there was one major problem.

The agent never asked him about his down payment, which was only 10%. As a minimum of 20% is required to purchase a property for over $1 million, his home purchase journey had just come to a dead stop. While his credit and income easily qualified him for the new purchase, his down payment did not. He had received bad advice from an inexperienced mortgage agent and was now in a tough position. As there was no availability of additional funds to make up the difference, there was no way he could complete this purchase and was forced to back out of the deal.

With down payments of 20% or greater, there are often alternative options. But with less than 20%, these options do not exist. The rules are set by CMHC… and there is no way around them.

THE MORTGAGE EXPERIENCE

Given that mortgages have so many moving parts, there is a lot that can go wrong. Issues can pop up at any time during the mortgage process and happen more often than you might think. At times, they can even arise a few days before closing, or even on the closing date itself. As you have so much money riding on your new home purchase, the mortgage arrangement process can get stressful at times; especially if there are complications along the way. This can lead to new levels of stress at a time when you should be excited about your new home. If you're dealing with a non-responsive mortgage professional, then you could be left in a very bad position.

Your mortgage professional should be easy to reach if you have any concerns, or if any complications arise. They can also give you the information you need along the way, to ensure everything runs smoothly. They should also have the experience and competence to address complications immediately and know what solutions to offer.

You can have a great experience with the process or it can be an absolute nightmare... and there is no guarantee your new home purchase will even close.

Having been in this business since 2007, I've heard my share of horror stories. If you read the introduction to this book, you heard my story about the bad advice I was given from one of the big banks prior to coming into this business. In fact, this was the entire reason why I entered the business to begin with. Ever since, the Paul Meredith Team's primary objective has been to give our clients a better experience than what can be found anywhere else.

Or you could just choose the person with the lowest rate and hope that everything will be okay. That will likely be us anyway, so why not have the best of both worlds?

CHAPTER SEVEN HIGHLIGHTS

- The person you choose to handle your mortgage can be more important than your choice of lender.

- When choosing a mortgage professional, there are two options: Dealing with the bank directly or dealing with a mortgage broker.

- A broker is one who brings the borrower and lender together and does not work for any one specific lender. Therefore, the mortgage specialist at your bank is not a mortgage broker.

- Talk to multiple banks and brokers and then go with the one you feel most comfortable with.

- Incompetence is something that is common in this industry and can be experienced equally on both the bank and broker side.

- Ask a lot of questions to ensure you're dealing with a knowledgeable and confident professional.

- One of the biggest mistakes you can make is choosing someone to work with based on rate alone.

The biggest challenge for an incompetent mortgage professional is a knowledgeable client. Arming yourself with knowledge will keep the mortgage professional on her toes, empowering you to make more discerning choices. It also enables you to evaluate their competence and suitability more effectively.

It really is amazing just how little some so-called 'professionals' in this industry actually know. On both the bank and the broker side. If you know more than they do... then why would you choose them to handle your mortgage for you?

Arm yourself with knowledge... and then shop with confidence.

8

THE MORTGAGE QUALIFICATION PROCESS

"Prepare yourself in every way you can by increasing your knowledge and adding to your experience, so that you can make the most of opportunity when it occurs."
~Mario Andretti

Whether you're a first-time homebuyer, or a seasoned home buying pro, purchasing a new home can be an exciting time. But before heading out on the hunt for your new dream home, you'll want to determine your borrowing power. There are some people who automatically assume they will qualify for the mortgage they need. Never make this assumption and always visit a mortgage professional first to get pre-approved.

I vividly remember a phone conversation I had with someone who was shopping around trying to find the lowest rate. He had just purchased a new home for $500,000. When discussing his qualifying eligibility, he advised that he made $45,000 per year. His wife was a homemaker, fully committed to taking care of their two small children full time. She had no plans to return to the workforce. Their down payment was only 5%, with no possibility of increasing it further. Knowing immediately that they would not come close to qualifying for the purchase, I asked if their offer was conditional on financing. He told me that it was, however, he had just waived it the day before. I asked him if he took the time to get preapproved or if he had checked with a mortgage professional before waiving the condition. Of course he hadn't.

The truth is, they would only qualify for a mortgage of $200,000 at best. He was looking for the lowest rate, when he should have been more concerned with just getting approved. I compassionately explained to him that they unfortunately wouldn't be able to qualify for the purchase. I was already quite surprised that someone would put themselves into this situation, but it was what he said next that was most shocking:

"Oh, because we also purchased a new construction home for $600,000 that is expected to close next spring. Do you think we'll have problems qualifying for that one as well?" Ummm... yeah.

Now, you would think that's where it ended right? Nope. He then starts asking me about the lowest rates once again. It does not matter who has the lowest rate if you don't qualify for the mortgage to begin with. And what was he thinking? The carrying costs for the property would have been greater than his after-tax earnings. Let alone, the carrying costs on the $600,000 property closing the following year.

I really wish I could tell you that I made up this story. But this actually happened, and no part of it was embellished for dramatic effect.

Applying for a mortgage is not like walking into a Tim Horton's and ordering a sandwich. But there are some who seem to believe that it is.

Qualifying for a mortgage is a process, and not everyone will qualify for the amount they are looking for. Even if you think you can comfortably carry the payments, the decision is up to the lender. This is why it's so important to go through the preapproval process before you start shopping for a new home... let alone, pulling the trigger on one.

HOW MORTGAGES ARE QUALIFIED

There are four key components that are considered when determining how much you'll qualify for.

- Down payment
- Credit
- Income
- Debt

Each of these components can be complex in their own way, so let's take a closer look at them in detail so you'll have a solid understanding of each one.

DOWN PAYMENT

As discussed in Chapter One, having a down payment of 20% or more will save you from having to pay mortgage default insurance (CMHC). It will also allow you to extend your amortization to 30 years. This will lower your mortgage payments, allowing you to qualify for a higher mortgage amount.

When asking about the down payment source, I've had some people challenge it by saying: "What's it to the lender? Why do they care where the money is coming from?" I remember speaking with a potential client where the conversation went something like this:

Paul: Please send us your bank statements covering the past 90 days.

Client: It's okay, the money is there.

Paul: Great, please send over the statements to confirm.

Client: I'm telling you the money is there, so we're good.

Paul: I completely understand that the money is there. I'm not questioning that. But a condition of your approval will be confirmation of down payment, which is why the bank statements will be required.

Client: You ARE questioning it! I'm not sure why you think I'm making this up. I'm telling you I have the money and that's all that should matter!

While the client may have had the money, simply telling us that 'it's there' will not fly with any lender. They are not simply going to take your word on it. Needless to say, this interaction didn't lead to a mortgage approval.

The source of your down payment is taken very seriously by all institutional mortgage lenders, including banks, credit unions, and monolines. This is because they must be in compliance with anti-money laundering legislation. More specifically, the Proceeds of Crime (Money Laundering) and Terrorist Financing Act. This is why all mortgage lenders are quite stringent when it comes to documentation to support your down payment. 100% of the down payment and closing costs need to be accounted for and documented. Should the lender be audited, they could face severe consequences if they didn't have adequate support for the down payment in your file.

Proving the source of down payment can be one of the biggest areas of frustration for home buyers. Usually when there are multiple accounts with money moving around, and deposits coming in from various sources. The more money moving around, the more complex it can be. By having a better understanding of what the lender is looking for, you can reduce the number of additional document requests. This can help the process to flow seamlessly, which eliminates frustration, giving you a better overall experience.

Acceptable forms of down payment include:

- Chequing / savings accounts
- RRSP / TFSA
- Gifts from immediate family (parents, grandparents or siblings)
- Proceeds from recently sold property
- Secured line of credit
- Credit cards or unsecured lines of credit (in some cases only).

Unacceptable forms of down payment include:

- Cash 'under the mattress'
- Gifts from friends or extended family
- Loans from friends or family (immediate or not)
- Bank loans
- Any money that can't be traced or explained (typically any amount over $1,000)

CHEQUING / SAVINGS / INVESTMENT ACCOUNTS

To support the down payment drawn from these accounts, lenders will require statements spanning the last 90 days from each relevant account. These statements are necessary to demonstrate the natural accumulation of the funds. Be prepared to explain any large deposits reflected in these statements, except for regular payroll deposits.

If a deposit lacks a satisfactory explanation or if you're unable to provide acceptable documentation to support it, then the lender will not consider those funds as part of your down payment. It is crucial for all significant deposits to be verifiable and compliant with the lender's criteria to be accepted.

Supporting documentation will be required. For example, if your statements indicate a $20,000 deposit from the sale of your shoe collection, make sure you have a bill of sale. A lender may also ask for a screenshot of the ad to provide additional support. While this scenario may seem unusual, it's a real life example from my own experience with a client.

It's quite typical for people to move funds between accounts. Even if you've consolidated all your funds into a single account, lenders will still require 90 days of statements from the other accounts involved prior to the transfers. This traces the origin of the funds and confirms that there are no undisclosed deposits not yet accounted for.

For instance, if a $5,000 transfer appears on a statement, the lender will then request a 90-day transaction history from the originating account to validate the source of those funds. Similarly, if the statements for the new account show an additional transfer, say $10,000, the lender would require a 90-day history for that account too. This process continues until the lender can clearly see the paper trail supporting your full down payment and closing costs.

This is where the homebuyer's frustration can begin.

"Why does the lender need so much from me? They tell me that they only need one more statement and then continue to ask for more!"

There is no doubt that this can be frustrating. But until your down payment is fully accounted for and documented, the requests will unfortunately continue. The lender has no choice... regardless of who they are.

By having a better understanding of what lenders are looking for, you can be better prepared to eliminate any additional requests from the beginning. By ensuring that the full down payment is supported with the statements provided, you should be able to get the down payment condition satisfied in a single shot. This alone can eliminate additional stress and make the mortgage arrangement process all that much more enjoyable.

RRSP / TFSA

If your down payment consists of funds held in registered accounts such as your RRSP or TFSA, then the same rules apply. A 90 day history of statements will be required, along with support of any deposits into these accounts. Funds from registered accounts should be withdrawn and deposited into your chequing account no later than 10 business days before your closing date. The lender will require the registered account statement confirming the withdrawal, along with the chequing account statement they were deposited into. As it can take several business days for transfers from registered sources to appear in your chequing account, I would recommend initiating the transfer no later than 15 business days before the closing of the new home purchase.

Account Ownership - Bank statements obtained from online banking portals usually provide all the necessary details that lenders require—except, quite often, they do not include the account holder's name. It might seem obvious, but lenders must verify that the bank statements provided actually belong to the applicant. Since statements from online banking might not include your name, they could, from the lender's perspective, belong to anybody. Typically, these statements will feature the account number, which becomes crucial for identification. Most online banking platforms offer a summary page that lists all your accounts, displaying your name alongside the account numbers. This summary page enables the lender to match the account number from the detailed, albeit nameless, statements to the account holder's name on the summary. This step provides the lender with the necessary assurance that the bank statements do indeed belong to you.

Smaller Deposits - Deposits below $1,000 are typically not scrutinized closely by lenders, but they may still inquire about them, particularly if there's a pattern of frequent, smaller deposits. For example, if your statements showed a $300 deposit every day for 30 days, this would be considered unusual activity. Although each deposit is under $1,000, the cumulative total is $9,000, which would trigger questions about the source.

GIFTS

One of the most common sources of down payment for first-time homebuyers is money given to them by relatives. Gifts are generally accepted from immediate family members only. Parents, grandparents, or siblings. Gifts from cousins, aunts, uncles, boyfriends, girlfriends and friends are generally not considered.

"But my aunt raised me and is like my mother!"

In certain situations, exceptions can be made, however, these would be accepted on a case-by-case basis. Take Emily for example. She had just received a generous gift from her aunt… the woman who raised her and whom she regards as her mother. While her gift doesn't come from what would typically be considered an immediate family member, it's still filled with the same love and support. Even the mortgage industry can be compassionate at times, and the human element still holds weight.

The donor will need to fill out a simple gift form (also referred to as a gift letter), stating that the funds are a gift and do not need to be repaid. You'll also be asked to provide a bank statement showing the gift being deposited into your account no later than 10 business days before closing. A 90 day history of bank statements from the donor is generally not required, however, lenders may still ask for them on occasion. This is rare when the donor resides in Canada, but I've seen the request.

If the donor is from outside of Canada, then the lender will need to know which country the gift is coming from. Some countries may be more scrutinized than others. For example, if the gifted funds are coming from a sanctioned country, then they may not be accepted for down payment use. In addition to the gift letter, you'll need to provide a copy of the wire transfer, along with your bank statement showing the funds being deposited. A 90 day history of bank statements will often be required from the donor account in these situations, but this requirement can vary from lender to lender.

RECENTLY SOLD PROPERTY

If part of your down payment is sourced from the sale of a recently sold property, specific documentation is necessary for mortgage approval. Firstly, you will need to provide a copy of the accepted offer on the property, including any relevant amendments and waivers. Additionally, lenders will request a mortgage statement for the sold property to verify the amount of equity available for use as a down payment.

For example, let's say you sold your home for $2.2 million and you have an outstanding mortgage balance of $1 million, leaving you with $1.2 million in equity. However, the total equity amount isn't available for your down payment. You must account for other expenses, such as Realtor fees, which will reduce the net amount of equity you can apply towards your new purchase. Mortgage lenders typically subtract a standard percentage from the sale price to account for Realtor fees and other expenses, even if the actual fees are lower or non-existent. If we take the previous example of a home sold for $2.2 million, lenders might deduct a standard 5% for Realtor fees, which reduces the usable equity to $1.09 million. This is $110,000 less than the total equity value and might be different from what you initially expected.

It's important to note that some lenders might deduct a higher percentage depending on their policies. Additionally, other expenses, like penalties for returning your current mortgage, should also be factored into the calculation of available equity. These deductions can significantly impact the actual amount you have for your down payment, so you need to account for them in your financial planning.

If the closing date for the sale of your current property is prior to the closing of the new purchase, you'll be asked to provide the trust ledger you received from your lawyer showing the amount of funds that were disbursed to you on closing. This is to be accompanied by a bank statement showing the funds being deposited into your account.

Sale of property or not, always be prepared to provide a 90 day history of bank statements showing the full paper trail for the period. It may still be required to support your deposit and/or closing costs.

SECURED LINE OF CREDIT

Funds coming from a secured line of credit, also known as a Home Equity Line of Credit, or 'HELOC', is also acceptable. However, as you're still borrowing the funds, it would be added as a liability. While HELOCs are generally interest only loans, meaning that the minimum payment is just the outstanding interest for the month, a higher payment is used for mortgage qualification. It's calculated using a 25-year amortization at the higher of the benchmark rate, or the actual rate. For instance, if the benchmark rate is 5.25% and the rate on the HELOC is 7.20%, then 7.20% will be used to calculate the qualifying payment. If you needed to draw $100,000 from the HELOC, then the actual payment would be $600 per month. However, when amortized over 25 years, the payment increases to $712.81, which is what would be used for qualifying purposes.

CREDIT CARDS / UNSECURED LINE OF CREDIT

If you're falling a little short on your down payment, it may be possible to make up the difference using your credit card or unsecured line of credit. This is often referred to as a Flex Down Payment. While this can sound intriguing, it's not something I would recommend. You're already going to have enough new debt from your new mortgage, so tacking on more may not put you in the best of positions. Unsecured revolving accounts, namely credit cards, can carry excessively high interest rates, making them less than ideal for home financing. Think about it for a moment... you're charging a portion of your new home purchase to your credit card. While there are always exceptions, it's best not to take on additional high interest debt right at the same time you're closing on your new home purchase.

While it's possible to take up to 5% of your down payment from a credit card or unsecured line of credit, there is only a small group of mortgage lenders who will accept it.

I'll be discussing Flex Down in more detail in Chapter 10.

CREDIT

Your credit history is the second vital component in determining mortgage qualification. Assuming that your credit is solid can lead to unforeseen complications. Credit reports can sometimes contain unexpected 'surprises'. For instance, you might discover collections on debts that you believed were already resolved. Unresolved issues can significantly impact your creditworthiness.

Additionally, errors on the part of creditors are not uncommon and may need rectification. Mistakes could range from incorrect reporting of payments to entries of credit cards or loans that don't belong to you. Regularly reviewing your credit report is vital to ensure its accuracy and to address any discrepancies promptly. These issues, if not corrected, can negatively affect your ability to qualify for a mortgage or secure favourable terms.

It's also possible that Equifax (the credit reporting agency used by most brokers and lenders) could have multiple files for you... meaning, multiple credit bureaus. Your mortgage professional should take the time to go over your credit report with you to ensure everything is accurate and that there is nothing missing. Should you be in a situation where there are multiple files under your name, your mortgage professional can generally get this corrected for you quite easily. However, there are still some situations where you may be required to contact the credit reporting agency directly.

Your Credit Score

Your credit score takes on different names depending on who retrieves it. When a mortgage professional accesses your credit report through Equifax, it's referred to as your FICO score. However, if you pull your own credit report directly, it's known as your Equifax score. It's important to note that these scores are calculated using different models, leading to potential variations between your self-accessed Equifax score and the FICO score used by mortgage professionals.

The distinction is important because in the context of mortgage applications, the FICO score is the only one that matters.

Lenders rely on your FICO score to assess your creditworthiness and make decisions about your mortgage application. The score ranges from 300-900, with 300 being the worst and 900 being the best.

What Determines a Good Credit Score?

Credit score rankings can be subject to interpretation as each financial institution may have their own internal classification systems. What one lender considers excellent; another may classify as good.

Equifax categorizes their credit scores as follows:

760 to 900 – Excellent
725 to 759 – Very good
660 to 724 – Good
560 to 659 – Fair
300 to 559 – Poor

The rankings are general to all credit applications... whether it be to lease an apartment, buy that new car, or apply for mortgage. While this classification system works on a broader scale, I'm going explain how it applies specifically to mortgage approval.

Qualifying for a new home purchase or mortgage transfer with an 'A' lender is possible with a score as low as 600 (refinancing requires a minimum score of 650). However, each application is evaluated individually, and approval would be considered on a case-by-case basis. The lender will scrutinize the contents of your credit bureau to determine why your score is so low. If there is a valid explanation, and if there isn't too much derogatory information reporting, then a lender may feel comfortable enough to mark your application as approved.

If your score is under 600 then you're out. Your only option would be to apply with a 'B' lender, which would generally be at much higher rates. I'll be discussing 'B' lenders in detail in Chapter Twelve.

Most mortgage lenders will approve you on credit with 650 credit scores or higher. Under 600, and no 'A' lender will touch you. This is why the fair ranking of 560 to 659 doesn't really make sense when it comes to mortgage lending. On one side you have no chance of qualifying with an 'A' lender and on the other side, qualification based on the score wouldn't be an issue... yet they are in the same ranking category.

Each lender can be a bit different with how they categorize your score. While the above may apply to most mortgage lenders, some may have their own requirements. For example, one lender might set their minimum acceptable credit score at 700, indicating a preference for a relatively higher creditworthiness. Another lender might be more flexible, accepting applicants with a score as low as 620. Meanwhile, a different lender could set their requirement at 680. While the minimum required credit score can vary from lender to lender, one thing that's consistent is that an 'A' lender's cut off is 600... which is a hard stop across the board.

How Important is Your Score?

While it's great to have a high credit score, it doesn't matter whether you're at 650 or a perfect 900 in most situations. You'll still qualify on score and may still be eligible for the lowest rates. In certain instances, a credit score of 700 might be necessary to qualify for a specific mortgage product, but this is not the norm. There is even one lender who won't offer their lowest rates unless your credit score is 780 or above. But that's just a single lender, who may or may not have the lowest rate when you're applying for a mortgage. And in most cases... they do not.

I cannot imagine a single situation in any type of credit approval where you would need to have a score higher than 780. Whether it's 760 or 900, it's excellent either way. There is not more than one category of excellent. There is no excellent one or excellent two. One thing cannot be more excellent than another. Excellent is excellent. Make sense? Excellent.

Credit score is important. There is no doubt that. But for the most part, having a particularly high score doesn't get you any special privileges. You either qualify on credit or you don't. There is no tiered qualification based on credit.

Thin Credit

While having a strong credit score is important, the score alone doesn't mean that you have solid credit. For example, you could have a very high score, yet still be declined for your mortgage based on credit.

WHAT? That doesn't make sense!

Many find this surprising, but it becomes logical once the reasoning behind it is understood. The credit score is only one component of your credit bureau. While it's the first thing a lender will assess, they'll also be reviewing the information contained within the report.

Think of credit as ice on a frozen lake. On one side of you, there is a lake with thin ice, and on the other side, one with thick, solid ice. Which lake do you think would have the lower risk of falling though? The thick ice of course.

Now imagine you're a mortgage lender, with the two lakes representing the credit profiles of potential borrowers. Which one would you feel more comfortable loaning money to?

A credit bureau with limited history, excessively small credit limits, or a single trade line is considered thin. And just like the ice, thin credit doesn't offer much support.

In cases of newer credit accounts, while there may be sufficient history to generate a strong credit score, it might not be adequate to convincingly demonstrate long-term credit responsibility. A credit history spanning just a few months, despite being well managed, wouldn't be enough to give the lender the reassurance they are looking for. They want to see a sustained track record of responsible credit use, which would then allow them to make an informed lending decision. A brief credit history doesn't give them enough data to fully assess the risk and stability of a borrower's financial habits over time.

But even an established credit history may still not be sufficient if the credit availability is limited. Consider someone who has only one credit card with a $500 limit. Even if it was effectively managed for several years, the modest limit doesn't provide the lender with enough evidence to make an informed decision. Higher credit limits give mortgage lenders more confidence in the applicant's ability to handle larger sums of credit effectively.

Minimum Credit Requirements

The general requirement is for mortgage applicants to have two active trade lines, each with a credit history of at least one year. However, it's worth noting that some lenders may look for a two-year history. Essentially, a trade line refers to any type of credit account, such as a credit card, line of credit, or loan, which appears on your credit report.

Ideally, at least one, if not both, of these trade lines should be revolving, meaning you can re-access the credit limit once it's paid down. Common examples of revolving trade lines include credit cards and lines of credit, which demonstrate your ability to manage ongoing credit responsibly.

> *The general requirement is to have two active trade lines, each showing a minimum history of at least one year.*

The limit on each revolving trade line should be at least $1,000, though higher limits are generally viewed more favourably by lenders. There is a common belief that too much credit is considered bad, and for this reason, some will try to keep their credit as thin as possible. While having excessive credit could be a concern for mortgage lenders, it would have to be quite excessive for you to be turned down based on available credit alone. The worst-case scenario would be the lender requiring you to close some of the accounts. There is a far greater chance of being declined for having too little credit vs. too much.

What's worse than having thin credit is having no credit at all. Picture this scenario: you've decided to close all your credit cards and currently have no active loans on your credit report. Even with a high score, the lack of active credit history can lead to a mortgage application decline.

Let's add another twist. Say you opened a new credit card with a $3,000 limit just three months ago. Despite this being an active trade line, the mere three months of history is still insufficient for mortgage approval. The key term is 'active.' It's not just about having a credit history; it's about having ongoing, current credit activity.

This can be baffling, especially if you've had multiple credit cards for over a decade, all managed impeccably, but closed them recently. In the eyes of lenders, these closed accounts, despite their perfect status, are irrelevant. They are closed and therefore old news. They need to see active, recent credit management. It's an aspect of the lending industry that may not seem logical, but it's a key factor in how lenders assess creditworthiness.

While there are still some lenders who will approve you, options will be more limited which could result in a higher mortgage rate.

Not All Tradelines are Created Equal

Revolving tradelines will carry more weight with a mortgage lender than a term loan. That is, a loan with a set date for it to be paid in full. A car loan for example. If the only tradeline reporting on your credit bureau is a loan, then your mortgage application may be declined. This is why you'll want to ensure that you have a minimum of one revolving tradeline reporting. Ideally two.

Mobile phone service providers such as Rogers, Bell, and Telus will all report to your credit bureau, however, they are not considered tradelines by mortgage lenders. If this is all you have reporting on your credit bureau, then this would be viewed as having no activity at all.

An interesting fact is that mortgages, despite being significant loans, only began appearing on credit bureaus in 2015. One might naturally assume that such large loans would be among the first to be reported. However, even though mortgages are now listed on credit reports, they are not classified as tradelines.

How Your Credit Score is Determined

Your credit score is influenced by a variety of factors, some of which are well-known, while others might be less understood or even surprising. In Canada, there are two major credit reporting agencies: Equifax and TransUnion. If you have ever come across Experian while doing any research, they operate only in the US, so that information wouldn't be applicable on this side of the border. These agencies may report different credit scores for the same individual due to their distinct algorithms for calculating the score.

Most mortgage brokers rely on Equifax, as do most lenders, however, some opt for TransUnion. It's not uncommon for lenders to pull credit reports from both agencies to cross-check for any inconsistencies between them. The variation in scores between the two agencies stems from their unique scoring models, although they both adhere to a similar framework in evaluating creditworthiness. This framework considers five different aspects of your credit history to determine your score:

- 35% - Payment history
- 30% - Ratio of current balances to available credit
- 15% - Length of credit history
- 10% - Mix of credit
- 10% - New credit / inquiries

35% - Payment History

The largest portion of your credit score is determined by your payment history. However, there's more complexity to it than just timely bill payments, although that certainly plays a significant role. This portion of your score can be comprised of any of the following:

- Total number and type of accounts
- The ratio of accounts with delinquencies to the total number reporting
- Details on late or missed payments
- Public records
- Collections

Number and Type of Accounts

It's not just the number of accounts that are paid on time, but the types of accounts as well. For example, a revolving account such as a credit card may have more influence on your score than a student loan.

Ratio of Accounts with Delinquencies

It's not just the delinquencies that influence your score, but their ratio to the total number of accounts. If you had ten accounts with 0 delinquencies, then the ratio is zero, which is ideal. If one account is delinquent, it would be 10%. If you have 9, it would be 90%. A high delinquency ratio suggests a pattern of unreliable credit management. The higher the ratio, the worse your credit becomes as it becomes more evident that you're not able to responsibly handle the credit extended to you.

Details on Late Payments

A late payment is a missed payment, and the two can be

used interchangeably. Even if you're one day late, you have missed that payment. This is generally tracked in increments of 30 days. In other words, a payment that is 60 days late will typically have a larger negative effect on your credit score than one that is only 30 days late. The severity of the impact reaches its peak when a payment is 90 days late. At this point, the late payment is considered a bad debt.

The tradeline will then be marked as 'written off' as the creditor is doubtful on your ability to repay the debt. This doesn't mean that you no longer owe the money. You're still responsible for the amount owed.

Such a categorization can substantially harm your credit score, as it signals a serious delinquency to lenders and credit agencies. It's a clear indication of financial distress or unreliability in managing credit obligations, which can have long-term implications on your ability to obtain credit in the future.

As soon as you know you have missed a payment, make sure that you make it promptly. If you pay the full balance prior to the next reporting period, then the creditor may not report the payment as being late. However, this is not something that you can count on, so you don't want to take the chance.

How much you choose to pay towards your credit cards is irrelevant as long as you at least make the minimum payment. An exception would be if the larger payment brings your balance below the 75% or 50% threshold (discussed in the next section).

Public Records

As the name implies, a public record refers to matters that are accessible by the public. They are generally legal or government matters, and can include municipal, provincial and federal documents.

Some examples of public records:

- Registered liens (against your home or car, for example)
- Civil judgements
- Past bankruptcies / consumer proposals

Collections

If a creditor doesn't receive payment they will register your debt with a collection agency, who in turn, registers it on your credit bureau. It may be reported to only Equifax, only Transunion, or both. I'm sure you don't need me to tell you that collections can have a big impact on your score. They essentially mean that you're not paying back the money you owe, and now they must chase you for it. Even if you disagree with the charge, you'll still want to find a way to make the payment.

Even with active collections, it's still possible that your score may fall within the qualifying range. In these situations, the lender may or may not ask for the reason behind the collection. This usually depends on its severity. If the lender is okay to proceed with your approval, they will require the collection to be settled. Even if it's still being disputed, the lender will require it to be paid before they release the funds on your closing date.

30% - Ratio of Current Balances to Available Credit

The second largest influencer of your credit score is the portion of your available credit that you're using. This generally refers to your revolving accounts. That is, the accounts that allow you to withdraw, repay and reborrow funds up to a predetermined limit, such as a credit card or line of credit.

The closer you get to your credit limit, the larger the negative impact on your score. Fully utilizing your available credit signals a high utilization ratio, which doesn't go over well with the credit scoring models. Your score will plummet... even if you're paying your bills on time. This is because maxing out all your credit cards can be a sign of potential financial strain or mismanagement of credit.

Credit scoring systems view lower utilization ratios more favorably, typically recommending using less than 75% of your available credit. However, keeping them below 50% will have a more positive impact. Keeping your credit balances well below your limits is key to maintaining a strong credit score.

Try to keep credit card balances under 75% of the limit if possible. Ideally... under 50%.

It's important to manage your overall debt levels responsibly. Even with a strong credit score and sufficient income, carrying an excessive amount of debt can be a red flag for lenders. In extreme cases, a high debt burden might lead to a mortgage application being declined, despite other qualifying factors being in place. While such instances are relatively rare, they do occur when the debt level appears alarmingly high. It's crucial to keep debt within manageable limits to avoid negatively impacting your mortgage application.

I remember reviewing a mortgage application for new clients who racked up their credit card balances to the tune of $125,000. With a combined household income of only $90,000, their current situation would keep them in debt for eternity. Their debt-to-income ratio was through the roof, and that alone was enough to shut the door on their dreams of buying the home they had their minds set on. When I advised them of the situation, they asked me with a glimmer of hope about how much they would qualify for.

The answer was a resounding $0.

Their towering credit card debt didn't just exceed the maximum allowable debt-to-income ratios... it blew past them like a runaway train zooming past the station. And with a down payment of only 5%, alternative options did not exist. Even if they did, the sheer magnitude of the debt would be a major point of concern for all lenders. As they were barely able to cover the minimum payments as it was, I advised them to speak with a bankruptcy trustee to discuss their options.

You may be wondering how they thought they would be able to make their mortgage payments given that they were barely able to meet the minimum payments on their credit cards. They were hoping to consolidate all their debt into the new mortgage, and therefore, lower their payment overall. In theory, this sounds like a great idea. However, the only way to consolidate debt into your mortgage when purchasing a new home is to deduct it from your down payment. As they only had the minimum of 5%, it was not possible.

Even if your debt-to-income ratios fall within acceptable limits, having an excessive amount of debt can be an issue for mortgage lenders. They might perceive it as a sign of over-dependence on credit, potentially leading them to reject your mortgage application.

15% - Length of Credit History

This is the length of time each account has been open and the date of last activity. Older credit accounts carry more weight than newer ones. The longer these accounts have been active, the more favorably they impact your credit score.

However, credit cards that have been sitting dormant for years will not have any positive impact on your credit. Your score may not suffer, but if all your credit cards have been collecting dust, then it weakens the overall strength of your credit profile. For example, let's say you have a total of three credit cards reporting and you haven't used them for a few years. You still may end up getting declined for a mortgage due to lack of recent credit activity, regardless of how high your score may be.

Older credit accounts carry more weight than newer ones. The longer these accounts have been active, the more favorably they impact your credit score.

This is why it's important to use your credit cards periodically, rather than just let them sit. Think of it as exercise for your credit. If you don't go to the gym periodically, your muscles will become soft and flabby. The same applies to your credit. Even charging $10 on a credit card once or twice a year will help keep your credit strong and healthy. If only the same could be said for going to the gym!

What many do not realize is that any time you close a credit account, it will also lower your score. It doesn't matter if it's a credit card or a car loan, your score is impacted. While it always feels great to make that final payment on your car loan, your score will drop as soon as that loan is paid in full.

It's quite normal for people to be apprehensive about anything that might cause their credit score to dip. However, it's important to understand that credit scores are dynamic and naturally fluctuate with regular credit usage. Closing an account might result in a drop to your score, but it's usually just a minor dip. If you have a strong credit score, this shouldn't be a cause for worry. The concern is more significant if your credit score is teetering on the edge of qualifying – that's when even a small decrease can have a bigger impact.

10% - Mix of Credit

It's good practice to have a variety of trade lines. For example, instead of having all credit cards, have a line of credit, a credit card, a car loan... etc. Mixing it up a bit shows diversification, which can demonstrate better credit responsibility.

10% - New Credit / Inquires

When adding new credit accounts, it's typical to see a minor dip in your score. These new accounts introduce a period of adjustment as the credit bureau's scoring system takes time to assess how effectively you're managing this additional credit. But as you consistently demonstrate responsible credit management with these new accounts, your credit score will recover and potentially even improve. Think of it as a brief 'getting-to-know-you' phase between your new credit accounts and the credit scoring system.

Many believe that their credit score will start plummeting the moment a potential creditor pulls your report. While it does drop, it's generally not a cause for concern, unless your credit is sitting right on the border. For example, if your score is 625 and then it drops to 615 after a couple of checks, then this could possibly mean the difference between qualification or a decline.

However, if your score is 775 and a couple of checks drop it to 765, then it's 100% irrelevant.

On the other end of the stick, if your score is 450, which is pretty bad, then there is no point in worrying about someone checking your score. The damage is done. It doesn't matter if your score is 470 or 420, you still won't qualify for a traditional mortgage.

In the above examples, I'm using a ten point drop for demonstration purposes only. The actual amount your score drops from each check can vary depending on your circumstances, however in my experience, it's typically minimal in most situations where credit is healthy.

Equifax will also permit you to have multiple cheques when shopping for a specific credit product. In this case, It's mortgages. You can have as many credit checks as you like within a 45 day window and it will only count as a single hit towards your score. Providing that the credit checks are specifically for mortgage application purposes.

Submitting Multiple Applications

This doesn't mean that you should be putting in mortgage applications with every broker, bank, and credit union. While your score won't take a hit, each check will be recorded and visible on your report. Anyone checking your score will know exactly where you have been shopping.

If you have concerns about your eligibility, a candid conversation with your mortgage professional can often provide clarity. They can provide guidance tailored to your particular situation and might be able to give you an idea of the expected rate in advance.

For those focused on finding the lowest rates, you can usually obtain a quote without a full application. Simply share your financial details and ask the mortgage agent for their best rate based on the information provided. Some mortgage agents may insist on completing an application before revealing their rates. However, competitive offerings are often available upfront from discount brokers, without the need to go through the entire application process just to receive a quote. This not only saves you a lot of time but saves the time of those you're applying with as well.

How to Maintain a High Credit Score

If you focus on every single component listed above, you'll end up pulling out all your hair from all the anxiety you create for yourself. While you want to ensure your score stays strong, it's not something that you need to obsess over. I'm going to simplify this for you substantially. All you need to remember is two things:

- Pay at least the minimum payment on time, ideally a few days before the deadline to be safe.
- Stay within 75% of your credit limits (50% is even better).

If you follow those two rules alone, your score will stay healthy.

I'll be discussing credit further in Chapter Twelve.

INCOME

The third component lenders use for mortgage qualification is your income. It's an important part of the mortgage approval process as it assures lenders that the borrower has the capacity to repay the loan. In other words, a steady flow of income high enough to support the overall debt, as well as a sufficient history of earnings. It doesn't matter how large your down payment is, or how much equity you have in your property. It's not about assets or equity. It's about the confirmation of sufficient income to ensure serviceability of the loan. In other words, income that will allow the borrower to comfortably make their payments on time.

Regardless of whether you're dealing with a major bank, credit union, or monoline lender, the documents required for income confirmation are similar. By having a better understanding of what mortgage lenders are looking for, it can help to eliminate additional requests, therefore giving you a better experience with the mortgage arrangement process.

The documentation required to support income can vary depending on whether you're employed or self-employed.

Employed Applicants

The basic documentation required for employed applicants is seemingly straightforward, but additional explanation may be helpful in giving you a better understanding of the exact requirements.

There are three main documents required:

- Letter of employment
- Recent paystub
- T4

Letter of Employment

A letter of employment (LOE) is essentially a snapshot of your work status, capturing the essential details for lenders. You can easily acquire this document from your HR department, payroll officers, or direct supervisor. To ensure its relevance, it should be recent... no older than 30 days.

This LOE must spell out three key pieces of your employment:

- The position you hold with the company
- The date you started
- Your annual income

For those who earn an hourly wage, the letter of employment should specify whether there's a set minimum number of hours you're guaranteed each week, as well as your rate per hour. If your hours aren't guaranteed, lenders generally want to see a two-year history with the same employer to establish a reliable income pattern. This is because, without a guaranteed minimum, it's challenging for lenders to establish a dependable income figure. So, even if you've been clocking in a steady 40 hours weekly for the past six months, lenders will look for a two-year average to determine your qualifying income. Remember, individual circumstances can vary. If your employment history is less than two years and your hours vary, it's important to discuss this early on with your mortgage professional who can advise you accordingly.

Your letter of employment (LOE) not only outlines your job details but also provides your lender with a contact for employment verification. To ensure a smooth process, it's wise to give your HR department or supervisor a heads-up that they might receive a call from your mortgage lender to confirm your employment status.

Recent Paystubs

At least one recent paystub will be required, however some lenders may ask for two. Your paystub should be dated within the last 30 days. A recent paystub is not required if on maternity/paternity leave, however, a lender may request the last paystub you received prior to going on leave.

T4

If you're salaried or are guaranteed a specific minimum number of hours, then your T4s may not be required. But if your earnings include variable components such as bonuses, overtime, or commission, lenders look for a stable two-year track record with the same employer. As these components are not guaranteed, the lender has no way to determine a useable income, so they will request your T4s from the past two years. If your income is increasing year over year, then they will use the two-year average. If the most recent year is lower, then only your income from that year will be considered.

If you've been at your job for two years (or close to two years), and you don't yet have the second T4 from the same employer, then no problem! Most lenders will allow us to average out the last T4 received with the year-to-date gross income on your most recent paystub.

Self-Employed Applicants

The income verification process for self-employed borrowers takes a slightly different turn. After all, writing your own employment letter might be amusing... but isn't exactly practical. As with non-guaranteed employment income, entrepreneurs need a two-year track record to demonstrate business stability and consistent earnings. And just as with non-guaranteed employment income, a two-year average is used.

There are four standard documents required when you're in business for yourself:

- T1 Generals
- Notice of Assessment (NOA)
- Articles of incorporation or business licence
- Financial statements (if incorporated)

T1 Generals

These are your tax returns, which will be required for the last two years. All income received will be broken down individually on a specific line number within the T1. In 2019, the CRA thought it would be fun to add a couple of extra zeros to each number. For example, what used to be line 150 is now line 15000. However, the original three-digit numbers are still used by most industry professionals, which is also what I'll be using in this section.

Your total income for the year will be reported on your line 150, however this won't necessarily be the income used for qualification. This is because it includes all income types, some of which may not be considered. For example, capital gains, rental income, RRSP withdrawals, or social assistance programs such as CERB, which was common in the pandemic years of 2020 and 2021. As these are not sustainable income sources, they would not be considered towards your qualifying income.

Incorporated vs. Sole Proprietor / Partnership

How your income gets reported on your T1s will differ depending on whether your business is incorporated. If incorporated, you can either pay yourself with a traditional salary, dividends, or a combination of both. Salary is reported on your line 101, whereas dividends are reported on your line 120. If you're paying yourself a salary, then you may issue yourself T4s for tax purposes. However, as these are generated by the company that you own, they wouldn't be accepted for income confirmation. Even if you pay yourself a base salary, the two-year average is still required by lenders. It's not uncommon for me to have incorporated clients tell me that they will just increase their salary. We have to give lenders a bit more credit here. They're aware that a business owner can change their salary at will. You could increase it to qualify for the mortgage you need, and then change it back once your new mortgage has closed. As you have full control over this as the business owner, the salary you pay yourself is irrelevant, so the two-year average is all that matters.

If you're a sole proprietor or in a partnership, income gets reported on lines 162 (gross income) and line 135 (net income). It's line 135 that will be considered. Depending on the type of business, your gross and net income may report on different line numbers, however, they are all found in the same section of your T1.

Note that mortgage lenders will require your full and complete T1 Generals. When you request these documents from your accountant, they will often send you summaries or condensed versions. Make sure specifically ask for the full and complete report, as this is what a lender will want to see. Even if it appears that all your income is included in the summary version, lenders will still want to see the full report. It's not so much that they want to see what's on the rest of the report, but they may want to confirm what's not on it. An undisclosed rental property for example.

Notice of Assessment

NOAs for the last two years will also be required to support the information on the T1. If there is an outstanding tax balance on your most recent NOA, then you'll need to provide confirmation that the balance has been paid.

NOAs are mailed to you by the CRA roughly six weeks after you file your taxes. They can also be accessed from your MyCRA account online, however, they will not show your name. From a lender's perspective, they could be from anyone. For this reason, lenders will require the version that was mailed out to you. If you do not have it available, you can request a new copy from the CRA. There are also some brokers who have the capacity to retrieve your NOAs, which can generally be done within 24 hours.

Articles of Incorporation / Business License

If you're incorporated, you'll be asked for your articles of incorporation. If a sole proprietor or partnership, then a valid business licence would be requested. These documents confirm your ownership of the business, as well as how long it has been established. However, it's understood that these documents aren't always available, as not all legitimate businesses have to be registered. You can legally operate a business under your own name for example. In these cases, the following documents will be required in addition to your T1s and NOAs:

- Notice of Return Adjustment/Summary from the CRA (GST return)
- Statement of business or professional activities (addendum to your T1)
- Financial statements for the past two years prepared and signed by an accountant.

Financial Statements

If incorporated, lenders will also require your corporate

financial statements for the last two years, prepared by your accountant. These include your balance sheet, income statement and statement of retained earnings. Financial statements are required to provide the lender with additional reassurance about the overall financial strength of the company, which provide additional support around the sustainability of your income in the future.

NON-QUALIFYING INCOME

It's not uncommon for self-employed applicants to have lower, declared income. This can be either due to tax write offs or due to having a larger cash component to the business, which is commonly found with trade workers. We all want to pay as little tax as we can, so those who are in business for themselves will try to keep their declared income to a minimum wherever possible. While this is great for paying taxes, it creates qualifying problems when it comes to mortgage approval.

It's common for incorporated applicants to keep as much money in their corporation as possible. Either in their operating company, or in a holding company. They'll pay themselves just what they need to get by, which results in paying the least amount of taxes. Their corporation may have earned $500,000 consistently for the past two years, while they may have only paid themselves $80,000. However, most lenders don't care about the corporate earnings. It's your personal declared income that you're being qualified on. This is one of the areas of the mortgage industry that seems to defy common sense. In this example, the business owner obviously has the ability to pay themselves significantly more and can do so at any time. If she feels she needs more money for day-to-day life, including making the mortgage payments on time, she can simply increase her personal income at any time. However, this is not how it works in the mortgage world unfortunately.

Before the US real estate crash in 2008, it was possible to do stated income mortgages with no evidence to support it at all. It was seldom even questioned, providing it was reasonable. Obviously if a self-employed hair stylist is stating $250,000 in income while only reporting $20,000 on her NOA, then this would of course be unreasonable. However, if the same hair stylist were stating $50,000 in income with $20,000 showing on her NOA, then it would be much easier to make a case for her. After all, she would get paid a certain amount in cash tips, not to mention all her write offs for items required in the day-to-day operation of her business.

The mortgage industry has since changed significantly and stated income mortgages are hard to come by. With the odd exception, they are generally available through alternative lenders only, which I'll be discussing in detail in Chapter Twelve.

DEBT

The last major factor considered in mortgage approval is your debt load. Any money owed on credit cards, lines of credit, car loans, personal loans, car leases, child support payments... and yes, existing mortgages are all considered debt. What's not considered debt is insurance, subscriptions (such as Netflix) and cell phone bills, to name a few. These types of expenses do not influence your borrowing capacity.

But it's not so much the amount of debt itself, but rather the cost of carrying it each month. For example, a $10,000 car loan with $600 monthly payment will more negatively influence your qualification than a $20,000 car loan with a $300 payment. Despite the higher balance, the lower payment will allow you to qualify for a larger mortgage.

Each type of debt can influence your maximum qualified amount in a different way. The actual minimum payment is often used, but this is not always the case. Here are common types of debts and the payment used on each for mortgage qualification:

- Credit card: 3% of balance
- Unsecured credit lines: 3% of balance
- Home Equity Line of Credit (HELOC): balance owing calculated at the higher of the current rate or the benchmark rate amortized over 25 years.
- Installment loans: Actual payment
- Car lease: Actual payment
- Student loans: 1-3% (depending on lender) of total borrowed if not yet in repayment. If currently in repayment, then the actual payment would be used.
- Mortgage(s) on current property owned (if not being sold): Actual mortgage payment.

This is equal across the board and doesn't change from one lender to the next. The only exception is with HELOCs, where some lenders will use a 30-year amortization, however, the vast majority use 25 years. There are also some lenders who will assess the HELOC as if it were fully utilized, right up to the limit, rather than on the actual balance owing, even if it has a zero balance. This alone can have a significant effect on what you'll qualify for.

There are some financing programs that offer a prolonged introductory period where no payments are required. When you snag those tempting no-payment deals on that plush sofa or the latest smart TV, remember, it's just a grace period before the repayment period begins. Lenders are ahead of the game—they'll calculate your mortgage eligibility using the eventual payment to be made. And if your temptation splurge lands on a credit card? Lenders are taking note there too, adding the standard 3% of your balance to the debt pile.

With some exceptions, having a modest amount of debt won't impact your mortgage qualification providing that your debt service ratios are within the maximum allowable limits.

DEBT SERVICE RATIOS

A debt service ratio is the amount of debt you carry in relation to your income level. In other words, your debt-to-income ratio.

There are two debt service ratios that are considered for qualification:

- Gross Debt Service Ratio (GDSR)
- Total Debt Service Ratio (TDSR).

These are more commonly referred to as the GDS and TDS.

GDS

The GDS is calculated by taking the sum of your mortgage payment including principal and interest, in addition to your property tax and heating costs (commonly written as PITH) divided by your gross income.

The formula looks like this:

$$\frac{\text{PITH (principal, interest, heat, taxes)}}{\text{Income}}$$

TDS

The TDS is the other key metric used for determining your affordability. This ratio includes your entire debt obligation: PITH, plus the monthly payment on all your other debt, divided by your income.

The formula for the TDS looks like this:

$$\frac{\text{PITH + debt payments}}{\text{Income}}$$

Both the GDS and TDS can be calculated monthly or on an annual basis. Either way, the results are the same.

While heating is often an unknown and unprovable variable, most lenders will use $100 or $125 when calculating debt service ratios. Some lenders will allow more or less than this, depending on the actual square footage of the property. Heat is the only utility that gets factored into debt service. Water, hydro, cable, internet, etc. are irrelevant and are never considered.

In cases where there is a condo or maintenance fee, the fee gets calculated into the debt service ratio at 50% of the actual amount. In other words, if the condo fee were $400, only $200 would be used in the qualifying calculation. If the maintenance fee includes heat, as it sometimes does, then heating costs can be omitted.

The maximum GDS is 39% and the maximum TDS is 44%.

Let's break this down and see how it looks using real numbers. Let's say John and Mary Smith require a mortgage of $650,000 on a freehold property with taxes of $6,000 per year. Their lowest mortgage rate is 3.99% and they'll be amortizing it over 30 years. Their combined gross household annual income is $144,000.

As they're required to pass the stress test as explained in Chapter Two, the payment used for qualification will be based on 5.99%... 2% above their actual mortgage rate.

Here are the relevant numbers used for the calculation:

Monthly household income: $12,000
Monthly qualifying payment (P&I): $3,862.29
Property tax (monthly): $500
Heat: $100
Total property related expenses: $4,462.29

Using these numbers, the formula for the GDS looks like this:

$$\frac{\$4,462.29 \ (PITH)}{\$12,000}$$
$$GDS = 37.19\%$$

Assuming acceptable credit, they will qualify based on GDS as the ratio is below the maximum of 39%.

Now, let's toss in some debt, just for the fun of it. We'll tack on the following:

Car loan: $650 / month
Credit cards: $60 / month (3% of a $2,000 balance)
Line of credit: $120 / month (3% of a $4,000 balance)
Total monthly debt = $830

The formula for the TDS looks like this:

$$\frac{(\$4,462.29 + \$830)}{\$12,000}$$
$$TDS = 44.10\%$$

Our beloved borrowers, John and Mary, will no longer qualify as their TDS is over 44%.

While there are some lenders who may consider making an exception to grant them approval despite the TDS being marginally over the maximum limit, the majority will not. However, all the borrowers would need to do in this case is payout their $2,000 credit card debt which would then bring their TDS down to 43.85%. While it's tight, they now qualify for the exact mortgage they were looking for.

ADDITIONAL DOCUMENT REQUIREMENTS

The mortgage arrangement process can seem simple and effortless, or it can be tiring and with one document requirement after another. If you have a better understanding of what a mortgage lender is looking for, and why they require certain documents, then the majority of those applying for a mortgage will find the process a breeze.

In addition to the down payment and income supporting documents explained earlier in this chapter, you'll also encounter a few more items on the checklist. These documents are the nuts and bolts that hold the structure of your application together, assuring lenders that you're a secure investment.

PURCHASES

- Agreement of Purchase and Sale (APS)
- Amendments and waivers (if applicable)
- MLS listing
- Current mortgage statement for any property currently owned (if applicable)
- Property tax bill for any property currently owned (if applicable)
- ID

MORTGAGE TRANSFERS OR REFINANCES

- Current mortgage statement
- Property tax bill
- Home fire insurance policy
- ID

Agreement of Purchase and Sale (APS)

This is what your Realtor draws up when you are putting in your offer to purchase your new home or condo. Once your offer has been accepted, it will be fully signed by all parties, which is the version that is required by mortgage lenders. Any amendments or waivers will also be required (if applicable). Sometimes an APS will refer to a specific schedule. For example, 'schedule B'. Any referenced schedules will also be required by the lender.

On a new build property, the APS can be as much as 50 pages or more. Lengthy as it may be, the entire document will be required, including floor plans, and Tarion warranty information.

The APS is a requirement as it provides the lender with the terms and conditions surrounding the purchase. This includes terms of the agreement including purchase price, deposit amount, closing date, and conditions.

If you are selling your current property, then the APS for the property being sold will also be required, along with any waivers, amendments, and schedules (if applicable).

MLS listing

The MLS listing is what your Realtor sends you prior to your purchase. It contains various information about the property, including the asking price, property taxes, lot size, etc, along with a description of the property. The MLS listing may or may not include the square footage (living space above ground) and age of the property, however, this information will be required prior to submitting your file through to a mortgage lender. If the listing is missing this information, then you'll generally be asked to obtain it from your Realtor.

Tip: You can eliminate some back-and-forth questions by sending this information to your mortgage professional along with the listing.

It's important that you send the listing you received directly from your Realtor, and not the listing sourced from a consumer-based site such as realtor.ca. The listings found on these sites will generally not have all the information required by lenders.

If you are purchasing a new build property, or a private sale, then there would not be an MLS listing available, therefore it would not be required.

Current Mortgage Statement

The mortgage statement is provided to you by your current lender. It outlines all the details of your mortgage including payment, payment frequency, maturity date, rate etc. Lenders will generally mail you out a paper copy of your year-end mortgage statement each January. This can often be acquired through your online mortgage portal as well, which is offered by most lenders. It's important that the statement shows the names of the registered owners, as well as the address of the property. The documents obtained from some online portals may not show the property address. If this is the case, then the lender will require you to provide a mortgage statement confirming the address which you may need to obtain by contacting your current lender directly.

Property Tax Bill

This is sent to you three to four times per year (depending on the city) by the municipal tax office. This is required for the new lender to confirm how much you're currently paying in property taxes. There are both interim tax bills, as well as a final tax bill. It's generally the final tax bill is required, as it's the final taxes that the lender needs to verify. If you don't have a copy of your final tax bill, then you may need to contact your municipal property tax office to obtain a copy.

Regardless of how low your debt-to-income ratios may be, the tax bill is required by all lenders. While the property taxes may not have any relevance to your approval if you easily qualify, lenders will still require confirmation of the amount to ensure accurate and precise debt-to-income ratios for compliance purposes. They cannot simply 'assume', regardless of how low your debt-to-income ratios might be.

Home Fire Insurance Policy

This is required to assure mortgage lenders that their security (your home) is protected in the event of a fire. The policy needs to be in effect at time of closing the new mortgage. It's not uncommon for an insurance policy to end on your maturity date. Your insurance provider will generally send out the new policy approximately 30 days before it expires. If you're starting the mortgage application process prior to receiving the new policy, you can simply send it into us once the new policy has been received.

If you live in a condo, then fire insurance is typically provided by the condo board. In this case, you will need contact them directly to obtain a copy of the policy.

ID

It's only natural that a mortgage lender will want to see your ID. After all, they are lending you several hundred thousand dollars, if not more.

You'll be required to provide two pieces of valid ID, one primary and one secondary. Many think that both pieces of ID are required to have your photo. However, only your primary ID needs to contain your photo. This is not a requirement for the secondary ID.

Here are some examples of both primary and secondary ID:

Primary ID

- Drivers license
- Passport
- Canadian citizenship card
- Canadian permanent residence card
- Government issued photo ID

Secondary ID

- SIN card
- Canadian birth certificate
- Credit card

Note that both sides of each piece of ID are required. The only exception is passports. Note that there is no mention of a health card on the lists. This is because it's not an acceptable form of ID. Unless an institution is involved in the provision of provincially funded healthcare, they are not permitted to collect or retain this information for identity verification purposes.

Ensure Your ID is Updated and Valid

Your ID will need to be valid at time of closing. If your

driver's license or passport is expiring in a week, then you'll need to have them updated. It's also important that your ID matches your current address entered on your application. If you have recently moved but have not yet updated your ID, then this can create complications at closing. Mortgage lenders will need to see confirmation that you're living at the address indicated on the application. This can sometimes be as simple as providing a cell phone or utility bill with your name and current address. However, it's still best to ensure your ID is updated, which will eliminate the possible requirement for additional documentation.

Note that additional documents can be required at any time during the process. A lender has the right to request them, which can be right up to your closing date. While it's rare for a lender to request a document this late in the game... it does happen on occasion.

CHALLENGING DOCUMENT REQUESTS

Most people are cooperative in providing the required documents. They realize that applying for a mortgage requires an in-depth qualifying process. However, there are some who will challenge even the most basic requirements.

Robert was applying to refinance this mortgage. He had a fair amount of debt that he wanted to consolidate as he had just gone through a large, self-funded renovation. During our discussion about the required documents, he was challenging every single one, going off on a long tirade about how the lender should trust him because he has sparkling credit and has never missed a mortgage payment. That the banks should be lining up to approve him for the mortgage he was looking for. "What do you mean I need to provide a job letter and a paystub? I told you how much I make. If the lender wants to verify, they can call my employer to confirm it. Why do they need me to provide so many documents?" he scorned.

I requested only the essential documents from Robert. The bare minimum that would be necessary anywhere he applied. But to him, it was excessive.

Having never missed a mortgage payment is not grounds for the lender to approve your mortgage. This does not make you special as they expect you to have made your payments on time. If you didn't, then you'd be hard pressed to find a lender to approve you at all... regardless of how much income you have or how cooperative you are with the document requests.

Mary had just purchased a new home, conditional on financing for five business days. She was cooperative, and promptly sent us her full document package. However, none of her bank statements had her name on them. We explained that the lender will require statements indicating her name so the lender can verify that the accounts belong to her.

"What do you mean? Who else would the accounts belong to?"

Is that the answer we are supposed to give to the lender?

I politely and clearly explained to Mary that while the ownership of the account is obvious to her, it's not to the lender. As she's an honest person, she can't relate to someone wanting to send the lender someone else's account information so they can qualify. That's completely unrelatable to her.

The lender on the other hand has been burned before. As has virtually every mortgage lender. The costs to them are significant. We were never doubting that Mary's accounts were hers. We just needed to prove that to the lender. If the lender were to be audited, and they see bank statements in the file with no confirmation of who they belong to, what do you think the auditor would say?

Sometimes you need to think like a lender.

If you were lending a large sum of money to someone you didn't know, would you want to ensure all the supporting documents were in place and were acceptable to you? When you understand the lender's perspective, the requirements can make a lot more sense.

> *Sometimes you need to think like a lender.*

ALTERED BANK STATEMENTS

When it comes to providing documentation for a mortgage application, clarity and transparency are paramount. Editing or redacting parts of documents, such as bank statements, will often raise red flags with lenders. It's crucial to understand that lenders require these documents unaltered to get a comprehensive picture of your financial behavior, which goes beyond just verifying your down payment source. Blacking out or concealing transactions, regardless of how inconsequential they may seem, can lead to concerns about undisclosed liabilities or questionable spending habits. It's not about prying into your personal expenditures; it's about presenting an unobstructed and trustworthy financial profile. Remember, lenders are not judging your shopping habits; they're assessing risk. Any form of document alteration, no matter how minor it may seem, casts a shadow of doubt and can hinder the mortgage approval process.

REMOVING DOCUMENT REQUESTS

There are times when a lender will ask for a document that might seem unnecessary. These requests may be based on sound reasoning, aligning with the lender's need to thoroughly assess risk. However, there are other times when they can seem utterly ridiculous... and believe me, sometimes they are.

If we feel a lender's request is excessive, we will challenge its validity and request for it to be waived. There are times when you may never even know that the request was ever made, as we'll shoot it down before it even makes its way through to you. However, there are also times when a lender may be unwilling to budge on our challenge with no way around it. The mortgage industry can sometimes defy logic and can even flat out defy what is seemingly common sense.

MORTGAGE FRAUD

Fraud is a serious problem in the mortgage industry and can result in significant financial losses to a lender. As they are trusting you with large amounts of money, they need to do their due diligence as they always run the risk that they may never see that money again.

Mortgage fraud involves intentionally attempting to mislead the lender to secure mortgage funding that would not have been approved had the truth been disclosed.

Here are just some examples of mortgage fraud:

- Providing false, misleading, or embellished information.
- Consciously omitting or concealing relevant information.
- Altering documents in attempt to mislead or hide things from the lender.
- Misrepresenting themselves or the information presented.
- Failure to disclose the intended use of a property. For example, stating that a rental property is owner occupied.

These practices can lead to misinformed lender decisions, breaches of trust, and in some cases, legal consequences. There are hundreds of thousands of dollars at stake, if not more. If the lender is going to trust you with their money, they are going to need a very specific set of documents before they are comfortable enough to part with their cash. There are also rules that they need to follow, and to be compliant with these rules, they need to have acceptable documents on file before they can fund your mortgage.

Yes, a lender can foreclose on a home if the borrower were

to default on the loan. But a lender has zero interest in pursuing this course which is something they would rather avoid. The only thing they do have an interest in is that you can make your payments on time.

They don't want to be chasing you.

They don't want force power of sale.

They don't want to foreclose.

Their only interest is that you make your payments on time. That's it.

CHAPTER EIGHT HIGHLIGHTS

- There are four basic components to mortgage qualification. Down payment, credit, income and debt.

- Never assume you will qualify for a mortgage.

- A 90 day history of down payment will be required, along with support for any large payments outside of your paycheques.

- Down payment gifts are only accepted from immediate relatives. Gives from cousins, aunts, uncles, and friends are not accepted.

- Having too much credit is better than not having enough credit.

- The general requirement is to have two active trade lines, each showing a minimum history of at least one year.

- It's possible to get declined based on credit, even if you have a strong credit score.

- There are two ratios used in calculating debt service. The Gross Debt Service Ratio (GDS) and the Total Debt Service Ratio (TDS).

- Sometimes you need to think like a lender to understand why a specific document might be required.

The more knowledgeable you are going into your first meeting or telephone call, the better chance you'll have at determining the experience level of the person handling your mortgage for you. A strong knowledge of how the approval process works combined with the information outlined in the last chapter will make your mortgage shopping much easier.

9

DOWN PAYMENT STRATEGY

"However beautiful the strategy, you should always look at the results."
~Winston Churchill

When considering buying a home, one of the most important elements is determining your available down payment. This is also one of the first things the mortgage professional will ask you about. While the concept of down payment might appear simple, it plays a pivotal role in the home-buying process. The size of your down payment can influence your rate, your maximum qualified amount, and can also shape your overall financial strategy for home ownership.

Do you put down the bare minimum?

Do you save up for more?

Do you go all in, depleting all your accounts by putting in every penny you have?

By the end of this chapter, you may have a completely different outlook when it comes to your down payment.

MINIMUM DOWN PAYMENT

The down payment requirements for buying a home can vary based on the home's purchase price. For homes priced at $500,000 or less, the minimum down payment is 5%.

However, for homes priced between $500,000 and $999,999, the calculation changes slightly. You'll need 5% for the first $500,000 and then 10% for the portion of the price over $500,000.

For instance, let's consider a home with a purchase price of $800,000. For this home, you'd need a 5% down payment on the first $500,000, which amounts to $25,000. For the remaining $300,000, a 10% down payment is required, which is $30,000. Therefore, the total minimum down payment for an $800,000 home would be $55,000.

For any purchase over $1,000,000, the minimum down payment is 20%.

As discussed in Chapter One, a purchase with a down payment of less than 20% is considered a high-ratio mortgage, therefore will require mortgage default insurance such as CMHC.

SHOULD MORTGAGE DEFAULT INSURANCE BE AVOIDED?

As explained in Chapter One, its sole purpose is to protect the lender in the event the borrower defaults on the mortgage payments. There are, however, two major benefits to the borrower. The first is that it allows them to purchase a home with less than 20% down payment. The second is that it usually results in a lower rate that can help to offset some of the premium cost.

I hear people trying to give advice on mortgages all the time. Everyone thinks they are an expert, and everyone is entitled to their own opinion of course. "Go with the lowest amortization possible, save up at least 20% before buying a home to save on the insurance premium!" While this strategy may be what's most suitable for them, it's not universal by any means.

There are two major benefits to the borrower. The first is that allows them to purchase a home with less than 20% down payment. The second is that it usually results in a lower rate that can help to offset some of the premium cost.

You'll want to observe how fast homes are appreciating in your area and compare that with how long you think it will take to save up the 20% down payment. Let's use the Greater Toronto Area as an example. From 2000 to 2014, the average home price in the GTA has appreciated an average of 6.26%, or $23,106 per year.

Let's say it's 2011 and Jim and Sandy are looking to purchase their first home in the GTA. They have 5% available for the down payment, but they've heard that it's a good idea to save up 20% to avoid paying the insurance premium. For this reason, they decide to wait until they have 20%, which takes them another three years to accumulate.

If they had purchased their home with 5% down in 2011 as they were originally considering, the average home price in the GTA was $465,014, which would have required a down payment of $23,250[8] (5%). The mortgage default insurance at the time was 2.75% (now 4.00%), which would have cost them $12,148 in insurance fees. As this gets added to the mortgage, the starting mortgage balance would have been $453,911.

The calculation looks like this:

Purchase Price – Down Payment + Insurance Premium
= Mortgage Amount

$465,014 - $23,251 + $12,148 = $453,911

Let's say the interest was 2.99% and they amortized over 25 years. Their monthly payment would have been $2,146 and their balance after three years would have been $415,487 (assuming monthly payments).

Fast forward to 2014. Jim and Sandy now have their 20% down payment and are ready to shop for their first home.

---

8   I'm leaving the pennies off throughout this example for simplicity, so actual numbers may fluctuate by a dollar in either direction.

The average home price in the GTA has now increased to $566,696[9]... over $100,000 more than it would have been if they had purchased in 2011. Their 20% down payment would be $113,339, which is $90,088 more than the 5% they would have put down in 2011. This means they would have had to save the equivalent of $2,500 per month over the last three years to avoid the insurance premium.

Their starting balance would be $453,357. Only $554 less than it would have been had they purchased the home three years earlier.

This is $37,870 more than they would have owed at this point if they had purchased in 2011 with only 5% down.

This assumes that they lived with their parents and didn't pay rent. But what if they had been paying a rent amount equal to the monthly mortgage payment, and were still able to save an additional $2,500 each month? If they applied the $2,500 monthly savings to their mortgage payment, their ending balance after three years would have dropped to $321,475.

This puts them $131,882 behind where they would have been if they had purchased the new home when they originally wanted to in 2011.

Here's a side-by-side comparison of the numbers:

---

9   Source: Toronto Real Estate Board

Details	Purchase in 2011	Purchase in 2014
Purchase price	$465,014	$566,696
Down payment	23,251	113,339
Insurance premium	12,148	0
Starting mortgage balance	453,911	453,357
Monthly payment	2,145.79	2,143.17*
Adjusted payment	4,645.79	n/a
2014 balance w/o increased pmt	415,487	453,357
2014 balance w/ increased pmt	321,475	453,357
Difference w/o increased pmt	$37,870	
Difference w/ increased pmt	$131,882	

*Assuming same rate of 2.99% with 25-year amortization

All this to save $12,148 in CMHC fees.

As you can see, delaying a home purchase can be quite costly in a rising housing market.

This is not the case in every situation however and saving up the 20% down payment to avoid the insurance premium can still be viewed as financially prudent. The above scenario was based on the Toronto market in a period that saw higher than normal appreciation. Many smaller markets will see significantly less. There are also periods where home prices can dip, depending on economic circumstances. You have to do what you feel most comfortable with and what you think makes sense for you.

....

Delaying a home purchase can be quite costly in a rising housing market.

....

BUT WHAT IF THE MARKET CRASHES?

Saving the mortgage default cost isn't the only reason why many suggest saving up the full 20% down payment. The other reason is to protect yourself against a market correction by having a larger equity position in your home. This way, if the market were to take a dive, you'll still likely end up in the black... meaning, your home is still worth more than what you owe on it.

Sure, it's possible that the market could correct. Anything can happen. If you purchase with only 5% down, and if the market were to correct right after purchasing, you will end up owing more on your home than it's worth. That is... until the market starts appreciating again, as it would.

There is no shortage of doom and gloomers that are always predicting a housing market catastrophe. "It's a bubble waiting to pop!" I've been hearing these predictions since 2006 and they haven't stopped straight through to the time of writing this update in early 2024. Anyone who listened to these people and either sold their homes, or waited for the big crash before purchasing would have missed out on six figure appreciation.

Will the market crash?

Anything can happen and no one can say for sure. Maybe it will or maybe it won't. All anyone can do is speculate.

From 1997 to 2023, the market experienced a 21-year upward trend in property values with only two instances of market decline. The first was in 2018, with a decrease of 4.21%, and the second in 2023, where the market saw a reduction of 5.69%.

TORONTO REAL ESTATE PRICES 1997 - 2023				
Year	Average Sale Price	Change ($)	Change (%)	Total Sales
1997	$210,695	+ $13,157*	+ 6.54%*	57,758
1998	216,017	+ 5,322	+ 2.53%	55,093
1999	228,372	+ 12,355	+ 5.72%	58,957
2000	243,255	+ 14,883	+ 6.52%	58,343
2001	251,508	+ 8,253	+ 3.39%	67,612
2002	275,231	+ 23,723	+ 9.43%	74,759
2003	293,067	+ 17,836	+ 6.48%	78,898
2004	315,231	+ 22,164	+ 7.56%	83,501
2005	335,907	+ 20,676	+ 6.56%	84,145
2006	351,941	+ 16,034	+ 4.77%	83,084
2007	376,236	+ 24,295	+ 6.90%	93,193
2008	379,080	+ 2,844	+ 0.76%	74,505
2009	395,234	+ 16,154	+ 4.26%	86,980
2010	431,262	+ 36,028	+ 9.12%	85,860
2011	464,989	+ 33,727	+ 7.82%	89,110

2012	497,073	+ 32,084	+ 6.90%	85,488
2013	$522,951	+ 25,878	+ 5.21%	87,047
2014	566,611	+ 43,660	+ 8.35%	92,776
2015	622,116	+ 55,505	+ 9.80%	101,213
2016	729,824	+ 107,708	+ 17.31%	113,040
2017	822,510	+ 92,686	+ 12.70%	92,340
2018	787,842	- 34,668	- 4.21%	78,017
2019	819,153	+ 31,311	+ 3.97%	87,747
2020	929,636	+ 110,483	+ 13.49%	95,066
2021	1,095,475	+ 65,839	+ 17.84%	121,712
2022	1,190,749	+ 95,274	+ 8.70%	75,047
2023	1,126,604	- 64,145	- 5.39%	65,982

Source: Toronto Real Estate Board / https://trreb.ca/files/market-stats/
market-watch/historic.pdf
*Average sale price in 1996 was $197,760

Average % increase each year: 6.78%
Average $ increase each year: $34,410

When you look at the rate of property value appreciation before each market downturn you can see the pattern. In the three years leading up to the 2017 correction, the market was on fire, with property values rocketing up by an average of 13.27% per year:

2015: +9.78%
2016: +17.31%
2017: +12.72%

That's a 45.15% increase in just three years. Following a brief stabilization, the market surged again starting in 2020, maintaining strong momentum for another two years. The average annual appreciation rate during this period was 13.34%:

2020: +13.49%
2021: +17.84%
2022: +8.70%

This led to a similar total increase of 45.36% over these three years. The nearly identical rates of appreciation preceding both corrections suggest a cyclical pattern of rapid growth followed by market adjustments. Given the long-term average increase in property values over the past 27 years, these corrections in 2017 and 2023 appear as natural responses to periods of unusually high growth.

The estate market is cyclical. After a housing market boom, it will eventually correct. But there is no way of knowing exactly when. A correction can come in the form of the market flattening out for a few years or it could be a much larger drop. The future is unknown and all we can do is speculate. Continual year over year appreciation is not guaranteed, nor is it expected. Eventually, the market will correct once again.

So, what do you do?

Deciding between purchasing a home with a minimal down payment or waiting until you have 20% hinges on what you feel most comfortable with.

Ask yourself this one important question:

What is the reason you are purchasing your home?

Is it to turn a quick profit within the next few years?

Or are you purchasing it to use as your primary residence for you and your family?

If you are just looking for a roof over your head, and the market were to take a dive, how is this going to affect you?

If a market correction leaves you in a negative equity position, where you owe more on your mortgage than what it's worth, the primary consequence is that you may need to delay the sale of your home. Sure, you have lost equity. But the market will eventually rebound, and your equity will return. You wouldn't lose a dime unless you were to sell during the correction period.

During the rebound, you'll continue to pay down your mortgage balance with each scheduled payment. If the thought of owing more on your home than what it's worth scares you, then you may want to consider increasing your payments to build equity faster. I'll be talking more about this in Chapter Eleven.

BENEFITS TO A SMALLER DOWN PAYMENT

Having the resources for a 20% down payment doesn't necessarily mean you should put down the full amount. As a mortgage broker, I see some people who can put down substantially more, yet they still choose to go with the minimum.

Why would anyone want to do this?

The rationale can vary, but primarily, it's about considering the alternative uses for the additional funds. In some situations, it might be beneficial to use them elsewhere, such as investing in higher-yielding opportunities, maintaining liquidity for emergencies, or funding other important financial goals.

Another thing to consider is the potential for higher returns on investments.

Recently, I received a call from Mai, a client halfway through her 5-year fixed mortgage term at a rate of 1.79%. With the current lowest 5-year fixed rate at 5.19%, she was exploring her prepayment options, aiming to reduce her mortgage balance as quickly as possible. She was concerned that rates would be higher at the end of her term, so she wanted to get the balance down as much as she could. After answering her questions, I asked her if this was something she really wanted to do.

Mai's fixed mortgage rate of 1.79% is exceptionally low. As it's well below the rate of inflation, it was like having access to 'free money'. Even the lowest risk investments could provide her with a higher return. There were high interest savings accounts offering returns as high as 4.00%, with GICs topping 5.00% in annual returns.

I advised Mai that everyone's situation can be different and that she has to do what she feels most comfortable with, but with guaranteed investments providing a much higher return than the rate on her mortgage, it seemed like a no brainer. At the end of her term, she could then cash out her investments and then pay a substantially higher amount down on her mortgage if she preferred.

I am not a financial advisor, nor do I pretend to be, so you're not going to see me venturing outside of my area of expertise with personal advice on how to invest your money. However, before making a final decision on down payment, I suggest speaking with a qualified financial advisor about your options. It's possible that you could end up with far more money at the end of your mortgage term than you would have if you had used the extra funds towards your down payment.

....

Before making a final decision on down payment, I suggest speaking with a qualified financial advisor about your options.

....

FINANCING 100% OF YOUR HOME PURCHASE

There used to be a time when just about anyone with a decent credit score could purchase a home with no money down. While options to purchase with no down payment are now much more limited, it's still possible. You're still going to need 5% down, however, you can borrow this 5% if you have a line of credit with a large enough limit. In essence, you would be financing 95% of the purchase with the mortgage secured against the home, with the remaining 5% borrowed against an unsecured line of credit.

Bingo!

You've just financed 100% of the purchase.

The payments for the borrowed down payment will need to be factored into the debt service ratios for qualifying. If you don't quite have 5% saved up and you are eager to purchase a home, then this can be an alternative providing everything makes sense for you.

But is this a good idea?

Many will advise against it, and I'm personally not a big fan of this strategy either. For that reason, I struggled with whether I should even include it in this book. As it is an option, and it's something that may work for certain individuals, I decided to include it.

But why isn't it recommended?

It's about having debt and being able to control it. Let's say you are purchasing a condo for $300,000 and are maxing out your line of credit with a $15,000 cash advance. Right off the bat, you have $15,000 in additional debt that you're now going to have to focus on paying off. Not the best way of starting out if you're struggling to make ends meet as it is.

Let's consider the following situation where this strategy may be an option to consider.

Jordan and Denise are looking at purchasing their first home, yet don't have any funds accumulated for down payment. They have about $10,000 saved up which they can use towards their closing costs, but they won't have anywhere close to the $20,000 they will need to purchase the $400,000 home they are interested in buying. The market is hot with values appreciating at an average of 8% per year. Waiting an extra year would mean they would have to spend an additional $32,000 to purchase a similar home.

Jordan is currently earning $50,000 per year as a resident physician; however, he'll be finishing his residency in one year, at which time he'll earn his full salary, which will be well into six figures. As his parents helped him out by paying for his education, he has no student loan and no other debt.

Considering the above situation, it's clear that Jordan is in a transition period in his life. Once he's making his full salary, he would easily be able to pay off the $20,000 owing on his line of credit, and he'll have saved $32,000 by purchasing the home a year earlier.

The above is just an example to demonstrate that there are times when it may make sense to purchase a home using borrowed funds.

Now let's look at another example on the opposite side of the spectrum.

Tyler and Marie have been dreaming about home ownership and it's something they are eager to get into. Their parents have been telling them that they need to buy a home as they are throwing their money away on rent each month. They've tried to save up, but with their $70,000 combined annual income, they haven't been able to accumulate much more than $7,000 over the past five years. Barely enough to cover their closing costs. Together they have accumulated about $15,000 in credit card debt. They found a condo they like for $200,000, however they don't have any money for the down payment. Their broker told them not to worry, as they can borrow the $10,000 they need from their line of credit. Coincidentally, that's the exact amount they have available, so if they max it out then they can make it work.

While it's great to own your own home, going deeply into debt to purchase a property can be a recipe for disaster. In this case, Tyler and Marie already have a high debt compared to their income. While they have managed to save $7,000 over the last few years, they haven't made a dent in their credit card debt. Now they are looking at borrowing an additional $10,000 giving them a total debt load of $25,000. This alone represents a large portion of their income. While they have managed to pay their bills on time, they struggled to save the money they have. Neither of their careers have any room for advancement, so they aren't expecting any notable increases to their income any time soon. Adding the additional $10,000 debt in this case would become excessive and will likely put them in a situation where they might never get it paid off. Their broker shouldn't have suggested for Tyler and Marie to borrow the down payment, even if they qualified for the mortgage. It was bad advice since it would have put his clients in a challenging financial situation.

As in the two examples above, you can see there are some situations where it might make sense to borrow the money for down payment and others where it doesn't. If you choose to borrow funds, it has to be from a source that has a verifiable payment structure such as a line of credit. Money borrowed from friends or family is not acceptable, as the repayment structure for the loan can't be confirmed.

The advice of an experienced, and ethical mortgage professional can be invaluable if you have any doubt at all.

Never let your emotions decide for you. The thought of purchasing a home can be exciting, so it can be easy to get carried away. Be conscious of this, and always know your limits. The excitement of owning a home can easily turn into a nightmare if you stretch yourself too thin by leaving yourself in a tough financial situation.

KEEP MORE MONEY IN YOUR POCKET

If you choose to put down the maximum your financial situation will allow, I always recommend holding back at least a bit of it. For example, some may have the resources to put down 40% and will put every single penny they have into their down payment, draining their savings right down to zero.

Always leave some room for additional expenses you may incur after taking possession. Unless you are okay with using old milk crates and the cardboard boxes from your move as temporary furniture, then you may want to hold something back. This way, you can furnish your home the way you really want to.

Other things you may need to purchase following closing:

- *Window coverings (particularly if it's a new build)* - Unless you like the idea of feeling like you're in a fishbowl where your neighbors can watch your every move, you'll likely want to cover up.

- *Lawn mower* - Unless you want your neighbors to think they're living beside the Clampett's, you'll need

PAUL MEREDITH

a mower if you're buying a house. Alternatively, you could always just buy a goat.

- *Cookware* - Moving into a new home may mean you'll want to upgrade some of your old cookware. Continuing to use the old frying pan your mom gave you when you first moved out may not cut it for the new home.

- *Towels* - You are moving into your new home! Time to cut up your old towels and use them as cleaning rags. Enjoy the new home experience to the fullest and buy yourself some new towels to go with it.

The list can go on. You won't have a full idea of exactly what you'll need until you've moved in. You also have no way of knowing if you're only a month away from your air conditioner or fridge conking out. Repairs and maintenance can be a costly part of home ownership, so you'll want to ensure you have some funds to pay any unforeseen circumstances that may arise.

Once you've gotten a feel for your new place and are content that you have everything you need, you can then put that extra money back into your mortgage using your prepayment privileges. I'll be discussing this in detail in Chapter Eleven.

PURCHASING A HIGHER VALUED HOME

Now we're going to move to the other end of the scale and discuss down payment requirements for higher valued homes. Unless you're new to the world of mortgages, most people are aware that the minimum down payment required to purchase a home is 20% for a conventional mortgage. However, what many are not aware of is that this rule only applies to homes valued up to a certain point. In other words, higher valued homes typically require a higher down payment. This can catch some off guard and throw a wrench into their plans.

On the higher priced homes, lenders will use a sliding scale to determine the minimum down payment they will accept on the purchase.

What is a Sliding Scale?

A sliding scale is where the minimum down payment changes once the purchase price reaches a predetermined threshold. A lender will accept the standard 20% down payment, but only up to a certain value. Once the purchase price exceeds this value, a higher down payment is required on the excess amount.

For example, a lender may accept a 20% down payment up to the first $1 million but may require a 50% down payment for any amount above $1 million. This is referred to as the sliding scale.

Why do Lenders Use a Sliding Scale?

It's directly related to their risk. The higher the purchase price, the more the value can fall if the housing market were to correct. A sliding scale gives the lender added protection, and therefore reduces their risk. When a market correction occurs, it does not correct evenly. Some areas will see a much larger drop than others. Higher valued properties may also see a larger correction. A $5 million home for example has much more room to fall than an $800,000 home. A $5 million home also appeals to a smaller demographic and can take longer to sell even in the hottest housing markets.

There are two major factors that can trigger the use of a sliding scale:

1. High purchase price
2. Property location

High Purchase Price

Sliding scale policies will vary from lender to lender, with the more stringent adhering to the example used above. They will allow a 20% down payment only up to the first $1 million of the purchase price, but will require a 50% down payment on the amount above $1 million.

This means the minimum down payment to purchase a $1.5 million property would be $450,000. $200,000 for the first $1 million (20%), and then another $250,000 for the additional $500,000 (50%).

While some mortgage lenders are this strict with their sliding scale policy, most lenders are more flexible.

What is the maximum purchase price you can hit without requiring a down payment greater than 20%?

The higher you go above $1 million, the fewer lending options become available. If you're purchasing in a major metropolitan area such as the GTA or GVA, you can purchase as high as $3.25 million with some lenders, without triggering a sliding scale. The higher you go, the fewer lending options become available. This doesn't mean you'll be paying a higher rate, and excellent mortgage rates may still be available to you.

Note that the sliding scale limits may be reduced for condos, and policies will vary from lender to lender. If you are purchasing a condo for more than $1 million, it's best to check with a mortgage professional before putting in an offer to purchase.

Property Location

Another major consideration is the location of the property. The further you purchase outside of a major centre, the more stringent the sliding scale may become. In some areas, the sliding scale may start as low as $500,000, which is not uncommon. If you were looking at purchasing a $750,000 cottage for example, the lender may only accept a 20% down payment up to $500,000, with a 50% down payment required for the additional $250,000. This would result in a minimum down payment of $225,000, or 30%. The sliding scale requirements can vary substantially depending on the location.

This is where it gets interesting.

If you are purchasing with LESS than 20% down payment in a rural area, you can go up to $999,999 without running into sliding scale issues. I know this sounds counterintuitive, and flat out defies logic. This is because a down payment of less than 20% requires mortgage default insurance such as CMHC. This gives the lender the additional protection they need and reduces their risk, therefore it eliminates the need for the sliding scale.

Lenders With a Sliding Scale Policy

It's not just 'some' lenders who have a sliding scale policy.

They all do.

It doesn't matter if you're applying to a major bank, credit union, or monoline lender. They all use sliding scales.

Anytime you are planning on purchasing a property, never assume you'll be okay because you have a 20% down payment. If you are purchasing in a well populated city, then you should be okay with a 20% down payment on a purchase up to $1 million with most lenders. But keep in mind that it can vary depending on the city, even within large centres such as the GTA and GVA.

CHAPTER NINE HIGHLIGHTS

- Minimum down payment to purchase a home is 5%.

- Homes over $500,000 will require 5% of the first $500,000 and 10% on the amount over $500,000.

- Homes over $1 million require 20% down payment.

- 20% is the minimum down payment needed to avoid mortgage default insurance.

- Always look at how fast homes are appreciating in your area and compare that with how long it would take you to save up 20% down payment. It may be cheaper to pay the insurance premium incurred from a lower down payment.

- Homes in the GTA appreciated for 21 straight years until we saw a minor correction in 2018.

- What is your purpose for purchasing a home? Are you looking for an investment or are you looking for a home for your family to live in?

- Speak with a financial advisor before putting all your money into your down payment.

- Keep some money aside for miscellaneous expenses, purchases, or repairs that may be required after closing.

- Always be conscious of a lender's sliding scale policy, which would require a down payment greater than 20%.

Like the choice between fixed and variable, the ideal down payment amount is a personal decision. It comes down to what you feel most comfortable with. Take the time to carefully outline your options and write out the benefits to each option. Speak with a financial advisor and then do what you think will be best suited to you and your family.

10

SECRETS TO SAVING ON YOUR MORTGAGE

"It's not how much money you make, but how much money
you keep, how hard it works for you, and how many
generations you keep it for."
~Robert Kiyosaki

If there is one thing we all have in common, it's the desire to save money. Everyone wants the lowest rate and there is a level of personal satisfaction and gratification that comes with finding the best deal. There is no question that rate is important. Very important. However, contrary to what many believe, the lowest mortgage rate doesn't always make it the best choice.

You'll first want to determine what's most important to you:

- Having the lowest mortgage rate.
- Having the lowest mortgage payment.
- Saving the most money over time.

If you could only choose one, which would it be?

At this point you're likely scratching your head with confusion as so many people are focused on the mortgage rate and nothing else. They use rate as the sole barometer for determining the overall cost of the mortgage.

As you read through this chapter, you'll gain a lot more clarity on why the lowest mortgage rate will not always save you the most money.

THE MORTGAGE RATE OBSESSION

Some people become so overly obsessed with finding the lowest rate on the market that they become completely consumed by it. They stress themselves out as they scour the internet, always on the hunt for a rate that's even a fraction lower. Their quest for the absolute lowest rate turns into a never-ending cycle, overshadowing other important aspects of choosing a mortgage. The search can become a mission for some, pouring in countless hours.

While being diligent in shopping for a competitive mortgage rate is a smart move, there's a fine line between research and obsession. If that same energy and passion were redirected towards wealth-building activities, you might discover new opportunities. These could provide more substantial long-term benefits than the comparatively marginal savings from a slightly lower mortgage rate.

It's great to find the lowest rate on the market, but it should never become an obsession... nor does it need to be.

Many tend to look at mortgages as a commodity, like buying

milk or sugar. However, there is a lot more to a mortgage than just the rate. Selecting a mortgage based solely on the interest rate can be a deceptive trap, one that might seem like a money saving move at first but could lead to unforeseen costs down the line. It's important to look beyond the allure of a low rate and scrutinize the fine print. Hidden clauses, stringent terms, and unexpected penalties often lurk within mortgage agreements. These overlooked details can transform what initially appears as savings into additional and unexpected costs down the road.

FOUR ELEMENTS TO CONSIDER WHEN SHOPPING FOR A MORTGAGE

While rate is an important component in making your choice, there are four elements that you need to consider which are listed in order of importance:

1. The person you choose to handle your mortgage
2. Terms and conditions
3. Mortgage rate
4. Lender

Let's review each one of these elements individually so you have a better idea of why I've put them in that order.

THE PERSON YOU CHOOSE TO HANDLE YOUR MORTGAGE

The value a quality mortgage professional can offer cannot

be underestimated. They play a key role in helping you to score a win on each of the other three categories on the above list. A proficient broker not only helps in acquiring a competitive mortgage rate but also saves you considerable time and effort by combing the market on your behalf, sparing you the hassle of shopping around for the best deal.

But there is a lot more to a mortgage than just rate and the savings that can be achieved through the quality of the advice provided by a seasoned mortgage professional can far surpass that of a lower mortgage rate at times.

Jaroslav and Irina were ecstatic when their offer to purchase their new dream home was accepted. They reached out to a mortgage professional who advised that they would have to return their existing mortgage, incurring a penalty of approximately $2,000. It also meant letting go of their current mortgage rate, which was an incredibly low 1.39% with $466,000 outstanding and 2.5 years left in the term. They were told that their only option was to accept a rate of 5.64% for their desired 3-year term. This significant jump in the interest rate was a tough pill to swallow, however, they had done their research on mortgage rates discovered that the new rate was the most competitive available at that time. For that reason, they figured they had no other choice but to accept it.

Even with the proceeds from the sale of their home, Jaroslav and Irina's down payment was well below 20%, meaning it would need to be CMHC insured. They asked the mortgage agent if there was anything that could be done considering that they also had to pay the premium when they purchased their current home two and a half years ago. The agent advised them that the insurance premium is specific to each transaction, and because they are now purchasing a new home, the full premium will apply in the amount of $28,000. The previous premium paid applied to the purchase of their current home only, and that no portion of it could be recovered considering that the previous purchase is viewed as old news.

Then they received the next piece of disappointing information.

They needed a new mortgage of $705,000 to make their new home purchase a reality. However, they were told that they would only qualify for a maximum of $640,000. While they had come to terms with the higher rate, they were now concerned that they would have to walk away from the purchase as they didn't have the additional $65,000 needed to qualify.

Jaroslav and Irina then decided to call us for a second opinion. After a thorough review of their situation, I advised them that they could port their existing mortgage to the new property. This option was a game-changer. Not only did it eliminate the $2,000 penalty for returning their current mortgage, but it also significantly reduced their interest rate from a steep 5.64% to a much more manageable 3.36%. The lower rate didn't just save them a boat load of cash, but it now enabled them to qualify for the mortgage needed to complete the purchase... no additional down payment necessary.

And since their original mortgage was also insured, I advised them that they could not just port the mortgage, but port the original CMHC insurance as well. Instead of paying the premium on the full $705,000, they now only had to pay the top up premium on the $239,000 increase. This brought the insurance premium from $28,000 down to a more reasonable $15,000, saving them an additional $13,000. As CMHC insurance premiums in Ontario are subject to 8% PST, the reduction also saved them an additional $1,000 in tax.

At the end of the day, their total savings amounted to a whopping $64,000:

$48,000 on the lower rate[10]
$2,000 on the penalty
$13,000 on the insurance premium
$1,000 on PST

$64,000 in total.

But most importantly, they were able to complete the purchase of the home they had their hearts set on.

This is just one of many examples of how a quality mortgage professional can save you money. I could fill an entire book with nothing but stories like this. They are endless.

A Mortgage is a Huge Financial Commitment

A mortgage represents one of the most significant financial

---

10 To calculate the savings between two mortgage rates, you match the payment from the higher rate option, then take the difference between the ending balance. On a $705,000 amortized over 25 years, the difference between 5.64% and 3.36% is $48,325.93 over the 36 month term.

commitments in a person's life. When you place a deposit on a new home, you're not just committing to a property; you're potentially risking tens of thousands of dollars or more. The financial stakes are high, making it essential to approach this decision with careful consideration.

When a lender approves your application, they will issue a commitment outlining all the terms and conditions. While it may seem like a solid assurance, it doesn't 100% guarantee approval. The only way to be absolutely sure that your home purchase will close without any hitches is if you have the full amount needed to buy the property outright. But when a mortgage is required to complete the purchase, there's always a degree of uncertainty, no matter how small, until the day you pick up the keys to your new home.

When lender issues a mortgage commitment (approval), it's not a legally binding document. You can cancel with that lender at any time, and you don't even have to give them a reason why.

However, this works both ways.

The lender can also cancel your commitment at any time, right up until the closing date. They also do not have to give you a reason why. It doesn't matter if you are dealing through a major bank, credit union, or monoline lender, the same rules apply.

There are many things that can go wrong with your mortgage prior to closing. The appraisal could come in low, requiring you to increase your down payment. Lenders could uncover details in your documentation that may have been initially missed, raising concerns or questions.

They could suspect misrepresentation of the information provided. As mentioned in Chapter Two, mortgage fraud is a huge problem in this industry, so a lender cannot have any doubts about the authenticity of the documents received.

In some cases, the issue might not even be with the borrower, but the property itself. Unexpected problems could surface that weren't initially apparent, creating complications. These issues are most commonly uncovered when people use a potential problem with the property as a bargaining chip to lower the purchase price after the offer has been accepted. I described this situation in detail in Chapter Two.

These are just some of the potential issues that can be encountered. There can be hundreds that could arise. A lender backing out of a commitment at the last minute is rare, however, you can minimize the risk by choosing the right person to work with.

When Jerome and Corina first reached out to us, the purchase of their first home was closing in just three weeks. As rates were dropping, they had held off on applying for a mortgage until that time. They had solid, confirmable employment, sparkling credit, 20% down payment, and their debt-to-income ratios were well within the maximum allowable limits. Everything looked solid and getting them approved was just a formality. It was a picture-perfect client with a picture-perfect application.

Following a detailed discussion about their options, we forwarded their application to their preferred lender and were able to secure an approval within just three hours. As they provided a complete set of documents upfront, the only remaining steps to finalize their approval involved obtaining an appraisal of the property and a verbal confirmation of their employment.

When Jerome and Corina returned the signed approval documents a few days later, the lender initiated the next step – verbally verifying their employment.

Cue major problem number one.

Jerome's employer informed the lender that he submitted his resignation the day before. This introduced a complication to what had appeared to be a straightforward approval. Jerome's income was essential for their mortgage qualification, and this sudden change put everything at risk. Naturally, I called him immediately. He explained that he had accepted a new position at another company, offering a higher hourly wage. He believed this wouldn't pose an issue, considering the increase in his income. In some situations, he would be right. But not in this one.

While switching jobs isn't usually a deal-breaker for mortgage approvals, as long as the new employment is properly documented and confirmed, this situation was different. All lenders will require a paystub from the new employer to validate the change in income. But given that he hadn't even started his new job, and with the closing date merely two weeks away, a paystub from the new employer wasn't going to be in the cards. This became a major stumbling block in finalizing their mortgage approval, putting their new home purchase at risk.

As if that wasn't challenging enough, the new employment wasn't exactly in the same field as he had been working in previously. Mortgage lenders typically prefer a consistent employment history within the same line of work, as it demonstrates stability and consistency in the borrower's career path. Employment in a new field introduces one additional layer of concern for a lender.

After extensive discussions with both the client and the lender, we were able to establish just enough of a connection between Jerome's new role and his previous position. By highlighting the transferable skills and relevant aspects of his career path, and leveraging my stellar relationship with the lender, I was able to get the new employment accepted... despite the lack of a paystub. I pulled a rabbit out of a hat.

Now, the final piece of the puzzle was the appraisal. For new construction purchases, mortgage lenders have a specific requirement: the appraisal report must not only confirm the value but also verify that the property is at least 97% complete. This percentage translates to essentially being fully finished, with the remaining 3% typically accounting for minor aspects like landscaping.

Cue major problem number two.

When we received the appraisal report just four business days before closing, it confirmed that the property was only 92% complete. The floors in the new home were not yet installed. Upon discussing the predicament with Jerome, he revealed an unconventional arrangement with the builder. They had struck a separate deal, outside the standard purchase agreement, to leave the floors unfinished. Jerome and Corina planned to install their own flooring after closing.

Now we have yet another colossal problem… and right before closing.

From the perspective of a mortgage lender, an unfinished property doesn't meet the criteria for a liveable space. For them to release the mortgage funds, the property must be fully completed and ready for occupancy.

After a series of in-depth discussions with Jerome, Corina and the lender, I presented a strong case, convincing the lender that the flooring would indeed be installed promptly after closing. Once again, I was able to get the lender to grant us yet another major exception and close the new purchase on time. Taddah!! Rabbit extracted from the hat once again.

There are times when a mortgage professional needs to be somewhat of a magician to work around issues that can arise. For Jerome and Corina, the closing process of their new home was riddled with stress and unexpected hurdles. Despite these challenges, they remained deeply appreciative of the expertise and unwavering commitment that ultimately got the purchase of their dream home closed on schedule.

I remember when I purchased my first home, just prior to entering the mortgage business. It was a new build property through Mattamy Homes. I asked them if they could deliver with home without carpet as I wanted to install my own flooring after closing. They advised me that they had to deliver the home fully completed… even if I was going to rip the carpet out immediately after taking possession. At the time, it didn't make sense, but I now understand why.

Saving on your mortgage extends beyond securing a

favourable rate or an optimal application structure. It involves not just tackling potential challenges but taking the necessary steps to prevent many of them from happening in the first place. Failure to meet a closing date can result in considerable extra costs for you. The expertise of an experienced mortgage professional is invaluable, particularly in steering you clear of costly pitfalls while minimizing your stress. Their deep comprehension of mortgages helps with working your way through complex scenarios, ensuring that the mortgage arrangement process remains smooth and free from unforeseen expenses.

Refer to Chapter Seven for a comprehensive guide on choosing a mortgage professional.

TERMS AND CONDITIONS

Once you have chosen the person you would like to handle your mortgage for you, the next most important consideration is the terms and conditions. The reason why this is more important than the rate is because it can significantly affect the cost over time. There is much more to a mortgage than just the rate.

Many look at mortgages as a one-size-fits-all article of clothing... where they are all the same. However, they are not all cut from the same cloth. A mortgage can contain hidden clauses that could come back to bite you down the road. While there are some that may be outlined in the mortgage commitment, the wording can sometimes be like trying to read hieroglyphics on the wall of an Egyptian pyramid.

Below is a list of common restrictions found with some mortgages that you should be aware of:

- High return penalties
- Bona fide sale clause
- Cashback clawbacks
- Inflated prime rate
- Variable rate compounding
- Limited prepayment privileges
- Collateral mortgages

High Return Penalties

One of the most important terms of consideration is how the penalty is calculated if you find yourself in a position where you need to return... or 'break' your mortgage early. There can be a significant difference from one lender to the next. The minimal monthly savings on rate wouldn't mean a whole lot if you are slapped with an additional $40,000 in penalties for returning your mortgage early.

I'll be discussing return penalties in detail later in this chapter.

Bona Fide Sale Clause

This restriction means that you cannot return your mortgage before the end of your term unless you sell your house... even with a penalty. With a bona fide sale clause, you're essentially marrying yourself to that lender for the full term, which is generally five years. At the end of the term, the restriction is irrelevant as the mortgage can then be transferred to another lender without additional cost. At this stage, it's no different from a mortgage without the clause.

Some products with a bona fide sale clause include BMO's

Smart Fixed Mortgage, MCAP's Value Flex, and CMLS's Rate Advantage.

Some do not fully understand the restriction when first explained to them. When told that they cannot return the mortgage unless they sell the home, they may respond by saying that they are okay with the clause as they don't intend to sell. However, selling the property is the only condition under which the mortgage can be returned before the term ends.

Note that some lenders may still let you refinance, but you are limited to the same lender. Other lenders may not let you refinance at all.

Most people won't face issues with a bona fide sale clause, often agreeing to it under the belief they won't need to return their mortgage. Yet, the unexpected can happen. For instance, if mortgage rates drop mid-term, creating potential savings, you might be tempted to return your current mortgage for a more favorable rate. However, with a bona fide sale clause in place, this wouldn't be possible, and you'd be left with no choice but to ride out your mortgage for the rest of the term. That is, unless you sell. As with any added mortgage restriction, your mortgage professional should take the time to point out and explain this restriction at the time they quote you the rate.

If you think there is a good chance that you may need to refinance before the end of the term, then you're best choosing a mortgage without a bona fide sale clause. Usually, I like to see a minimum discount of 0.10% - 0.15% on the rate to justify the clause. Even then, you are committing to a more restrictive mortgage, so if this is something that is even slightly concerning to you, then I would opt for a mortgage without this clause.

Cashback Clawbacks

Cashback mortgages can be extremely profitable for banks, so it's not uncommon for some to push them. As the name implies, a cashback mortgage will pay the borrower a certain amount of cash back at the time of closing.

While there are many cashback mortgages that do not have any strings attached, there are some that carry a higher interest rate. It's not 'free money' in these situations. If you return your mortgage early, not only will you be facing a penalty, but you'll also have to pay back the cash as well. Most lenders will pro-rate this, however, some do not. In fact, some banks will require 100% of this cash to be paid back to them, regardless of how late into the term you return the mortgage. It could be in the final month of your term, and you'll still have to pay 100% of it back to that bank. In that case, you'll have paid the higher interest rate for nothing.

Note that not all cashback mortgages have a clawback clause, so it's best to confirm with your mortgage professional before you ink the deal.

Inflated Prime Rate

This applies to variable rate mortgages only. For the most part, the prime rate is the same across the board, regardless of which lender you choose. However, TD has a special 'mortgage' prime rate, which is 0.15% higher than virtually all other lenders. For example, let's say the prime rate is 7.20%. If TD is offering prime -1.00% while another lender is offering prime -0.85%, it can sound like TD is the better deal given the larger discount off prime. But as TD's mortgage prime rate is 0.15% higher at 7.35%, the mortgage rate will be 6.20% with both lenders.

Here's where it can get even more confusing. If you were to visit TD's website, you'll see that their prime rate is the same as all other lenders. This is because TD uses two different prime rates, so it's important to distinguish between the two. There is the TD prime rate, which is the same as the rest of the industry. Then there is the TD mortgage prime rate, which is the one that they use specifically for mortgages.

But what fun would it be if they didn't add yet another layer of complexity?

If you're applying for their Flexline product, which includes a HELOC, then they use the standard prime rate on both the amortized mortgage portion as well as the HELOC portion. It's only on their standard mortgage products where the higher prime rate is used.

When you're quoted a variable rate mortgage, the mortgage professional should be providing you both the discount off prime as well as the actual rate itself. It's the actual rate that is most important as it's the one that your initial payments will be calculated from.

Variable Rate Compounding

While the interest on fixed-rate mortgages is always compounded semi-annually, regardless of lender, it can be compounded either monthly or semi-annually with variable rate mortgages. This is something that few people even think about, however, it can be an important consideration when choosing a variable rate mortgage as it has an impact on its overall cost.

You might have two lender options to choose from, both with the same rate, but with different compounding periods. This means that the options will appear the same when presented to you, however, there will be a difference in the payments between the two.

For example, let's say you need a $500,000 mortgage with a 25-year amortization. You have two options, both at 4.00%. Here's the monthly payment on each:

Semi-annual compounding: $2,630.10
Monthly compounding: $2,639.18

Same rate.

Same mortgage amount.

Same amortization.

Yet the monthly payment on the option with monthly compounding is $9.08 higher.

In the above example, a 4.00% variable rate with monthly compounding would be equivalent to having a rate of 4.03345% with semi-annual compounding.

However, it doesn't remain constant for the term as the difference in payment and equivalent rate will vary depending on the rate itself. For instance, if the rate was 7.00%, there is a greater difference in payment:

Semi-annual compounding: $3,502.08
Monthly compounding: $3,533.90

The monthly payment difference on the same $500,000 mortgage grows to $31.82 with an equivalent rate of 7.1029%. In other words, if you were offered 7.1029% by a lender with semi-annual compounding and 7.00% by another with monthly compounding, it would sound like you're getting a better deal by choosing the lower rate of 7.00%. However, based on that rate, they are 100% identical in terms of payment and cost. Of course, your mortgage rate will only have two decimal places, so if we round the semi-annual compounded rate down to 7.10%, you would actually be saving 10 cents per month compared with the lower rate 'deal' at 7.00%. However, this is only if the rate were to remain unchanged.

Now let's look at the monthly payment difference using a rate of 2.00%:

Semi-annual compounding: $2,117.26
Monthly compounding: $2,119.27

With the lower rate, the difference in monthly payment drops to $2.01 with an equivalent rate of 2.00834%. It didn't even crack two decimal places.

Few people consider these compounding differences. Always remember to ask about compounding when choosing a variable rate mortgage product.

Limited Prepayment Privileges

All mortgages will allow you to pay your mortgage off faster through their prepayment privileges. While the majority of lenders are quite flexible in this department, there are some which are quite limited. If your goal is to aggressively pay down your mortgage, then you'll want to ensure your lender of choice has prepayment privileges that are flexible enough to accomplish your goal. I'll be discussing prepayment privileges in detail in the next chapter.

Collateral Charge Mortgages

If researching collateral mortgages, you'll likely find your fair share of conflicting information. This is because it used to be a bigger issue than what is today, however, it's still worth noting. There was a time when the only way to move a collateral mortgage to another lender was to refinance. In many situations, refinancing rates can be higher than what you could find if you were doing a straight mortgage transfer. In these cases, the additional cost created from a collateral mortgage could easily get into the thousands. Fortunately, mortgage regulations have changed, and now the additional cost involved with transferring a collateral mortgage is far less severe, if anything at all. I'll be discussing collateral mortgages in detail later in this chapter.

MORTGAGE RATE

The third most important thing to consider when choosing a mortgage is the rate. People generally look for the lowest rate as it's the simplest concept to understand. Mortgage rate is extremely important of course. The lower the rate, the less interest you'll pay and the more you save. However, the lowest mortgage rate will not always be the best choice for the reasons mentioned above.

A competent mortgage professional plays a crucial role in this scenario. They should be transparent about any restrictions or special terms associated with a mortgage product right from the start. This information allows you to make an informed decision, balancing the appeal of a lower rate with the practicality and flexibility you need in a mortgage. In some cases, you might find that the lowest rate is available without significant restrictions, or perhaps with terms that are manageable for your specific situation. Ultimately, the goal is to find a mortgage that aligns with not just your immediate financial needs but also your long-term financial health and goals.

LENDER

While the choice of lender is important, it's at the bottom of this list. I've already discussed rates and terms and conditions, which can often be used to rule out certain lenders. Some lenders may also have better service departments than others. I would personally never put a client of mine with a lender that I would not feel comfortable dealing with for my own mortgage, or if I were doing one for a close family member, such as my mom, brother, or sister. My reputation is far too important to me to take that chance. While there are some lenders who fall into this category, most lenders are pretty good to deal with.

Some believe that it's better to deal with a major bank, solely because they are familiar with the brand name. However, familiarity with a lender's name doesn't necessarily make them the best option for your mortgage needs. Conversely, not recognizing a lender's name doesn't automatically make them a poor choice. Keep in mind, it's the lender who is loaning you the money, not the other way around.

When choosing a lender, it's important to evaluate them based on their mortgage products, terms, rates, and service quality, rather than just their brand recognition. Smaller or less well-known lenders may have more competitive rates compared to larger banks. Ultimately, the decision should be based on which lender is best suited to your specific financial requirements and circumstances.

There are many myths about non-bank lenders, most likely spread by the big banks themselves. Sometimes banks will try to make it seem as though their money is of better quality than the money coming from other lenders. Some mortgage specialists may even resort to providing flat out false information in attempt to deter you from taking your business elsewhere. If you're getting conflicting information, it's best to research it yourself to determine if what you're being told is accurate.

I discussed lender differences in detail in Chapter Six.

HOW TO GET THE BEST DEAL

Exploring your mortgage rate options with various banks or brokers can be highly beneficial. It's surprising how often people overlook this simple step, which could involve just a few emails or phone calls. By not investigating, you might miss out on significantly lower rates, sometimes as much as 0.30% lower... or even possibly even lower than that.

So how does this translate into real numbers?

Let's say you have a $300,000 mortgage amortized over 30 years. Lender X is offering a 5-year fixed rate of 2.89% while lender Y is offering 2.59%. The savings with lender X works out to $4,491.72 over the five-year term. [11] This is money that could be in your pocket as opposed to the bank's.

In Chapter Seven, I gave you a list of questions to ask your broker and one of them was to determine exactly how many different lenders they deal with. If they are putting their business predominantly with a single lender, then there is a good chance they may not be getting you the best available rate. Not every broker has access to every lender. A broker very well may be giving the lowest rate they are able to, however, lower rates might be available through another lender that they may not deal with regularly.

If they are putting their business predominantly with a single lender, then there is a good chance they may not be getting you the best available rate.

Regardless of whether you choose to go with a bank or a broker, speak to at least three different industry professionals so you can get a better handle on what's available. It also doesn't hurt to do a quick Google search, however, you can't always believe every rate you see online unfortunately. Usually, online rates are for high ratio mortgages only, meaning they are not available to everyone. As explained in Chapter Three, rates are very heavily dependent on down

---

11   Total savings is calculated by using the payment from the higher rate for both options and then calculating the difference in ending balance.

payment percentage, property value, transaction type, etc. We no longer live in a world with one-size-fits-all mortgage rates. I don't see anything wrong with promoting low rates online, as long as there is a clear disclaimer outlining the circumstances in which that rate can be provided.

WHAT YOUR BANK MAY NOT BE TELLING YOU

In Chapter Six, I discussed how any one specific lender such as a major bank, can only offer their own products. For example, if you walk into BMO, they aren't going to come out and tell you if CIBC happens to have a product that better suits your needs, or vice versa.

Back when I used to work in retail more than twenty-five years ago, we had a rule of thumb that we had to follow. SWAT. It stood for Sell What's Available Today. If we didn't have an item in stock, we were to present the product that we did have available at that time, which would increase our chances of making the sale on that day. Banks are going to employ a similar system to SWAT by only selling the products they have available to them.

Makes sense of course, right?

Why would one lender try to sell you another lender's products?

They wouldn't.

As they are only going to sell their own products, they may not be so quick to tell you about any potential disadvantages they may have. They know that telling you may result in you going elsewhere for your mortgage. While the same logic can be applied to brokers, their ability to source mortgages from many different lenders gives them a much larger pool of mortgage products to offer.

This is why it's so important to become a knowledgeable mortgage shopper. Fortunately, you're reading this book, so you will now have a significant edge when shopping for your next mortgage, regardless of whether you choose to go through your bank, or through a broker.

STANDARD CHARGE VS. COLLATERAL CHARGE

A mortgage is an amortized[12] loan secured by collateral on real estate. Since your home serves as collateral, the lender can extend a lower rate compared to an unsecured loan, where no collateral is offered. Should the borrower default on the mortgage, the lender has rights associated with the property it was secured against.

The mortgage gets secured to the property with what's called a charge, which is similar to a lien. There are two types of charges that can be used:

- Standard charge
- Collateral charge

---

12   Amortized meaning that the principal of the loan gradually gets paid down to zero through scheduled payments of principal and interest.

Let's take a look at each one in detail to give you a better understanding of what the different charges mean to you.

STANDARD CHARGE

Most mortgages are registered as standard charges, offering you the flexibility to transfer your mortgage to another lender at the end of your term, often with minimal to no additional cost. This process usually involves legal fees and sometimes an appraisal fee, but these are typically covered by the new lender. Regardless of whether it's a standard or collateral charge mortgage, a small discharge fee is incurred in most provinces when the lender is fully paid off. While a few lenders might absorb this fee, most do not, leaving the option to either roll the discharge fee into your new mortgage or pay it upfront during the transfer process.

COLLATERAL CHARGE

With a collateral mortgage, the lender does not always cover the legal and appraisal fees, which is the biggest drawback. The legal fee can range from $600 to $900, depending on the province. When required, the appraisal fee generally ranges from $300 to $400, however, this number can be higher in less populated areas. There are some lenders who will cover some, or even all these costs for you, however, the rate is often 0.05% higher than it would be if the borrower were covering the costs.

How does this work out in real numbers?

Let's say you need a $500,000 mortgage amortized over 25 years and would like to proceed with a 5-year fixed term. You have two options:

1. 3.64% with fees of $1,100 added to the mortgage balance.

2. 3.69% with fees paid by the lender.

Which do you think is the better choice?

The answer is they are almost identical with a negligible cost difference of $53.61over the term in favour of the slightly higher rate of 3.69%. The more the mortgage amount falls below $500,000, the more you'll come out ahead with the lender covering the fees at the higher rate. Over $500,000, the lower rate with the borrower paid fees would be the better choice.

The legal fee can be added to the mortgage balance, so you would not need to pay this out of pocket. If an appraisal is required, then you would need to pay it up front since the appraisal report would be required prior to the closing of the new mortgage. The cost of the appraisal can often be reimbursed to you after closing, however, every situation is a little different.

In some cases, the fees can be covered for you without any rate premium at all, which would make the collateral charge insignificant.

A transfer will convert your mortgage from a collateral charge to a standard charge mortgage. This can potentially lower the cost of switching at the end of the new term.

Additional Credit Secured by a Collateral Charge

Another drawback to collateral mortgages is that any credit cards, lines of credit, overdrafts, or loans that you have with the same lender can also be tied to your mortgage. Most people are likely not aware of this, if they are even aware that their mortgage is a collateral charge in the first place. If you have a collateral mortgage and a credit card with the same lender, and if that credit card were to go into default, then your mortgage could be considered in default as well... even though you haven't missed a single mortgage payment. This is rarely, if ever an issue, but it's still worth mentioning. If you happen to fall behind on a credit card that is secured by the equity in the home, then it would be an easy situation to rectify. Make the minimum payment and problem solved.

The Benefit to a Collateral Charge Mortgage

Lenders who offer collateral mortgages will generally give you the option to register them for up to 125% of the property value. In other words, if you are buying a home for $1 million, you can choose to register the mortgage for $1.25 million, regardless of the actual mortgage amount. This would allow you to borrow additional funds against your home as it appreciates. Because your mortgage was already registered for a higher amount, there is no need to register additional security. This would eliminate the legal fees involved with borrowing more money. Otherwise, it could cost roughly $600 to $1,000 to obtain this secondary financing.

Sounds okay, right?

Well, the problem is that you still need to qualify for the additional financing. If the lender were to decline your application, then you would be out of luck as the lender has tied up all your equity. If you were in a bad position where you were in dire need of funds, then you would have no choice but to refinance the entire mortgage and pay the associated penalty. This means you could potentially be giving up a lower mortgage rate in exchange for a much higher one, which would not be a good position to be in. (I've had clients in this situation).

If you do qualify, then great, you 'potentially' saved yourself $1,000 in set up costs. However, at the end of your term, you'll still find that options are more limited if you want to switch to a different lender at no additional cost.

How do You Know if your Mortgage is a Collateral Charge?

Any multi-component or hybrid mortgage will also be collateral, regardless of how it's divided. Below are some examples:

- Mortgage + HELOC
- Part variable rate / part fixed rate
- 3-year term + 5-year term

It doesn't matter if your lender is TD, CIBC, MCAP, B2B Bank, or whoever. If it has more than one component registered on the same charge, then it will be a collateral mortgage. Period.

Any freestanding HELOC (without any amortized mortgage attached to it) would also be registered as a collateral charge. This applies regardless of lender.

There are a few lenders who will register ALL their mortgages as a collateral charge, which include TD, Tangerine, and

National Bank. Note that if you switched in from another lender, then it's possible that your mortgage with these lenders may still be registered as a standard charge.

Also, TD did not start registering all their mortgages as collateral until October 18, 2010. If you arranged your current mortgage with TD prior to that date, and you have not refinanced since, then you likely have a standard charge mortgage.

You can sometimes tell if your mortgage is collateral simply by the product name. Some of these include:

- Home Power Plan (CIBC)
- STEP (Scotiabank)
- HomeLine (RBC)
- ReadiLine (BMO)
- Fusion (MCAP)

The above would all be registered as collateral mortgages, regardless of whether you have a second component attached to it.

Should Collateral Mortgages be Avoided?

Most borrowers will not benefit from a collateral charge. Does this mean that it should always be avoided?

Not at all.

There are some cases where they are required. It depends on your needs, as well as the offering. Some people require a HELOC, in which case a collateral mortgage would be the only option. It can be set up where the limit on the HELOC increases as the mortgage is paid down. This type of set up can be important to investors for example, and a standard charge mortgage would not be best suited to their needs.

Sometimes the rate offering from the collateral mortgage can be attractive, which would make the disadvantages insignificant. If lender X is offering a rate of 2.99% with a collateral charge and lender Y is offering 3.29% with a standard charge mortgage, then the choice is a no brainer. Since the savings seen from the lower rate would more than cover the possible costs when transferring the mortgage, it wouldn't make any sense to avoid the collateral charge.

I've seen some people go out of their way to avoid a collateral mortgage, regardless of how much lower the rate might be. In their mind, a collateral mortgage is bad, so they avoid it like the plague. They don't know why, and when asked, they can't explain it. They just know they don't want it.

I remember overhearing a mortgage 'professional' saying that they would never put their clients into a collateral mortgage under any circumstances. While there may be some cases where it makes more sense to opt for a standard charge mortgage, a blanket statement like this is nothing short of bad advice.

The only considerable disadvantage of a collateral mortgage is that there could potentially be some added fees to transfer it to another lender.

Any mortgage with more than one component will be registered as a collateral charge.

Conventional vs. Collateral

Many consumers will often refer to a standard charge as a conventional mortgage. I've even seen some banks use this terminology, but this is incorrect. Any mortgage that does not require default insurance such as CMHC is considered a conventional mortgage, regardless of the type of charge.

For example, let's say you inquire with a lender that registers all their mortgages as collateral charges. You tell them that you have 20% down and that you would like a conventional mortgage. They can assure you with confidence that you will in fact be getting a conventional mortgage. However, they may not tell you that this conventional mortgage will also be registered as a collateral charge. They aren't misleading you here either. They are simply answering your question... and answering it correctly. The simple fact that your mortgage doesn't have a default insurance premium is what makes the mortgage conventional. Therefore, you can have a conventional mortgage that is also a collateral charge.

If you want to ask about the type of charge then ask flat out if it's a collateral mortgage, just to ensure there is no confusion. Even in these cases, I've had many clients present this question to their bank who were told that their mortgage is not collateral, only for them to find out later that it is. In fact, this happens quite regularly.

This is why it's always a good idea to ask a lot of questions as I outlined in Chapter Seven. Get an idea of that individual's experience level so you know you're getting the right answers. In the end, if you're getting a new mortgage with TD, National Bank or Tangerine, then your mortgage will be a collateral charge. The only exception to this is if you're transferring your mortgage from another lender at the end of your term. In this case, the standard charge would remain intact.

UNDERSTANDING MORTGAGE PENALTIES

When you select your mortgage product, you're entering into a contractual agreement with the lender for a specific closed term. Should you find yourself needing to return the mortgage early, you're essentially breaching your contract with the lender. Consequently, the lender will then impose a penalty for breaking it early.

Think of this as the lender's return policy. If you're purchasing something that you're not 100% sure you'll want to keep, you'll want to learn about the store's return policy. When you break your mortgage, you're essentially returning the borrowed funds to the lender.

How the penalty is calculated can vary significantly from one lender to the next.

One of the biggest opportunities to save money on your mortgage is by choosing a lender with a consumer-friendly formula for calculating your penalty. It's amazing how many people will tell me that they don't plan on returning their mortgage early, so they are not concerned about the return penalty being high.

The problem is that circumstances change.

Things come up.

Life throws you curveballs.

Anything can happen in a five-year period. Many don't plan on returning their mortgage, but people don't plan on getting divorced either. But it happens. As a result, many borrowers end up returning their mortgages before the end of the term. If they knew they would be in this situation, then they would have chosen a more suitable mortgage product.

....

Many borrowers end up returning their mortgages before the end of five years.

....

VARIABLE RATE PENALTIES

Variable rate mortgage penalties are generally limited to three months' interest, regardless of the lender you are dealing with. The formula is straightforward:

Mortgage balance x interest rate ÷ 4

For example, if you have a $400,000 mortgage at 5.00%, formula would look like this:

$400,000 x 0.05 ÷ 4 = $5,000

Most lenders will use the contract rate to calculate the penalty (the rate your payment is based on). However, some use the prime rate, which would result in a higher penalty. It's best to ask your broker or the bank to confirm which rate your penalty is based on.

It's important to note that there are some exceptions to the standard three months' interest penalty. There are a few variable products that come with a substantially higher penalty, typically around 2.75 or 3.00% of the balance. When returning a mortgage at 2.25% with a $300,000 balance, the three months' interest penalty would be $1,687. At 2.75%, the penalty would be $8,250. Huge difference.

So why would anyone choose a variable rate that comes with such a high return penalty?

Most of the time, these products are at lower rates, which makes them seem more attractive. However, the potential downside is the significant cost involved if the mortgage is returned before the end of the term. While the lower rate promises savings over time, the savings can quickly be outweighed by the hefty penalty for early termination.

To justify going with a variable rate with an excessively high return penalty, I like to see a rate difference of at least 0.15%. There also must be reasonable certainty that the borrower will be content with their home for the full five-year term. Even then, it doesn't come without strong warning.

An example of this would be a couple who has been married for 25 plus years with a great relationship, kids moved out, and no plans to ever move out of their home.

The opposite would be a couple in their twenties who have been dating for two months and purchasing their first home.

See the difference?

FIXED RATE PENALTIES

Regardless of which lender you choose, the penalty to return a fixed rate mortgage is typically the <u>greater</u> of three months' interest or the interest rate differential (IRD). The IRD is the difference between your current rate and the new rate the lender says they can get when they re-lend the money after you have returned it. The IRD compensates the lender for lost profit if their reinvestment rate is lower than your rate when re-lending the money for the remainder of your original term.

The simplest way to explain the concept is if the rate for a similar term to what you have remaining is the same or higher than your current rate at the time you return, then you would pay three months' interest. If it's lower, you would pay the interest rate differntial... if it's greater than three months' interest. That explains the concept, however, the actual calculation is not that simple.

Let me further explain. The lender compares the interest rate on your mortgage with their current rate for a term closest to the time remaining on your term. In other words, if you have a 5-year fixed and you return it after three years, then there are two years remaining. The lender's 2-year fixed rate is what they use to calculate your penalty, as it matches what you have remaining on your current term. This would be considered the reinvestment rate.

For example, let's say you have a 5-year fixed at 3.99% and choose to return it after three years. The lender's current 2-year fixed is 2.99% (reinvestment rate). The two-year rate is used as it's the closest term to what's remaining on your current term. This means the lender will be collecting 1.00% less interest when they re-lend the money you are returning. It's that 1.00% difference that the lender will use to ensure they are compensated due to the lower reinvestment rate.

The further the reinvestment rate drops below your contract rate, the higher your penalty may become.

All lenders use similar wording: The greater of three months' interest or the interest rate differential. This can lead you to believe that the penalty would be the same with each lender. However, nothing could be further from the truth.

Interest Rate Differential (IRD) Calculation Methods

When it comes to the IRD, all penalties are not created equal. It can be calculated in different ways, with each providing a substantially different figure:

1. Based on the contract rate
2. Based on receiving a discount off the posted rate
3. Reinvestment rate tied to bond yields

1. Based on the Contract Rate

This is the best and most fair way for a lender to calculate the IRD penalty. This is the method used by lenders such as First National, MCAP, MCAN, RFA and most other monoline lenders. These are known as fair penalty lenders.

The reason why they are considered fair penalty lenders is because their reinvestment rates tend to be at market rates or higher. The higher the reinvestment rate, the lower the IRD. This is because the lender can relend or 'reinvest' the returned funds at a higher rate of return.

Note that dealing with a fair penalty lender does not mean

that your penalty will be low. If the reinvestment rate is significantly lower than your contract rate when you return your mortgage, then you could end up with a high penalty regardless of lender. Just not quite as high as it could be with a harsher penalty lender.

2. *Based on Receiving a Discount Off the Posted Rate*

This is the method used by all the big banks, as well as some credit unions. They calculate the IRD penalty by applying your original discount off the posted rate to their closest comparable posted rate.

As these lenders give you a "discount" off an inflated posted rate, it drives down their reinvestment rate, which in turn, drives up the IRD. This can result in a substantially inflated penalty. The larger the discount, the lower the reinvestment rate... and the lower the reinvestment rate, the higher the IRD penalty.

3. *Reinvestment Rate Tied to Bond Yield*

A small number of lenders will use a reinvestment rate that's tied to bond yields. This is one of the harshest formulas used to calculate the IRD penalty. It can create an extremely low reinvestment rate, resulting in a much larger IRD. Once again, the lower the reinvestment rate, the higher the IRD.

As the reinvestment rates are lower, the lender would then earn a smaller 'perceived' return when relending or 'reinvesting' the returned funds.

Regardless of the method being used, the penalty will never fall below three months' interest unless there are fewer than three months remaining on the term.

The penalty to break a fixed rate mortgage with a harsher penalty lender such as a major bank can be as much as 900% higher than most of the non-bank lenders. This could mean the difference between a $5,000 penalty or a $45,000 penalty. Just to be clear, there is not always this big of a difference in penalty. While a 900% higher penalty is possible, it's not that common. What is common is a penalty that is 300-500% higher. Either way, the difference can be substantial.

RETURNING WITHIN THREE MONTHS OF MATURITY

If you're returning your mortgage with less than three months to your maturity date, most lenders will charge a penalty equal to what's remaining on your current term. For instance, if you have six weeks remaining, they will only charge you the interest for those six weeks. However, there are some lenders who will still charge the full three months' interest… even if returning your mortgage with one week left in the term.

HOW TO LOWER YOUR PENALTY

Your remaining amortization plays a key role in determining your IRD penalty. The lower your amortization, the less interest you'll pay to the lender over the term. If you lower it prior to returning your mortgage, your penalty will drop. There are two different ways to do this:

1. Change from monthly to accelerated payments.

2. Make a lump sum payment.

3. Time your prepayment.

1. Change From Monthly to Accelerated Payments

If you're on a monthly payment schedule, you can reduce your amortization simply by converting to accelerated biweekly or weekly payments. This results in a slightly higher payment which reduces your amortization, and in turn, your penalty.

2. Making a Lump Sum Payment

You can also make a large, lump sum payment which will also reduce your amortization. As you're reducing your balance, you're reducing the time it would take to pay the mortgage down to zero (amortization). The penalty would also be calculated on the lower balance, therefore reducing your penalty further.

Note that some lenders will not allow prepayments within 30 days of breaking your mortgage... or even longer in some rare cases. If you're planning on returning your mortgage early, it's best to contact your lender to confirm their policy on prepayments prior to paying them out in full.

3. Time Your Prepayment

The timing of your prepayment can also make a difference on your penalty.

As mentioned, lenders will calculate your IRD penalty by comparing your current rate with the rate they would charge for a mortgage term closest to your remaining term. If you return your mortgage right before reaching the halfway point on a five-year term (for example, 29 months), the lender will compare your rate with their 4-year fixed. But if you wait until just after the halfway point, say at 31 months, then most lenders will then use their 3-year fixed rate to calculate the penalty. If the lender's 3-year fixed rate is higher than their 4 year, which it generally would be, then this would reduce your IRD penalty.

REASONS FOR RETURNING YOUR MORTGAGE

Many people are convinced that their mortgage will suit their needs for the full term, and therefore, won't need to return it. But there are several reasons why people may need to head to the exit before the end of the show:

- Change in family / living situation
- Change in financial situation
- Drop in mortgage rates
- Increase in mortgage size
- Selling your home

CHANGE IN FAMILY / LIVING SITUATION

Housing needs can vary greatly depending on individual circumstances. For example, a single person residing in a 300 sq. ft. bachelor apartment in downtown Toronto might find it perfectly suitable for her current lifestyle. However, life changes can rapidly alter housing needs. Suppose she meets her ideal partner and they decide to move in together; their combined needs could make the small apartment feel cramped. Furthermore, if they plan to have children, the need for additional space becomes even more pressing.

Life can be unpredictable, as exemplified by the story of good friends of mine. They initially planned to have just one child, but life had a different plan, and they ended up with triplets. Just over a year later, they were surprised with the arrival of a fourth child. Such unexpected turns in life can drastically change one's housing requirements, often triggering the need for a larger home to accommodate a growing family.

It's also quite common where a couple may enter a relationship with the intention of staying together for life, holding onto the belief that their deep love will be unshakeable. For some fortunate ones, this romantic ideal becomes a reality. However, life often has its own plans, and what's expected does not always become reality. Unfortunately, separation and divorce are quite common, leading to situations where couples are compelled to sell their homes earlier than expected.

Even in cases where one partner wishes to buy out the other's share, financial complications often arise. Typically, this process involves refinancing the mortgage to access the necessary funds. However, a significant hurdle is that many individuals find they do not qualify for a new mortgage on a single income. This financial limitation can leave them with no choice but to sell the property.

Life's unpredictability can impact housing and financial decisions. The divergence between what we plan and what actually happens can lead to difficult choices, especially in the case of shared homeownership.

Change in Financial Situation

Financial circumstances can shift in various ways, sometimes improving and other times deteriorating, and both scenarios could lead to returning your mortgage. On the positive side, you might be lucky enough to win a lottery or receive a substantial inheritance from a distant relative. In situations where you have come into a large sum of money, the penalty to return your mortgage early doesn't seem as concerning. In fact, it's not a bad problem to have!

On the flip side, there are instances where financial situations take a turn for the worse. This could be due to a range of reasons like job loss, accumulating significant debt, a business failure, or simply losing control of your finances. Life has its unpredictable moments, and sometimes it can deal you a bad hand. Facing critical illness, disability, or the loss of a family member are all profound events that might necessitate returning your mortgage. This could involve selling your home or refinancing to withdraw equity to cover the expenses.

Drop in Mortgage Rates

If mortgage rates drop substantially in the middle of your term, then this could represent a huge opportunity to potentially save thousands.

In this case, four things need to be considered:

1. Current rate
2. New rate
3. Time remaining on term
4. Penalty

The first and most important factor is the difference between your current rate and the new, lower rate now available. Naturally, a lower rate translates to less interest paid. However, returning your mortgage early will incur a penalty.

The key question is: Will the savings from the new, lower rate outweigh the penalty costs over the remaining term of the mortgage?

The more time remaining on your term, the easier it becomes to offset the penalty. In other words, there is a much greater chance of coming out ahead if you're returning the mortgage with three years remaining on the term compared with six months. If you're in the last six months of your term, then the difference will need to be enough to offset that penalty for the remaining six months. If not, then it may make sense to wait until you're within the 120 day rate hold period. This is the window during which you can secure a new rate that will take effect on your mortgage's maturity date, allowing you to bypass the penalty altogether.

The higher your starting rate, the lower the chances of saving money by switching your mortgage in the middle of the term. In other words, if you're starting off with a rate of 6.50%, there will be much less opportunity to save by switching mid-term than if your starting rate was 3.00%. This is because the minimum penalty will never be less than three months' interest. The only exception is when there is less than three months remaining on the term. The lower the starting rate, the smaller the penalty and the easier it will be to come out ahead by making the move.

....

The lower the starting rate, the smaller the penalty and the easier it will be to come out ahead by making the move.

....

For example, if you're returning a $500,000 mortgage at 5.50%, the lowest possible penalty is $6,875, which is three months' interest. If the lowest available rate dropped to 5.00% with two years remaining on your term, then the rate difference only amounts to a savings $5,015. Quite a bit shy of the $6,875 penalty. It would obviously make the most sense to stay with the current mortgage at the higher rate.

Conversely, if you're returning the mortgage at 3.00%, then the lowest possible penalty drops to $3,750. As the penalty is $3,125 lower than the previous example, it becomes easier to make up. If rates dropped to 2.50%, then the difference over the remaining two years is $4,905, or $1,155 higher than your penalty. While you're not saving thousands, you're at least in the black.

The more time remaining on the term, the greater the chances of coming out ahead as illustrated in the chart below:

Remaining Term	5.50% to 5.00%		3.00% to 2.50%	
	Difference before Penalty	Total Savings	Difference Before Penalty	Total Savings
2 years	$5,015	-$1,860	$4,950	$1,155
3 years	7,637	762	7,345	3,595
4 years	10,353	3,478	9,791	6,041

Same 0.50% drop in rate, yet two completely different outcomes. The starting rate is a crucial component in determining if switching to a lower rate in the middle of the term would be a practical move.

Waiting for the Lowest Rate Can be Expensive

If you're in a fixed rate mortgage, it's not quite as simple. Everyone wants the lowest rate, so when rates are declining, the logical thing to do is to wait for rates to reach rock bottom before making the move. However, this is where it gets a bit counterintuitive. Waiting for rates to reach their rock bottom can be an expensive decision. With fixed mortgage rates, the more rates fall below your current rate, the higher your penalty may become. It can easily get to the point where the penalty becomes too large to offset with a lower rate. So, the goal isn't to switch when rates are at their lowest. It's to switch when there is the right combination of rate and penalty.

....
The goal isn't to switch when rates are at their lowest. It's to switch when there is the right combination of rate and penalty.
....

For example, let's say you're in a fixed rate mortgage of 4.79% with $650,000 owing and three years remaining on your term. Rates are declining fast, so you wait to see how far they drop. Rates have now dropped to 2.79%, so you decide to make the move. Over the remaining three years of your term, the difference based on rate alone would be a whopping $38,543. However, such a large difference in rate has driven your IRD penalty up to $45,000[13]. As the penalty has now exceeded the savings, the most cost-effective approach is to ride out your current mortgage until the end of the term. Switching to the lower rate would be a costly move.

But let's say you decide to make the move when the rates drop just 0.50% to 4.29%. The difference based on rate alone works out to $9,822 over the remaining three years. If you're able to return the current mortgage with a three-month interest penalty, then you'd be looking at a penalty of $7,784. In this situation, you'd be coming out ahead by $2,038 if you were to make the move.

The question is... what are the odds that you'll be able to return the mortgage with a three-month interest penalty?

Remember, with fixed rate mortgages, the more the rate falls, the higher the penalty can become. But since all lenders don't move their fixed rates simultaneously, there can still be options to return your current mortgage with a penalty of three months' interest, despite the 0.50% rate drop.

....

With fixed rate mortgages, the more the rate falls,
the higher the penalty can become.

....

Your initial step should be to contact your current lender to confirm your penalty. Note that a lender will only quote

---

13   This is just an example to illustrate the point and not necessarily the actual penalty.

penalty based on returning the mortgage on that specific day, however, the penalty can change by the time the transfer is completed. If your current lender reduces their rate in the interim, then you could be facing a much larger penalty than the one initially quoted. If it turns out to be higher than anticipated, then you are not obligated to proceed with the transfer, even if you have already signed the mortgage commitment.

Capitalizing the Penalty

On mortgage transfers, most lenders will allow you to include up to $3,000 of the penalty into your new mortgage. Let's say you're transferring a mortgage with a $400,000 balance and your return penalty is $4,000. The new mortgage can increase to a maximum of $403,000. The remaining $1,000 would need to be paid out of pocket when the new mortgage closes.

The only way to increase the size of your mortgage would be to proceed as a refinance which I'll be discussing in detail shortly.

Blend and Extend

This is an option to consider when mortgage rates decrease and you're not selling your home. It involves renegotiating your mortgage with your lender to blend your current rate with the lower market rate, resulting in a new, lower rate. Additionally, you'll be extending the term of your mortgage, hence the name "Blend and Extend." It's a strategy that can be beneficial if market rates have dropped significantly, but as with any financial decision, it's important to evaluate its cost-effectiveness for your specific situation.

This strategy can be employed in two different scenarios: either when refinancing your mortgage to access the equity in your home, or simply to capitalize on lower mortgage rates. In the case of the latter, it's the extension that enables you to benefit from the reduced rates.

For instance, imagine you are two years into a 5-year fixed at 4.99% with a remaining balance of $850,000. Your current lender is offering a new 5-year fixed rate at 2.99%. With the "Blend and Extend" approach, your existing mortgage rate of 4.99% would continue for the remaining three years of your original term. The new lower rate of 2.99% would then be applied to the entire loan amount for the additional two years that you're adding. In this scenario, the resulting new blended rate for the extended five-year term would be 4.19%.

Although the new blended rate isn't the lowest available on the market, it offers two distinct advantages:

1. You can avoid any penalties associated with breaking your current mortgage.
2. You see an immediate reduction in your monthly payments.

For instance, if your mortgage initially had a balance of $900,000 with a 25-year amortization period, your starting monthly payment would be $5,229.32.

After applying the Blend and Extend option at a rate of 4.19%, your monthly payment would decrease to $4,559.15. This change results in a monthly savings of $670.17, which is a substantial reduction and can be seen as a financially beneficial move.

However, this is not always the cost-effective option. In some cases, the penalty may still apply, but could be hidden in the new rate offered. This doesn't necessarily make it a bad as it's still possible to come out ahead. As every situation can be a bit different, it's best to discuss your options with your broker.

INCREASING THE SIZE OF YOUR MORTGAGE

There may be times when you need to borrow additional funds and tapping into your home's equity is usually the most cost-effective option for doing so.

There are several reasons why one might need to access the additional cash:

- Renovations
- Debt consolidation
- Investment opportunities
- Purchase an investment property
- Travel
- University education for your kids
- Financing larger purchases such as a car or boat

This can be done by adding a HELOC (Home Equity Line of Credit) or by increasing the size of your current mortgage through refinancing.

Adding a HELOC

The first way of accessing your equity is by adding a home equity line of credit. This can often be added separately from your existing mortgage, which would keep it intact; no penalty or breaking your mortgage required. This approach can be particularly helpful if you have a low mortgage rate that you would like to preserve.

The biggest drawback is that HELOC rates are substantially higher than that of a traditional amortized mortgage. It comes down to how much money you need and what you need it for. A big advantage to HELOCs is they allow you to draw the funds when you need them, which can be particularly handy when completing a renovation.

The primary disadvantage of a HELOC is that its interest rates are substantially higher compared to those of a traditional, amortized mortgage. The feasibility of adding a HELOC depends on how much money you require and the specific purpose for which you need it.

For a more comprehensive discussion on HELOCs, including their intricacies and how they operate, refer to my detailed explanation in Chapter Four.

Refinancing

Refinancing involves increasing the size of your mortgage and/or increasing your amortization period. This is often the most economical way to access your home's equity. Refinancing can be done at any time in the middle of your term, or it can be done at your term's end. If the latter, it would be done without penalty since your current mortgage has matured. This would ideally be the best time to refinance. But if you need the funds sooner and you're in the middle of your term, then waiting for your renewal date may not be practical. This would generally involve returning your mortgage and paying the penalty. However, it may be possible to refinance with the same lender without penalty using blended rate mortgage as described earlier in this chapter. It's important to note that not all lenders offer blended rates on refinances, and some may not offer cost-effective refinancing options at all. In these cases, the only option is to return the mortgage and pay the penalty.

Opting for a blended rate doesn't always result in maximum savings. In many cases, it may be more economical to return your existing mortgage, pay the associated penalty, and secure a completely new mortgage.

Opting for a blended rate doesn't always result in maximum savings.

The most cost-effective option depends on factors such as the rate on your current mortgage, the new rate being offered, the availability of blended rate options, and so forth. Each situation is unique, and therefore, it's highly recommended to have a detailed discussion with a mortgage professional who can provide tailored advice based on your specific circumstances.

SELLING YOUR HOME

One of the main reasons for returning a mortgage is due to homeowners deciding to sell their property. It could be due to a growing family, relocation for work, or simply just for a change of pace.

Porting Your Mortgage

If you're facing a large penalty for returning your mortgage, you may be able to avoid it altogether by porting it to a new property. This can effectively reduce what could have been a substantial penalty down to zero.

Porting your mortgage involves transferring your existing mortgage over to the new property. This process not only saves you from paying a penalty for returning your mortgage early but also allows you to keep your existing interest rate, which can be particularly beneficial if it's favourable.

For example, let's say you owe $300,000 on your mortgage with a fixed rate of 3.99% and two years remaining on your term. You need to borrow an additional $200,000 to make your new home purchase a reality, however, rates have now increased to 5.99% for a 5-year fixed. You could then port the existing $300,000 mortgage, persevering the current rate for the remaining two years of your term. The additional $200,000 required would be at the new rate of 5.99%. At the end of the initial two-year term, the entire mortgage balance of $500,000 will then adjust to the higher rate of 5.99% for the remaining three years of the term. This is all blended together to form a single rate and payment. This is referred to as a blended rate mortgage, which is the same concept previously explained. It's a simplified way of managing the different rates over the term. In this case, the blended rate would be 5.51% which would be your rate for the full five years.

Porting a Variable Rate Mortgage

When it comes to porting a variable rate mortgage, the

process differs notably from that of a fixed rate mortgage. With most lenders, only the existing balance of a variable rate mortgage can be ported. This means you can transfer your current mortgage to a new property, but you cannot increase the loan amount while maintaining the same terms.

If, like many homebuyers, you need to increase the size of your mortgage when moving to a new property, porting a variable rate mortgage likely won't be an option. In such cases, you're required to return your current mortgage and pay the three months' interest penalty. A completely new mortgage will be required for the full loan amount.

....

While variable rate mortgages are typically portable, most lenders will only let you port over the current balance.

....

Another strategy to consider is to convert your variable rate into a fixed term which would then allow you to increase the size of your mortgage and blend the rate. However, this is not always the best choice as the rates offered are generally not the lowest available in the market. In many situations, it may make more sense to return your mortgage, pay the penalty, and secure an entirely new mortgage at a lower rate. It all comes down to the most cost-effective option. A skilled mortgage broker can be instrumental in this process, as they can analyze different scenarios from various lenders. They can advise you on the most cost-effective approach, allowing you to make a well-informed decision that aligns with your financial goals and circumstances.

Competitive Rates When Porting

When porting your mortgage, don't expect a deal on the new rate. Your lender knows that it's going to cost you money to leave, so they may not offer a competitive rate on the new portion of the loan. What makes porting so attractive is that it enables you to retain your existing, potentially lower interest rate in comparison to current market rates... while avoiding the penalty at the same time.

Plus, there is typically no cost involved with porting. If you are facing a particularly large penalty, porting can come across as a no brainer. However, this isn't always the case. Never assume that porting is the best course of action solely because you save on the penalty. In many situations, it can be more cost-effective to simply pay the penalty and go with a different lender altogether.

Never assume that porting is the best course of action solely because you save on the penalty.

There are a few things you need to consider before you make your final decision:

- Your current mortgage rate
- Current balance
- Time remaining on your original mortgage
- Amount of additional money required
- Rate on the additional funds

For example, let's say you have a $300,000 mortgage at

2.99% with six months remaining on the term. You need to borrow an additional $250,000, which you are being quoted 3.79% by your current lender. It's important to remember that your current rate of 2.99% is only valid for another six months. After that, you'll be paying the 3.79% on the entire balance for the remaining 4.5 years. Your lender offers you a blended rate of 3.75%. However, you're being offered 3.39% by another lender which would require you to return your current mortgage, incurring a penalty of $2,542.50.

In this example, porting your mortgage would result in an additional cost of $5,885 compared to paying the penalty of $2,542 on your current mortgage and securing a new mortgage with a lower rate of 3.39%. Despite the immediate cost of the penalty, securing a lower rate with a new mortgage can lead to greater savings over the term. This is why it's important to consider the overall cost differences between both options before making your final decision.

Some people hear the word penalty and become fearful, envisioning additional costs that they will do anything to avoid. I've seen people commit to a mortgage costing them thousands more... just so they can avoid the penalty. This decision effectively means choosing to pay significantly more in the long term to save a smaller amount now. In the above scenario, it would cost you $5,885 to eliminate the $2,542 penalty. You'd be amazed at how many would choose to save the penalty as the math was not outlined for them. (Note that the $5,885 savings already has the penalty factored in).

Common Porting Restrictions

Just as there can be restrictions with the mortgage you

choose, there can be restrictions with porting as well. There are four that you need to be aware of:

- Purchase limited to $1 million
- No blended rate offerings
- Time limit
- Term length

Purchase limited to $1 million - In some situations, porting may not be available if the purchase price on the new property is greater than $1 million. This is directly related to the insurability of the mortgage, which I described in detail in Chapter Three. This is more common with monoline lenders and some credit unions.

No blended rate offerings - Some lenders may not offer blended mortgages and may simply add a second component instead. This can sound great to a less savvy mortgage shopper; however, it can be costly. Let's say you need to port your mortgage with 3 years, 7 months remaining and you need to increase it by an additional $200,000. The lender adds a second component to your mortgage consisting of a 5-year term for the additional money you need while keeping your current term intact; no blended rate involved. Now you have two components to your mortgage, with two different maturity dates. This means that you will NEVER be able to get out of this mortgage without paying a penalty. If you have one mortgage component maturing on June 1st, and the other doesn't mature until September 17th of the following year, you'll always have this misalignment. As a result, you'll always pay a penalty on one component or the other. Unless you see one of the terms through to completion with the same lender. This alone would likely be a costly choice.

Time limit - If you have sold your home, but have not yet found a new one, you can still port your mortgage, however, the clock is ticking. Most lenders will give you 90 days to port your mortgage after your home has been sold. Some lenders may give you as little as 30 days, while others might be as long as six months. You would pay the full penalty at the time of closing on your sale, but this would then be reimbursed to you once your new home purchase closes.

Term length - The term you are porting to must be equal or greater to the years remaining on your current term. For example, if you have three years remaining, you cannot port your mortgage into a two-year term. The options would only be for three years or greater. This will suit the needs of most borrowers, however if you are looking for a shorter term of 1-2 years, your only option would be to return your current mortgage and pay the penalty. While this is common with the majority of mortgage lenders, some will only offer porting on five-year terms.

BRIDGE LOAN STRATEGY

A bridge loan is a short-term financing solution that helps cover your down payment when the closing date of your new home purchase is earlier than the sale of your current home. For instance, if you sold your current home with a closing date of June 15th and the closing date on your new home is June 1st. Since the proceeds from the sale of your existing home won't be available in time for the earlier closing of your new home, a short-term loan (known as the bridge) is required. This covers you for the portion of the down payment coming from the proceeds of the sale which would then be paid out once the sale has closed.

To be eligible for bridge financing, the sale of your current home must be firm, meaning all conditions have been removed prior to closing on your new purchase.

Note that lenders will want to build in some cushion. For example, if you sold your home for $1.4 million with $800,000 owing on your mortgage, the full difference of $600,000 would not be available to you in the form of a bridge loan. There are other expenses such as Realtor fees, legal expenses, as well as the penalty to return the current mortgage. It's best to know these costs up front, which will help you with your planning. Your mortgage professional will be able to help you sort this out.

Cost of a Bridge Loan

Rate on a bridge loan can be anywhere from prime +2.00% to prime +5.00% and can carry a fee anywhere from $0 - $500 in most cases. In other words, if the prime rate is 6.00%, then you're looking at a bridge loan rate of 8.00% to 11.00%. Don't get thrown off by the rate, as these are annual rates and bridge loans are intended for short term only. Anywhere from a couple of days to a few weeks for most situations.

No payments are required for the bridge loan since the interest will be settled upon repayment of the loan from the sale proceeds of your current home.

Note that your lender may require the bridge loan to be

registered, particularly if it's a larger loan. Your lawyer will charge you for a 2nd mortgage registration, generally less than $100. When the bridge loan is discharged, you'll also be charged a discharge fee which can vary depending on your province. This can be anywhere from zero to $400 in most situations.

Most lenders will accept a maximum bridge of 30 days, however, longer may be available if needed. There are some lenders who will allow up to one year, however, it would be an extreme case to require such a long bridge. Not to mention, it would be extremely pricey. Keep in mind that the rate for the bridge is quite high, so you'll want to keep its length as short as possible.

The rate for the bridge is quite high, so you'll want to keep its length as short as possible.

HOW TO SAVE MONEY ON YOUR BRIDGE LOAN

It wasn't that long ago when Raj and Fatima reached out to me to discuss mortgage options for the purchase of their new $2.2 million home. They advised me that their down payment was coming entirely from the sale of the current property which was closing 28 days later. The amount needed for their bridge loan was $1.2 million.

Raj and Fatima were ecstatic with the favorable rate I secured for their $1 million mortgage through a major bank. However, they were concerned about the cost of the bridge loan given its high interest rate of 11.20%. This was fully understandable. It was a huge bride and a long one at that.

Over the 28 days of the loan, the interest would amount to $10,310. As a client in their position, I too would be looking for ways to minimize this cost. So, I suggested a strategy to do just that.

Although Raj and Fatima hadn't originally considered a mortgage with a HELOC, I proposed that we add one for $760,000 in addition to the $1 million mortgage they were looking for... which brought the total amount borrowed up to 80% of the purchase price... the maximum possible.

I suggested that we fully utilize the HELOC at closing to reduce the bridge loan by $760,000. This brought it from $1.2 million down to $440,000. I was able to secure the HELOC at the prime rate, which was 7.20%. Far lower than the 11.20% bridge loan. This saved them $2,332.06. That's money that would now be left in their pocket, as opposed to the banks.

Here's the comparison of both scenarios side-by-side:

Bridge Details	HELOC + Bridge	Bridge Only
HELOC	$760,000.00	n/a
Bridge loan	440,000.00	1,200,000.00
28 days interest on bridge (11.20%)	3,780.38	10,310.14
28 days interest on HELOC (7.20%)	4,197.70	n/a
Total Interest Paid	7,978.08	10,310.14
Savings	2,332.06	0.00

When the sale of their current home was completed, the

proceeds from the sale paid off the bridge loan and brought the HELOC balance down to $0.

A few months after closing, Raj and Fatima used the HELOC to fund an investment that is earning them a locked rate of 11% per year. That's a net return of 5.80% amounting to $28,880 in annual investment income... after interest on the HELOC was paid. At the time of writing in early 2024, the prime rate was expected to drop considerably over the next two years, which will increase their net return on their investment income. And just think... they didn't want the HELOC originally.

As the HELOC is now being used to fund an investment, the interest becomes tax deductible.

HOW TO REDUCE YOUR MORTGAGE PAYMENTS

Sometimes finances can get tight, and any bit of relief can help. It might be particularly relevant during periods like maternity leave, or any other circumstance where there's a need for increased cash flow. Additionally, this kind of financial flexibility can also boost your preapproved amount for the purchase of a new investment property, giving you more purchasing power so you can explore more options in the property market.

There are two possible options:

1. Switch to monthly payments
2. Increase your amortization

SWITCH TO MONTHLY PAYMENTS

The perception of accelerated biweekly payments is often misunderstood. Many believe that choosing this payment frequency is equivalent to the monthly payment, just paid more frequently. For example, if the accelerated biweekly payment is $2,000, they might think of it as paying $4,000 per month. However, this is not accurate. With accelerated biweekly payments, you're making the equivalent of one extra monthly payment annually. This is because there are 26 biweekly periods in a year, which is equivalent to making 13 full-sized monthly payments annually.

If we multiply the $2,000 accelerated biweekly payment by 26 and then divide by 12, it's equivalent to making a monthly payment of $4,333.33, which is $333.33 higher than the monthly payment option. This extra payment is what contributes to the faster payoff of the mortgage as it's applied directly to your principal.

If you want to increase your monthly cash flow, all you need to do is change your payment frequency to a monthly schedule. If you prefer to continue making payments on a weekly or biweekly basis to line up with your paycheques, you can request your lender to remove the accelerated feature.

Implementing any of these changes will result in a monthly cash flow increase of $333.33 in this example. Most lenders will allow this at no cost. While this might seem like an obvious solution, there are many who are currently on accelerated payment plans while facing financial challenges.

Switching to a monthly or non-accelerated payment

structure is the simplest way to lower your payments. It can provide immediate financial relief without the need for more complex financial restructuring.

Most lenders will have an online portal where you can make the change without having to contact them.

INCREASE YOUR AMORTIZATION

Amortization refers to the length of time it takes to pay off your mortgage in full, assuming consistent payments throughout the period. Essentially, the longer the amortization period, the lower your payments. If your current mortgage is set to a shorter amortization schedule, you can reduce your payments by extending your amortization up to a maximum of 30 years.

The only way to extend your amortization is by refinancing your mortgage. If done in the middle of your term, it would involve paying the penalty and getting an entirely new mortgage with a new rate and term. This can be done with the same lender or with a different one. It would come down to who has the best deal at the time.

When you're refinancing a mortgage, you can also increase the total loan amount to include your return penalty and can even add more funds if needed. This can be beneficial if you have any additional debt that you would like to consolidate as it can significantly reduce your overall monthly payment obligations. This is due to the typically lower interest rates of mortgages compared to other forms of debt like credit cards or personal loans. You also have the flexibility to withdraw some extra cash for other uses, which can offer a sense of financial security and peace of mind.

....

*Refinancing can be beneficial if you have any additional
debt that you would like to consolidate as it can significantly
reduce your overall monthly payment obligations.*

....

Let's use Tony and Juliana as an example. Like many, they have a goal of paying their mortgage off as quickly as possible. Thanks to the combined strength of their dual incomes, they have the financial flexibility to afford larger mortgage payments. With this in mind, they decided to amortize their $475,000 mortgage over 15 years at a variable rate of 5.70%, giving them a monthly payment of $3,307.37.

The mortgage payments were quite manageable for Tony and Juliana initially. However, their financial situation changed significantly with the arrival of their first children - twins. This unexpected but pleasant surprise no doubt brought considerable adjustments to their life. They decided that Juliana would permanently leave her job to dedicate herself to raising the twins full-time.

While they could get by on Tony's income alone, they quickly found that their finances became uncomfortably tight. Like many new parents, Tony and Juliana discovered that the costs of raising children were higher than they had anticipated. This new reality, combined with the loss of one income, put a strain on their budget. What were once manageable mortgage payments now became a financial challenge.

I advised them that they could substantially reduce their payments by refinancing with a 30-year amortization. Their penalty to return their mortgage was $7,119, including discharge fee. The refinance would also incur a legal fee of $800, which brings the total new mortgage required to $482,919. They decided to go with a 3-year fixed rate at 4.99%, which was the lowest available at the time. This reduced their monthly payment to $2,574.41 which increased their monthly cash flow by $732.96. This substantial reduction in payment brought them a great sense of relief.

Then we addressed their debt.

They had a car loan with an $850 monthly payment and $10,000 owing, along with $15,000 in credit card debt which they had only been able to cover the minimum payment of roughly $250 per month. I suggested increasing the new mortgage by another $25,000 to $507,919 which would pay off the debt. This increased the monthly mortgage payment by $133.27 to $2,707.68 while eliminating the $1,100 in monthly debt payments.

Here's the breakdown of their financial situation before and after the refinance:

FINANCIAL DETAILS	OLD SITUATION	NEW SITUATION
Mortgage balance	$475,000	$507,919
Amortization	15 years	30 years
Car payment	$850	$0.00
Credit card payment	$250	$0.00
Mortgage payment	$3,307.37	$2,707.68
Total payments	$4,407.37	$2,707.68
Monthly cash flow increase	n/a	$1,699.69

They increased their monthly cashflow by roughly $1,700 per month, putting them into a significantly better position financially. But proceeding with the refinance, they virtually eliminated all their financial stress and worry.

While refinancing to a longer amortization can provide immediate relief by lowering your monthly payments, it's important to consider the long-term implications, such as increased interest costs over the life of the mortgage. But in this case, we're not talking about maximizing your savings over time. We're talking about how you can reduce your payments to ease financial stress. It really comes down to your goal and everyone's situation can be a bit different.

CHOOSING A VARIABLE RATE AND SWITCHING TO FIXED MID-TERM

Most variable rate mortgage products offer the flexibility to convert to a fixed rate at any point during the term, usually without cost. In scenarios where variable rates are higher than fixed, converting to a fixed rate can be a quick way to lower your mortgage payments. While it sounds tempting, it's not necessarily the best choice. It heavily depends on market forecasts and your individual financial circumstances. If you find yourself in a situation where meeting your current payments is becoming challenging, switching to a lower fixed rate can provide some much-needed relief. But it can be a costly move, particularly if the prime rate is expected to drop. Locking in would shut you out of the expected rate cuts to come.

However, fixed rates are seldom higher than the variable rate options. In most markets, variable rates are lower than fixed. This can make a variable rate quite tempting for many. After all, the rate is lower, so why not go for it? But as I explained in Chapter Four, variable rate mortgages are not for everyone. Many worry about rising rates, asking if choosing a variable rate with the intention of converting to a fixed is advisable. Particularly when there is media coverage on rising rates.

Choosing a variable rate mortgage with the intention of switching to a fixed rate mid-term is not something I would typically suggest. The main reason is the unpredictability of the market and the challenge of timing the switch correctly. This concept is similar to the stock market where you ideally want to buy low and sell high. While it sounds good in theory, the difficulty lies in accurately predicting market movements. When fixed rates are higher than variable rates, converting to a fixed rate means you are accepting an immediate increase in both your interest rate and payment. Consequently, many people tend to put off the move for as long as they can, hoping for a clear sign that it's the right time to convert. However, this often results in waiting too long, and by the time they decide to make the move, fixed rates may have already increased.

When considering converting from a variable rate to a fixed rate mortgage with your current lender, it's important to manage expectations regarding the interest rate you'll receive. Typically, the rate your lender offers you will not be the lowest on the market. Often not even the lowest that they would offer to a new customer. They will generally offer you their standard fixed rate at that time, which could

be 0.10% to 0.20% higher... or even more in some cases.

You're also taking a gamble that the prime rate will continue to increase since your new rate and payment would typically be higher than it would be if you just accepted the increase on your variable.

Many with variable rate mortgages will ask if it's a good time to lock in at the first word of a potential rate increase. When choosing a variable rate, it's understood that your rate can change in either direction at any time over your term. At times when years pass without an increase, many become complacent. This was the case when we went almost seven years without an increase between September 2010 and July 2017. In these situations, many become comfortable with thinner spreads, as rate increases are not something they are accustomed to. For this reason, some people tend to panic when they hear chatter about a possible rate increase.

When choosing a variable rate, it's understood that your rate can change in either direction at any time over your term.

The truth is, if you don't like being exposed to market fluctuations, or if the thought of an increasing rate and payment scares you, then variable rate was likely not the best product choice in the first place. If you have a variable rate mortgage, then I'll generally suggest staying put and riding it out for the term in most situations. But there are always exceptions. If you have anxiety to the point where you are fraught with worry and are having trouble sleeping at night, then you'll want to do what will set your mind at ease. In many situations, it may be more cost effective to pay the three months' interest penalty and switch to another lender. It all depends on what rates are being offered. If they are low enough, you could potentially save thousands, over and above the penalty, therefore making it worthwhile to make the move.

Before making a final decision, it's important to assess the difference between your variable rate and the fixed rate being offered. If this spread is narrow, say around 0.25%, then that's a bit of a different situation. In cases like this, switching to a fixed rate might be a sensible option, especially if there's an expectation of further rate hikes in the near future.

However, you would still be betting on further increases to the prime rate by proceeding with the conversion, so it really depends on the person. Anyone taking a variable with a very thin spread could potentially consider this, but in these cases, a fixed rate mortgage may have been the better choice to begin with.

The future of interest rates is uncertain and unpredictable. No one knows for sure. Maybe the rate will increase or maybe it won't. Maybe it will drop next year, or maybe it will remain unchanged for the rest of the term. It's all speculation. Regardless, choosing to lock into a fixed rate at the first sign of a rate increase is generally not the best strategy. But as always, every situation can be a bit different. With some exceptions, I suggest staying with your variable rate for the entire term, rather than choosing variable with the intention of switching halfway through.

MAXIMIZE YOUR SAVINGS AT RENEWAL

Your mortgage rate applies only to your current term. In other words, a mortgage with a five-year term would have a rate valid for five years. When you reach the end of your term, your mortgage then becomes due and payable. There are three options available to you at that time:

- Pay off the mortgage in full.
- Renew with your current lender.
- Switch to a different lender.

PAYING THE MORTGAGE OFF IN FULL

For most people, this isn't a practical or feasible option... unless you've won the lottery or received a significant inheritance. However, if you are nearing the end of your mortgage's lifespan, then paying off the balance could be considered. It would free you from any further mortgage payments, providing financial relief and a sense of accomplishment in owning your home outright. Mortgage freedom!

RENEW WITH YOUR CURRENT LENDER

As you approach your maturity date, your current lender will send you a renewal document outlining the new rate offers for your next term. This is the easiest option. You are not required to requalify, and do not need to provide any documentation. All you need to do select your desired mortgage product from the list of options, sign the form and send it back to your lender.

That's it. You're done. It couldn't be easier!

While this is the easiest option, it can also be costly.

For many of us, time is precious, and the path of least resistance can be enticing. There are some that are so busy that they don't care how much they will save. They just want to get it done and over with, so they sign the form regardless of rate. Banks are aware of this common behavior and may even send you the renewal form with their posted rates. Just to give you an idea of what this means, the difference between a bank's posted rate and the lowest mortgage rates available could be as much as 3.00% or even higher. On a $500,000 mortgage, this works out to a difference of roughly $73,000 over a five-year period.

The difference can be SIGNIFICANT.

It's rare to see a lender try to gouge with such a high rate offering at renewal, however, I've seen it done.

Simply signing the renewal form and sending it back to the lender without doing any research is tantamount to opening your wallet and emptying it into the trash. It doesn't take much time to do a quick Google search or reach out a broker to find out what rates you're eligible for. Respectable savings are not only possible, but likely.

....

Signing the renewal form and sending it back to the lender without doing any research is tantamount to opening your wallet and emptying it into the trash.

....

While some lenders will put their best foot forward and offer you competitive rates at renewal, higher rate offerings are common. I've seen some consciously renew with their current lenders knowing that they could save more than $5,000 by switching. But they are okay with this, as they don't want to spend the extra time to apply for a new mortgage.

But how much time do they think this will take?

How long would it take them to save up $5,000... after taxes?

While the savings can vary from none at all, to significant amounts, this is always something that should explored before signing your mortgage renewal.

Still think you're too busy?

All you need to do is ask your current lender for a lower rate and they will usually oblige. It's as simple as that. Even then, I wouldn't just accept your bank's discounted rate either. At least, not without doing further research. There are often lower rates to be found. And in many cases... much lower, even after you have negotiated the lowest renewal rate with your current lender.

This is exactly why you'll want to shop around at the end of your mortgage term.

SWITCH TO A DIFFERENT LENDER

While not as simple as renewing your mortgage, switching to a different lender is a fairly easy process. It involves completing a new mortgage application and providing some basic documentation. The process can be started once you're within 120 days of your maturity date and can take anywhere from 21 to 30 days to complete. The clock starts when your application is submitted to the lender for approval. A 21-day window is really tight, and some lenders may still require the full 30 days, so it's best to allow plenty of time.

If you're within 30 days of your renewal date, then it's likely that your new mortgage will close late. However, no need to panic! You should promptly contact your current lender and request to be put into an open mortgage as of your renewal date. While most lenders will automatically do this, it's not universal practice. The only way to be sure is to contact them with the request. This should be done in writing, which ensures clarity while having a record of the request. Some lenders will automatically renew you into a 6-month closed term, which means that a penalty would apply... even if closing a day late.

....

Some lenders will automatically renew you into a 6-month closed term, which means that a penalty would apply... even if closing a day late.

....

Open mortgage rates are significantly higher than the lowest fixed rate options, sometimes by as much as 4.00% or more. For instance, if the lowest available fixed rate is 4.74%, an open mortgage rate might be around 8.74%. At first glance, this may seem exorbitantly high, which it is. But it's important to remember that this is an annual rate, and you shouldn't need it for more than a few days to a few weeks at the most.

People will naturally associate the higher rate with a proportionately higher cost. However, in this context, the additional cost isn't the full 8.74%. It's the difference between the open mortgage rate and the rate on your new mortgage. The temporary nature of the open mortgage means that the higher rate is only in effect for a short period, resulting in a smaller financial impact than the annual rate might suggest.

For example, let's say you have $400,000 owing on your mortgage at renewal. The rate on the new mortgage is 4.74%, and the rate on the open mortgage is 8.74%. This is a difference of 4.00%, which is the rate used to determine the additional per diem (daily) cost. This would be calculated as follows:

$400,000 x 0.04 / 365 = $43.84 per day.

If you end up missing your renewal date by four days, then the additional cost would be $43.84 x 4 = $175.36 using this example. If you missed it by 10 days, then the additional cost would be $43.84 x 10 = $438.40. It can add up, so be sure to allow enough time when starting the process. Even with the additional costs, switching lenders can still lead to significant savings, however, every situation is unique and should be evaluated individually.

Cost to Switch Lenders

On the majority of mortgage transfers, legal and appraisal fees are covered for you. The only other fees are a small government fee of around $80, and a discharge fee from your current lender. These fees will be added to your new mortgage, so nothing needs to be paid out of pocket.

Discharge fees generally range from $0 to $450, depending on your province. In Ontario, they can range from roughly $275 to $450 depending on the lender. While most mortgage lenders will not cover the discharge fee for you, there is a small handful who will. If you're working with us for your new mortgage, we'll let you know exactly what's covered for you when we present you with your options, so you'll know what to expect before making your decision.

Switching a Collateral Mortgage

If you have a collateral charge mortgage, then the legal and appraisal fees may not be covered for you. The legal fee can range from around $600 to $900, depending on your province (around $800 in Ontario), and appraisal can range from around $275 – $400 (or sometimes even higher). Many lenders are now covering these fees for you, but there are still some who are not.

What Happens if You Don't Qualify?

Life is unpredictable, and sometimes unforeseen challenges can arise. You may find yourself in a difficult situation, such as being between jobs or experiencing a downturn in your credit score, just as your maturity date rolls around. If you're facing these kinds of difficulties, then you are likely not going to qualify and your only viable option may be to re-sign with your current lender. However, this doesn't mean you're without leverage. Even under these circumstances, you can still negotiate with your current lender for a lower rate than what they initially offer. Providing you aren't taking out any additional funds, there is no need for them to re-approve you. You're already approved!

This means no credit check.

No employment confirmation.

Nothing.

Even if you've recently lost your job or declared bankruptcy, your current lender is likely not aware of these changes. Before your renewal, it's a good idea to research the market to understand the rates currently being offered by other lenders. Armed with this information, you can approach your current lender and ask if they are willing to match these competitive rates. As your current circumstances will not enable you to switch lenders, this is a bluff. But you might be surprised by how often lenders are willing to negotiate to retain your business. They may not want to lose a customer and could be open to offering you a better rate than initially proposed.

This strategy of making a simple phone call and negotiating can potentially save you a significant amount of money. A few minutes of discussion could lead to a reduced rate on your mortgage renewal, which can amount to substantial savings. It's still entirely possible that the lender may not reduce your rate by as much as you were shooting for, however, they should at least come down from their original offer. In either case, your only option will be to accept their offer given your current circumstances.

But what happens if your credit has plummeted and you need to take out additional funds? There is hope here as well, which we'll discuss in Chapter Twelve.

THE TRAP OF EARLY MORTGAGE RENEWAL

There are times when your bank might contact you with a "special" renewal rate six months before your maturity date. They may present this as an exclusive, limited time offer, often giving you just a few days to a week to sign the renewal documents. If you haven't committed to them by that time, then the offer is off the table.

There will always be instances where rates may genuinely be on the rise, necessitating prompt action to secure a lower rate. However, this brief window of opportunity presented in early renewal offers is often a strategy crafted by the bank to prompt a quick decision. Banks are aware that many people are more likely to act on an offer if they believe it's a limited-time opportunity. This is similar to a child who may not show interest in a toy until it's about to be taken away. By presenting an offer with a tight deadline, banks aim to entice customers to commit early, leveraging the psychological concept of FOMO (fear of missing out). It may not even be an attractive offer, but it may be presented in a way that makes it seem irresistible. They know that other lenders will not be able to lock a rate until you're 120 days before your renewal date. Getting to you a couple of months in advance can essentially eliminate their competition. They then throw in the tight timeline to accept their offer in attempt to get you locked in at the new rate before you have a chance to shop.

As soon as you sign the early renewal documents, the new term typically comes into effect immediately. If the new rate offered in this early renewal is higher than your current rate, you end up immediately switching from your lower rate to a higher one. This means you lose out on the potential savings you could have had during the last six months of your existing, lower-rate mortgage term.

If the early renewal rate offered is lower than your current rate, the bank's case becomes more compelling. They may argue that your payment will decrease due to the lower rate, allowing you to benefit from the new, reduced rate right away. Additionally, they'll offer to waive the penalty for breaking your current mortgage term early. This proposition can seem quite attractive because it presents immediate savings. Given the perceived value of the deal, it can be tempting to accept this "special, exclusive offer."

There are times when it may be cost effective to take advantage of the offer, but there are often lower rates available. Jumping on your bank's promotional offer could potentially be costing you thousands of dollars when compared to what you might have secured by exploring other options.

Jumping on your bank's promotional offer could potentially be costing you thousands of dollars when compared to what you might have secured by exploring other options.

It may make sense to wait until your closer to the end of the term. However, if there's an indication that rates might rise, one strategy is to lock in a rate with a different lender using a 120-day rate hold. This approach would bring you to within two months of your renewal date. At that point, you can compare the rate you've secured with other available options leading up to your renewal date. If it turns out that the rate you have locked is the best option, you can consider transferring your mortgage to that lender and finalizing the deal. You would incur a penalty, but in most cases, it would only be the interest for the remaining term–which is two months in this case.

The rate offered by the new lender should be low enough cover the penalty, while still providing you with additional savings over your current lender's renewal offer.

It's not to say that you should always reject your lender's early renewal offer. If market trends suggest that interest rates are likely to rise over the next six months, accepting an early renewal could be a wise decision. However, it's important to first explore other available rates prior to making the move.

CHAPTER TEN HIGHLIGHTS

- Always take the time to explore your options before choosing a mortgage professional to work with.

- The most important consideration to make is choosing the right person to handle your mortgage for you.

- A seasoned mortgage professional may have suggestions on how to structure your mortgage to achieve maximum savings, over and above your interest rate.

- Decide what is most important to you: having the lowest mortgage rate, lowest payment, or saving the most money over time.

- The lowest rate does not always translate into the most savings long term.

- Choosing a mortgage based on rate alone can be a deceptive trap.

- Be aware of your mortgage's terms and conditions and what they mean.

- A true mortgage professional can steer you clear of hidden traps by advising you on the fine print, lender differences, while setting you up with a competitive rate.

- When choosing a variable rate, it's understood that your rate can change in either direction over the term.

- While variable rate mortgages are typically portable, most lenders will only let you port over the current balance.

- Any mortgage with more than one component will be registered as a collateral charge.

- The only considerable disadvantage to a collateral mortgage is that there could potentially be some added fees to transfer from one lender to another.

- Penalties to break your mortgage early can vary substantially from one lender to the next.

- Few people expect to break their mortgages early, yet so many do.

- Always take the time to research the lowest mortgage rates available to you before signing the renewal agreement with your current lender.

- Switching lenders at time of renewal can result in significant savings.

Securing the lowest mortgage rate is just one piece of the puzzle when it comes to saving money on your mortgage. Many get fixated on the rate, overlooking the broader goal of maximizing long-term savings. Through strategic planning and structuring of your mortgage, you can unlock savings that significantly outweigh the advantages of a low rate alone... accelerating your journey to mortgage freedom.

11

THE JOURNEY TO MORTGAGE FREEDOM

"Once you replace negative thoughts with positive ones, you'll start having positive results."
~Willie Nelson

A common goal for many mortgage borrowers is to pay their mortgage off faster with the ultimate goal of becoming mortgage free. But before we can say farewell to your mortgage payments, we need to explore strategies to expedite your journey to Champagne Day... the day you become mortgage free!

PAYING YOUR MORTGAGE DOWN FASTER

While all the lower rate mortgages are closed, meaning there is a penalty to return them early, they all come equipped with prepayment privileges. These are what allow you to pay a specified amount towards your mortgage each year without penalty, over and above your scheduled payments.

Prepayment privileges can vary among lenders, with some being flexible, and others that are more restrictive. This is why it's important that you're choosing a lender with terms that allow you to reach your prepayment goals.

Let's take a closer look at how they work.

There are two components to prepayment privileges:

1. Payment increase
2. Lump sum payments

They are written as a fraction. 20/20, 15/15, or 100/15 to give a few examples. The first number represents the maximum percentage by which you can increase your scheduled payment. The second number is your annual lump sum allowance.

For instance, if your mortgage offers 15/15 prepayment privileges then you can increase your payments by up to 15%, or you can pay up to 15% of the original mortgage balance as an annual lump sum payment. This is over and above your scheduled payments. With most lenders, you can do a combination of each, providing you don't exceed the maximum lump sum limit.

In other words, if you have a $300,000 mortgage, you have the option to pay up to $45,000 (15%) annually toward your mortgage in addition to your regular mortgage payments. However, if you choose to prepay the full $45,000, then you would generally not be able to increase your payments by 15% as well. This is the policy with most lenders.

If you only chose to prepay $20,000, for example, then you can still increase your scheduled payments up to the maximum limit. However, the combination cannot exceed the $45,000 annual lump sum limit.

While there are a select few lenders who will allow you to fully utilize both lump sum and payment increase privileges, they are few and far between.

STACKING YOUR PAYMENT INCREASES

Many are not aware that the payment increase privilege is stackable. In other words, if your privileges allow you to increase your payments by 15%, you're permitted to increase them by an additional 15% each year based on the already increased payment. For example, let's say your monthly payment is $1,000. If you max out the increase in the first year, your payment would then be $1,150. You can then increase the $1,150 by another 15% the following year, and so on.

The payment structure would look like this:

Year 1 - $1,150
Year 2 - $1,322.50
Year 3 - $1,520.88
Year 4 - $1,749.01
Year 5 - $2,011.36

This is how prepayment stacking works with most mortgage lenders. Some lenders, however, will only allow increases each year based on the original payment amount. In this case, the structure would be as follows:

Year 1 - $1,150
Year 2 - $1,300

Year 3 - $1,450
Year 4 - $1,600
Year 5 - $1750

The payment structures outlined above apply only if you are progressively increasing your payments each year. For instance, you can't jump from your original payment amount directly to a payment of $1,750 in the fifth year if you haven't been incrementally raising your payments in the preceding years. Each year's increase builds on the previous year's adjustment, so consistent annual increases are necessary to reach the higher payment levels in subsequent years. If you only use a portion of the payment increase privilege, then the 15% in the following year would be based on what you used. For example, if you increase your monthly payment to only $1,200 in the first year, then you would only be able to increase it to a maximum of $1,380 in the second year ($1,200 =15% = $1,380).

Most lenders give you the option to return to your original payment amount at any point during your mortgage term, which can be helpful if you need to improve your cash flow. However, it's important not to assume this is universally true. Always verify with your lender, as some may only allow you to go back to the increased payment amount from the previous year. For instance, if you're in the fourth year of your mortgage with a payment of $1,600, your lender might only permit a reduction to the $1,450 payment from year three, not all the way back to the original $1,000 payment. It's advisable to consult with your mortgage specialist to understand your lender's specific policy on payment adjustments.

Lump Sum Payment Frequency

Lenders often have different policies regarding the frequency of lump sum mortgage payments. Some restrict you to making a single lump sum payment per year, whereas others may allow up to three. However, most lenders offer greater flexibility, allowing you to make multiple lump sum payments as long as they align with your scheduled payment dates and don't exceed the maximum annual limit.

Let's say you have a mortgage with an original balance of $400,000, amortized over 30 years at 2.99% with monthly payments and 20/20 prepayment privileges. Your lender gives you the flexibility to make any number of lump sum payments, providing they fall on a scheduled payment date. This would allow you to pay $80,000 towards your mortgage each year in addition to your regular payments. If your mortgage is set up on a monthly payment frequency, you will have 12 payments per year, which means you could increase each payment by an additional $6666.67. As with all additional payments, it would be applied directly to your principal. When added to your regular monthly payment of $1,680.28, you'd be paying $8,346.95 per month.

This would result in an effective amortization of only four years, three months, and a few days. In other words, your mortgage would be paid off in just over four years. The original amortization is meaningless.

Lump sum payments do not need to be made evenly. You have the option to vary the amounts according to your financial situation. For example, you could make a $5,000 lump sum payment one month, $8,000 another month, and then $15,000 a few months later. It's up to you how you want to structure the payments. You can make only one lump sum payment if you like... or you can choose to make no lump sum payments at all if that suits your financial plan better.

Paying an additional $80,000 per year toward their mortgage is not an option for the vast majority of homeowners, but it gives you an example of what's possible.

Now let's look at a scenario that is a little more realistic. Using the same mortgage above, let's say you make an additional lump sum payment of $5,000 once per year on the anniversary date. This strategy would drop your amortization down to 27 years, 4 months and would give you a projected savings of $28,654.82 in interest. This is based on the first five years alone. If you were to carry this strategy on throughout the life of your mortgage, the amount of savings would increase significantly.

LUMP SUM PREPAYMENT RESTRICTIONS

When aiming to aggressively pay off your mortgage, you'll want to ensure that your lender's prepayment privileges align with your goals. Some lenders restrict you to just one lump sum payment per year. For instance, they might permit a maximum annual lump sum of $100,000, but if you make a single payment of $5,000, they won't allow any further payments until the following year. This limitation means you would miss the chance to utilize the remaining $95,000 of your allowable lump sum for that year.

LUMP SUM PAYMENTS VS. DOUBLING PAYMENTS

When a lender allows for a 100% increase in mortgage payments, it can be written as a numerical representation,

100/20 for example, or it can be referred to as a "double up". 100 refers to the ability to increase your original payment by up to 100%, effectively allowing you to double it.

There are some who specifically search out a lender offering the double up feature on their payment increase privilege. However, this is not necessary providing that you're working with a lender who doesn't limit the frequency of your lump sum payments.

For example, let's say you have a mortgage of $850,000 at 3.69% with a 25-year amortization. The regular monthly payment will be $4,329.48. If your lender is offering 20/20 prepayment privileges, then the 20% increase would bring it to $5,195.38 if you were to max it out. Doubling it would bring it to $8,658.96 which is notably higher. If the lender has a 20% lump sum privilege without a restriction on the frequency, then you would have the ability to increase your payment by an additional $14,166.67. This would bring the maximum possible monthly payment to $18,496.15 which is more than four times the original monthly payment in this case. A double up privilege is meaningless if the lender is flexible with their allowable lump sum payment frequency.

Reaching Your Prepayment Limit

If you have maximized your prepayment privileges for the year, you will need to wait until the next year for them to reset. The reset timing depends on your lender's policy; it could be based on the calendar year or the anniversary year of your mortgage.

If your lender allows for a maximum lump sum payment of say $150,000 per year, and you make this full payment on the last day of the relevant year (either calendar year or anniversary), you are eligible to make another $150,000 payment on the very next business day of the new year. However, after making this payment, you would then have to wait another full year before you can utilize your prepayment privileges again.

Maxing out your privilege doesn't mean that you cannot pay anything more towards your mortgage. You still can, however, you would pay the penalty on the overage. For instance, if your limit was $150,000 and you wanted to pay $160,000, you still can, but the penalty would apply to the additional $10,000. So many people are afraid of the word 'penalty'. After all, we don't want to be penalized for anything. For this reason, many will wait until the following year before they make another payment. But depending on the situation, this can be costly.

Maxing out your privilege doesn't mean that you cannot pay anything more towards your mortgage.

Sanjay and Nisha have a goal to get their $585,000 mortgage paid off as quickly as possible. They have a fixed rate mortgage at 4.00% with an annual lump sum prepayment privilege of 15%.

Two months into the second year, they have it paid down to $550,000. They recently collected an inheritance of $150,000 which they want to apply to their mortgage. However, their lump sum privilege limits them to paying a maximum of $87,750 per year which they pay immediately, bringing their balance down to $462,250. Since they've reached their annual prepayment cap, Sanjay and Nisha wait another ten months for their privileges to reset, allowing them to pay the remaining $62,250 without penalty.

But the penalty would have been only $622.50, equivalent to three months' interest. By waiting to make the full payment, they effectively incurred a "penalty" by paying ten months of interest on the $62,250 when they could have got by with only three.

In Sanjay and Nisha's case, their effort to save on the penalty ironically led to a higher overall expense. I cannot stress enough the importance of considering all aspects of the mortgage, rather than individual elements like rate or penalty alone. In the end, it's the overall cost of the mortgage that is most important.

LEVERAGING YOUR PAYMENTS WITH VARIABLE RATE MORTGAGES

Deciding between a fixed rate and a variable rate mortgage can be challenging with multiple points of evaluation as I detailed in Chapter Four. But if you're still uncertain about which option is best for you, then you may want to consider choosing a variable rate, but then set your payment as if you had chosen the higher fixed rate. This would be done using your prepayment privileges. Since you're already considering the higher payment associated with the fixed rate, this method allows you to pay down your mortgage faster while taking advantage of the lower interest rates that are typically found with variable rate mortgages. Needless to say, this strategy works when the variable rate options are lower than the fixed, which is the case with most markets. However, if the variable rate is higher than the fixed rate options, then the strategy can be reversed.

If you were to start off with the higher rate option, then 100% of the payment difference would be applied to interest. But using this strategy, 100% of the payment difference is applied to principal, therefore rapidly accelerating the payoff of your mortgage, and putting you ahead of the game. This way, when rates do increase, you may have a higher rate, but it will be on a lower balance, resulting in you paying less interest.

For example, let's say you need to borrow $450,000 amortized over 30 years and are trying to choose between two options:

5-year variable rate at 2.50% with a monthly payment of $1,775.02
5-year fixed rate at 2.99% with a monthly payment of $1,890.32

If you chose the variable rate but set your payments at $1,890.32 to match the fixed rate payment, the $115.30 difference will be applied directly to your principal. Over the 5-year term, this amounts to a significant reduction in principal, totalling $10,988.68, assuming no changes to the variable rate over that period.

However, it's important to note that the likelihood of the prime rate remaining constant throughout the period is quite low. It can move in either direction, which will influence the results. Historically, there have only been two instances of a five-year or longer period without any movement in the prime rate:

The first was from the establishment of the Bank of Canada in March 1935 until February 1944. This was largely influenced by the economic conditions of the era, which included the Great Depression and the early years of World War II.

The second period spanned from February 1944 to October 1950, which covered the latter part of World War II and the significant economic recovery in post-war years.

There has also never been a period in history where the prime rate has increased, but not decreased within the same five-year period.

This strategy will generally fall within the prepayment allowances of most lenders. Given that the payment increase in the above example is roughly 6.5%, and most lenders will allow a payment increase of 15 to 100%, you would still have room to increase your payment even further. If it's comfortable for you, then I would recommend doing just that. Every additional $1 you add to your payment is one less dollar that you'll need to pay interest on... starting with your very next payment.

....

Consider choosing the variable option, but increase your payments to match the payment on the 5-year fixed rate.

....

This strategy also offers a degree of flexibility to your mortgage. If rates stay low, or decrease, you're paying off your mortgage faster, without feeling the financial strain. If you're in an adjustable rate mortgage (ARM), where payments change with the prime rate, then you can choose to enjoy the lower payments and increased cash flow when the rate drops; or you can maintain the higher payment to reduce your balance all that much faster.

If interest rates rise, you're already accustomed to the higher payment, which you can maintain to keep it in line with what you were previously paying. That is, as long as the prime rate doesn't rise to the point where your payment becomes higher than what you were previously paying. But even in this situation, the payment increase would be far less than what it would have been if you started without increasing your payment at all.

This strategy gives you ultimate flexibility and is a great way to maintain a comfortable payment, while accelerating the payoff of your mortgage at the same time.

MORTGAGE RATE INFLATION HEDGE STRATEGY

One of the most common questions I get from my clients is about my predictions for the direction of mortgage rates in coming years. Usually from those who are undecided on the ideal term length or uncertain about whether to choose a fixed or a variable rate mortgage. This is an important consideration when choosing your ideal mortgage product.

If rates are expected to decrease in the coming years, clients might be inclined to choose a shorter-term mortgage or a variable rate product. This is so they can capitalize on the anticipated lower rates to come. If respectable decreases in rates are expected, then this can be a strategic financial move, even if the initial rates for these shorter-term or variable products are higher than those for longer-term fixed options. Clients choosing this path are essentially betting on the forecast that rates will drop, allowing them to renew at a lower rate sooner, or ride a variable rate down as the prime rate drops.

If the outlook suggests that rates are likely to increase, most will prefer to lock in a longer fixed-term mortgage. It's a protective measure against the potential financial strain of rising rates in the future. By choosing a longer fixed term, they effectively secure a consistent interest rate over an extended period, providing a sense of stability and predictability, leading to greater peace of mind.

In either situation, the decision involves a level of risk and speculation, as interest rate forecasts can be uncertain and influenced by a myriad of economic factors. Therefore, it's important to consider your risk tolerance and overall financial situation when making this decision.

Interest rate forecasts can be uncertain and influenced by a myriad of economic factors.

The truth is no one knows for sure what's going to happen with rates. All we can do is speculate. In other words... we're guessing. Even Canada's top economists often get it wrong. From September 2010 through July 2017, we experienced one of the longest streaks in history without an increase to the prime rate. From 2011 through to 2014, I would consistently hear economists predicting that we would see an increase to the prime rate 'next year'.

What eventually happened?

The prime rate dropped early in 2015. Twice.

At the beginning of 2022, it was forecasted that the prime rate would rise four to five times over the year, with each move being the standard 0.25%. This would have meant a total increase of 1.00% to 1.25%. Instead, we saw seven increases totalling 4.00% by the end of the year.

In late 2022, four out of the big six banks predicted that the Bank of Canada would not increase its rate in 2023. The remaining two banks forecasted a 0.25% hike in the first quarter. Contrary to the forecasts, there was a 0.25% increase in January, followed by two additional hikes by mid-summer, totalling 0.75%.

The only certain method to predict future interest rate movements is to have a high-quality, sparkling crystal ball at your disposal. (As for mine, it's currently being professionally polished).

Given the uncertainty of future mortgage rates, one can implement a hedge strategy. It's not about shielding yourself from rising rates, as that's impossible. Rather, the goal is to strategize in a way that makes the impact of rising rates less painful. Specifically, this involves hedging against the potential increase in mortgage rates.

What is a hedge?

I'm not talking about a row of small shrubs (although planting some may help with your resale). A hedge is a way of protecting yourself against financial loss. In this case, the idea is to get a head start against rising rates by artificially increasing them yourself.

Huh?

Let me better explain.

This strategy involves utilizing your mortgage's prepayment privileges to voluntarily increase your payments, as if they were already based on a higher interest rate. You start in year one, then progressively raise your payments in the second, third, fourth, and fifth years. As your income grows annually, you correspondingly increase your mortgage payment. This way, when rates do start to increase, you're already accustomed to payments based on a higher rate. The additional payments are applied directly towards your principal. Consequently, by the time rates increase, you'll have already paid your mortgage down further. This means the higher rate will be calculated on a lower balance, which will result in you paying less interest.

This works equally well for both fixed and variable rates.

HEDGE STRATEGY WITH FIXED RATES

Let's take a look at an example to give you a better idea of what I'm talking about by examining the following mortgage:

Mortgage amount: $300,000
Amortization: 25 years
Rate: 2.89%
Term: 5-year fixed
Monthly payment: $1,402.86

Let's hypothesize that the 5-year fixed mortgage rate will reach 3.99% by the end of a five-year period. While this prediction is entirely speculative, the suggested strategy is effective regardless of how rates actually move in the future. By sticking to your regular monthly payment schedule without making any extra payments, you would owe $255,879.53 at the end of the five-year term.

If you were to renew for another five years, the new mortgage would look like this:

Mortgage amount: $255,879.53
Amortization: 20 years
Rate: 3.99%
Term: 5-year fixed
Monthly payment: $1,544.82

This represents a payment increase of $141.96 compared to what you were accustomed to paying during your first mortgage term.

Now here's where the fun begins!

Since we're using a five-year term in this example, we are going to divide the future payment increase by five and then increase the mortgage payment by that amount. This works out to be an increase of $28.39 per year.

Here's what the payment structure would look like along

with the ending balance each year when implementing the $28.39 increase right from the very first payment.

$28.39 Annual Payment Increase

Year	Payment	Mortgage Balance
1	$1,431.25	$291,329.68
2	1,459.64	282,061.79
3	1,488.03	272,178.91
4	1,516.42	261,663.16
5	1,544.81	250,496.10

At the end of five years, you'll be used to paying the equivalent of a 3.99% rate, which will remove the shock of having such a large payment increase as a result. This scenario represents an interest savings of $273.23 at the end of five years. Now, $273 may not exactly get your birds chirping, but it's still $273 that you won't have to pay to the bank. You will also have eliminated the shock of having to make a higher payment if the rates did increase to this level.

If your rate remained unchanged until the mortgage was paid to zero, and you maintained the $1,544.81 payment, you would save a total of $14,143.87. That being said, this is not a realistic scenario. It's just not going to happen. But I thought I'd include this example for anyone who may be interested in the 'but what if' scenario. Plus, it's fun to dream!

This will also shorten your effective amortization from 25 years down to 22 years, 1.5 months based on the first five years alone. Following this simple strategy, at the end of five years your ending balance will be $5,383.43 lower than it would have been if you just stuck with your regular scheduled payments.

Here's how it would look if your rate actually did increase to 3.99% at the end of your term. If you had implemented the hedge strategy, the new mortgage at renewal would look like this:

Mortgage amount: $250,496.10
Amortization: 20 years (Based on it being 5 years later)
Rate: 3.99%
Term: 5-year fixed
Monthly payment: $1,512.32

The first thing you may notice is that the monthly payment is lower than the $1,544.82 we used for the hedge strategy. By implementing the hedge strategy and increasing your payments, you effectively reduced the balance of your mortgage. Consequently, when you start a new term, the payment required is lower due to this reduced balance. The payment projection in the hedge strategy was based on the assumption of no proactive action being taken. However, since you've employed the hedge strategy, you'll now have a lower payment for your new mortgage term.

You can reapply this hedge strategy for the next five-year period and continue it throughout the duration of your mortgage, until it is fully paid off. If interest rates were to decrease, this strategy positions you even further ahead. In such a scenario, you could potentially save thousands of dollars, as you would have already reduced your principal balance, leading to even lower interest costs over the life of your mortgage.

HEDGE STRATEGY WITH VARIABLE RATES

This hedge strategy is also highly effective for variable rate mortgages. It's an excellent approach for individuals who are interested in variable rates but are uncertain about whether it's the right choice for them. The primary concern with variable rate mortgages is the possibility of rate and payment increases at any time. This uncertainty is why many people choose fixed rate mortgages, which is also a completely valid decision. By using this strategy with a variable rate mortgage, you can prepare for potential rate increases by incrementally raising your payments, thereby reducing the impact of any future rate hikes.

To illustrate the inflation hedge strategy on a variable rate, we'll use different numbers from the fixed example, just to keep things fun. Similar to the strategy we used for fixed rates, we will be artificially increasing the variable rate as well.

We'll use the following mortgage for our example:

Mortgage amount: $425,000
Amortization: 30 years
Rate: 2.15%
Term: 5-year variable
Payment: $1,600.90 (scheduled monthly payment)

Let's consider a scenario where the prime rate increases by 0.50% each year for the next five years, implying two increases per year. Of course, there's no certainty that this will actually occur, but the key point of this strategy isn't to accurately forecast future rate movements. It's to prepare for unforeseen changes, thereby reducing the potential for future payment shock. By proactively adjusting to higher payments through this strategy, you can better position yourself to handle any unexpected increases in mortgage rates, making them more manageable should they occur.

If rates increase, you're prepared to manage the payments comfortably. If rates stay the same or decrease, you've accelerated your principal repayment, reducing your amortization and total interest paid. Essentially, this approach positions you to be in a better financial situation regardless of how the prime rate fluctuates. In either case, you're a winner.

There are of course a million potential scenarios that could be taken into consideration. We'll however keep things simple by analyzing just three of them. I'll leave the other 999,997 up to you.

The actual outcome of future mortgage rates will always be speculative. The main purpose of this strategy is to help protect you against the shock of suddenly increasing payments in an environment where prime rate is steadily increasing.

....

The main purpose of this strategy is to help protect you against the shock of suddenly increasing payments in an environment where prime rate is steadily increasing.

....

Scenario One

The first scenario outlines how your payment structure

would appear if you continued with your scheduled payments without any increases, under the assumption that the prime rate remains unchanged throughout the term.

Standard Payment Structure

Year	Rate	Payment amount	Mortgage Balance
1	2.15	$1,600.90	$414,786.23
2	2.15	1,600.90	404,351.69
3	2.15	1,600.90	393,691.60
4	2.15	1,600.90	382,801.08
5	2.15	1,600.90	371,675.15

This provides a clear, preliminary picture as it would appear on paper before implementing any changes or strategies. As we're maintaining the original payment structure, it doesn't provide a cushion against potential future rate increases, leaving you more vulnerable to payment shock if rates rise unexpectedly.

Now it's time to start the fun stuff!

Scenario Two

In the second scenario, we'll also assume no change to the prime rate. However, this time we'll apply the hedge strategy be incrementally increasing the payment as if there were a rate increase of 0.50% per year, starting in the second year.

Payment Increases to Simulate a 0.50% Annual Rate Hike

Year	Rate	Payment	Mortgage Balance
1	2.15	$1,600.90	$414,786.23
2	2.65	1,706.11	403,076.69
3	3.15	1,811.67	389,834.25
4	3.65	1,917.25	375,026.68
5	4.15	2,022.55	358,622.98

At the end of five years, you'll be used to making payments as if the rate were 4.15%. This effectively prepares you for a situation where the rates might increase to this level, thus eliminating the shock of suddenly higher payments. This scenario represents a savings of $403.78 at the end of five years. Moreover, it reduces your amortization to only 17.77 years, a significant decrease from the initial 30-year amortization period outlined on paper. This result demonstrates the effectiveness of the hedge strategy in not only preparing you for potential rate increases but also in accelerating the payoff of your mortgage.

That means your balance at the end of your term would be $13,052 lower than it would have been had you maintained your regular payment schedule.

Scenario Three

The third scenario illustrates the financial outcome if the hypothetical situation of steadily increasing rates materialized. For simplicity, I've implemented the 0.50% increase at the beginning of each year.

Payment Increases With a 0.50% Annual Rate Hike

Year	Rate	Payment amount	Mortgage Balance
1	2.15	$1,600.90	$414,786.23
2	2.65	1,706.11	405,128.44
3	3.15	1,811.67	395,935.88
4	3.65	1,917.25	387,126.55
5	4.15	2,022.55	378,625.41

In this example, your payment increases would total an additional $12,647.76 over five years. Simultaneously, your ending mortgage balance would rise to $378,625.41, compared to $371,675.15 if you had maintained your initial payment and the rate had stayed constant.

In essence, you would have paid an extra $12,647.76, and your ending balance still increased by $6,950.26. Combining these figures, the rate increases in this scenario would have cost you an additional $19,598.02 over the five-year term.

This outlines the value of utilizing your prepayment privileges. By increasing your payments in anticipation of potential rate hikes, you can mitigate the impact of such increases on your overall mortgage balance and interest paid. This way, when rates start to increase, you'll be paying the higher rate on a lower balance and will therefore be paying less interest.

MANIPULATING YOUR AMORTIZATION

The definition of amortization is the amount of time it would take to pay your mortgage down to zero while maintaining equal payments. Therefore, any increase in your regular payment or making a lump sum payment towards your mortgage directly reduces your amortization period. Essentially, once you start making these additional payments, the original amortization schedule you began with becomes less relevant. This is because the schedule was based on a fixed payment over a set period, and any changes to the payment amount alter the timeline for paying off the mortgage. This is how additional payments can significantly accelerate the reduction of your mortgage balance, leading to an earlier payoff than initially planned.

When adhering to your original payment schedule, portion of the payment allocated to principal will increase with each payment, while the interest portion proportionately decreases. The chart below illustrates the standard payment structure on a $400,000 mortgage at 2.99%, amortized over 30 years.

Original Payment Schedule

Pmt #	Interest	Principal	Total Pmt	Balance
1	$990.51	$689.77	$1,680.28	$399,310.23
2	988.81	691.47	1,680.28	398,618.76
3	987.09	693.19	1,680.28	396,534.05
4	985.38	694.90	1,680.28	397,230.67
5	983.66	696.62	1,680.28	396,534.05
6	981.93	698.35	1,680.28	395,835.70
7	980.20	700.08	1,680.28	395,135.62
8	978.47	701.81	1,680.28	394,433.81

9	976.73	703.55	1,680.28	393,730.26
10	974.99	705.29	1,680.28	393,024.97
11	973.24	707.04	1,680.28	392,317.93
12	971.49	708.79	1,680.28	391,609.14

In this example, the amount applied to principal increases by approximately $1.70 each month and then continues to increase a penny or so every couple of months. The interest portion of each payment then decreases by an equal amount.

Now let's take the same mortgage, but we'll increase the payments by 15%.

Payment Schedule with 15% Payment Increase

Pmt #	Interest	Principal	Total Pmt	Balance
1	$990.51	$941.81	$1,932.32	$399,058.19
2	988.18	944.14	1,932.32	398,114.05
3	985.84	946.48	1,932.32	397,167.57
4	983.50	948.82	1,932.32	396,218.75
5	981.15	951.17	1,932.32	395,267.58
6	978.80	953.52	1,932.32	394,314.06
7	976.43	955.89	1,932.32	393,358.17
8	974.07	958.25	1,932.32	392,399.92
9	971.69	960.63	1,932.32	391,439.29
10	969.32	963.00	1,932.32	390,476.29
11	966.93	965.39	1,932.32	389,510.90
12	964.54	967.78	1,932.32	388,543.12

The portion of your payment applied to principal jumps from $1.70 to $2.33 from your very first payment. While we are just talking pennies, these pennies start to add up very quickly.

Applying a 15% increase to your monthly mortgage payment amounts to an additional $252.04 per month. Over the span of a five-year term, this results in a total extra payment of $15,122.40. By choosing this strategy, the balance remaining on your mortgage at the end of five years will be $16,281.96 lower compared your regular payment schedule.

This means you'll come out ahead by $1,159.56 when compared with the regular payment schedule (no increase to payments). By increasing your payments by 15%, you will have also shaved almost six years off your projected amortization in the first five years alone. Not bad.

CHOOSING THE RIGHT PAYMENT FREQUENCY

Choosing your payment frequency is typically the final decision made before your application is sent to a lender for approval. Some lenders issue your initial set of approval documents with monthly payments, allowing you to change it when finalizing the paperwork. Others will issue the documents with your preferred frequency right from the beginning. Regardless of the approach, the ultimate choice of how often you make your mortgage payments is up to you.

There are six different payment frequency options:

- Monthly

- Semi –Monthly
- Biweekly
- Weekly
- Accelerated Biweekly
- Accelerated Weekly

Monthly

Monthly mortgage payments are straightforward and simple to understand. As the name suggests, you will have a single mortgage payment each month, due on the same date. For example, if you purchase a property that closes on the 15th, then your payment will fall on the 15th of each month. If the purchase closes on the 31st, then your payment will generally fall on the last day of each month. For instance, February 28th.

Some lenders prefer to collect payments on the first of each month, leading them to adjust the timing of your first full payment accordingly. For example, if your closing was April 20th, then a lender may schedule your first payment for June 1st.

Why such a long gap?

A lender is only able to collect a complete mortgage payment once the interest for the entire payment period has accrued. If your closing was on April 20th, then only 10 days have passed by May 1st, falling significantly short of a full month. The lender will make a partial withdrawal on May 1st to account for the interest accumulated over these first 10 days, which is referred to as an interest adjustment.

This is not an extra charge or an additional cost. It simply covers the interest owed to the lender leading up to May 1st, which is known as the interest adjustment date. The payment schedule is now on track for your first full mortgage payment to be withdrawn from your account on June 1st.

Note that some lenders may deduct the interest adjustment from the funds advanced to your lawyer at closing, meaning, you would need to make the payment as part of your closing costs.

SEMI-MONTHLY

Semi-monthly mortgage payments are made twice per month for a total of 24 payments per year. A common misconception is that a semi-monthly payment is half of the monthly, which is the information you'll find on most websites. However, this isn't entirely accurate. While dividing the monthly payment by two offers a rough estimate, the actual semi-monthly payment will be slightly lower. For example, if we use a $500,000 mortgage at 3.99% amortized over 25 years, the monthly payment will be $2,627.39. If you divide this by two, you'll get a semi-monthly payment of $1,313.70. But the actual payment would only be $1,312.61, or $1.09 less per payment.

This is because you're making a payment 15 days earlier than you would under a monthly payment schedule, resulting in paying slightly less interest. Once a payment is made, you're no longer paying interest on the principal portion of that payment. This is why the principal portion increases and the interest portion decreases with each payment made. The earlier a payment is made, the quicker the principal balance decreases, which means less interest is charged over time. However, the difference is marginal. Choosing a semi-monthly payment frequency will only save you $129.67 in interest by the end of a 5-year term.

BIWEEKLY

Biweekly payments are made every two weeks, which may initially seem like making payments twice per month. However, semi-monthly payments are made 15 days apart, resulting in two payments per month for a total of 24 payments in a year. In contrast, biweekly payments are 14 days apart, totalling 26 payments annually. There are two months per year that have a total of three payments. Note that this doesn't mean you're paying more overall as each biweekly payment will be smaller than that of a semi-monthly payment.

You can get a rough idea of your biweekly payment by multiplying your monthly payment by 12 and then dividing it by 26. But just as with semi-monthly payments, the actual payments will be marginally lower for the same reason explained above. By the end of the 5-year term, you'll have paid $139.74 less interest when compared with monthly payments. Just marginally better than the semi-monthly payment option.

Biweekly payments are not to be confused with accelerated biweekly, which I'll be explaining shortly.

WEEKLY

As the name implies, weekly payments are made once per

week. Most online resources explain the calculation as your monthly payment multiplied by 12 and then divided by 52. Once again, this will only give you a rough idea of the payment, as the actual number will be slightly lower.

Choosing a weekly payment frequency will result in paying $199.50 less interest by the end of the 5-year term when compared with a monthly payment structure.

While semi-monthly, biweekly and weekly payments all result in paying marginally less interest, the difference will not reduce the time it will take to payoff of your mortgage. This is where accelerated payments come into play.

Accelerated Biweekly

Accelerated biweekly payments are accurately determined by dividing your monthly payment in half. The payment is then made every two weeks for a total of 26 payments annually. This results in a higher payment than the non-accelerated option, which is how it's beneficial. On a $500,000 mortgage at 3.99% with a 25-year amortization, your regular biweekly payment will be $1,211.57. If accelerated, it increases to $1,313.70. The difference is applied to your principal, therefore 'accelerating' the payoff of your mortgage.

Accelerated Weekly

Instead of dividing your monthly payment in half as you would with accelerated biweekly payments, you would divide it by four. The payment is then made every week for a total of 52 payments per year. As with biweekly, the accelerated payment will be a little higher than the non-accelerated option.

To be consistent with true mortgage industry fashion, what fun would it be if there wasn't an additional layer of confusion to add into the mix? Not every lender offers standard weekly or biweekly payments and will only provide accelerated options. However, they may refer to them as just weekly or biweekly... but they are in fact accelerated. They just haven't attached that label to them.

The Mechanics of Accelerated Payments

By simply accelerating your payments, you'll be making the equivalent of one additional monthly payment per year, which is applied 100% towards your principal. This results in a noticeable reduction to your amortization which will vary based on interest rate. The higher the rate, the larger the reduction, and vice-versa.

For instance, a mortgage at 2.99% with a 30-year amortization would automatically become 26 years, 5.5 months. If the rate were 3.99%, it would drop to 25 years, 10.6 months.

If starting with a 25-year amortization at 2.99%, accelerating the payment reduces the amortization to 22 years 2.8 months. At 3.99%, it would become 21 years 10.6 months.

The extra monthly payment with an accelerated structure is distributed evenly across 26 or 52 payments respectively. This makes the additional amount more manageable. One thing to note is that accelerated payments will cut into your cash flow, as they result in paying a bit more each month. In situations where money is tight, monthly, semi-monthly, or non-accelerated weekly/biweekly payments may be a better choice.

Making the Decision

Let's look at how the payments will vary for each payment frequency. For simplicity, we'll stick with the same numbers we've been using throughout this section: a $500,000 mortgage at 3.99% amortized over 25 years.

Frequency	Payment	Pmts /Yr	Annual Payments	Int Paid After 5 Years	Interest Paid vs. Monthly	Amrt (yrs)
Monthly	$2,627.39	12	$31,528.68	$92,837.18	$0	25
Semi-Monthly	1,312.61	24	31,502.64	92,707.51	-129.67	25
Biweekly	1,211.57	26	31,500.82	92,697.44	-139.74	25
Acc. Biweekly	1,313.70	26	34,156.20	91,306.41	-1,530.77	21 yrs/ 10.6 mths
Weekly	605.55	52	31,488.60	92,637.68	-199.50	25
Acc. Weekly	656.85	52	34,156.20	91,234.84	-1,602.34	21 yrs/ 10.4 mths

The majority of borrowers tend to choose accelerated biweekly payments, as it's the easiest way to pay their mortgage down faster... without having to give it any thought.

When it comes to selecting the best payment option, there's no right or wrong answer. It depends on what aligns best with your personal financial situation and comfort level. Many people find it convenient to synchronize their mortgage payments with their payroll schedule, setting their payments to fall on the same dates they receive their paycheques.

For those who are still uncertain about which payment

frequency to choose, I generally recommend starting with monthly payments. This is a standard option that's simple and easy to manage. Then once you start getting a feel for your overall monthly expenses, you can change to an accelerated payment structure if you prefer. Most lenders provide the flexibility to make the change at any point during the term, usually without any additional cost.

Alternatively, you can maintain monthly payments and take advantage of your prepayment privileges. This provides a balance between regular, manageable payments and the opportunity to pay your balance down faster when your financial situation allows. Ultimately, the key is to select a payment strategy that fits comfortably within your budget while helping you achieve your long-term financial goals.

CHAPTER ELEVEN HIGHLIGHTS

- Leverage your prepayment privileges to pay your mortgage down faster.

- Prepayment privileges have two components: Increase to payments and lump sum payments.

- Some lenders will limit you to a single lump sum payment per year, while others will let you make them on any scheduled payment date.

- You don't need a double up payment feature if you have flexible lump sum prepayment privileges which are far more powerful.

- It can sometimes be more cost effective to exceed your prepayment limit and pay the associated penalty, rather than waiting for your privileges to reset.

- If trying to decide between fixed and variable, consider choosing a variable rate, but set your prepayment privileges to match the higher fixed rate.

- Implement the mortgage rate inflation hedge strategy to maximize savings and eliminate the payment shock from potentially higher rates in the future.

- Your effective amortization drops every time you use your prepayment privileges.

- Choosing accelerated weekly or biweekly payments is the easiest and most popular method to pay your mortgage down faster.

Your prepayment privileges can be a powerful tool in expediting your journey to mortgage freedom. It can also help you to feel a sense of power knowing that you are in control of your mortgage, rather than having your mortgage in control of you. If simply choosing an accelerated payment structure can knock a 25-year mortgage down to roughly 22 years, imagine what would happen if you increased the payment even further?

With a little discipline and commitment, you can pay your mortgage down to zero at a rapid rate. And each additional payment you make will put you one step closer to popping the cork.

12

ALTERNATIVE MORTGAGE LENDING

"I learned there are troubles of more than one kind. Some come from ahead, others come from behind. But I've bought a big bat. I'm all ready, you see. Now my troubles are going to have trouble with me".
~Dr. Seuss

L ife is full of ups and downs. There are times when things can become tough even for the most credit worthy and financially stable individuals. I've dealt with clients who were as solid as solid can be when arranging their mortgage. Then, a few years later, they contact me after life threw them a curveball sending their financial situation spiraling downward.

There are a number of things that can cause someone's finances to turn south:

- Loss of job
- Disability
- Divorce
- Business venture turned bad

- Legal issues
- Unexpected expenses, etc.

It's a harsh reality that even good people can face difficult times, and this happens more often than we'd like. It can be next to impossible to get a mortgage through traditional sources when your credit has taken a beating.

There are also some who have solid credit and income, yet still struggle to qualify for their required mortgage amount due to stringent lending criteria.

Fortunately, there are alternative lending solutions to service these markets.

WHAT IS ALTERNATIVE MORTGAGE LENDING?

An alternative mortgage lender is one that specializes in situations where the applicant does not qualify through an 'A' lender, such as a major bank. That is, a lender specializing in qualified applicants. Any lender who specializes in mortgages that don't fit within the general qualifying criteria of an 'A' lender would be considered an alternative.

The following are some of the typical situations that would require alternative lending:

- Bad credit

- Non-confirmable income[14]
- Non-qualifying income
- Refinancing above 80% LTV
- Specialty properties

TYPES OF ALTERNATIVE LENDERS

There are two types of alternative lenders. 'B' lenders and private lenders.

'B' LENDERS

A 'B' lender, often referred to as an equity lender, caters to applicants who are unlikely to be approved by an 'A' lender. While 'A' lenders focus on the creditworthiness and income of their applicants, 'B' lenders place more emphasis on the specific property and its available equity, or in the case of a purchase, the size of the down payment. These lenders are more flexible with their qualification criteria, making them a suitable alternative for those who don't meet the stringent requirements of traditional 'A' lenders.

....

'B' lenders place more emphasis on the specific property and its available equity.

....

---

14   In some cases, non-confirmable income can still be done with an 'A' lender, depending on the situation. See Chapter Six for more information on stated income found in the section on self-employed borrowers.

Given the higher risk associated with these borrowers, 'B' lenders generally require a larger down payment. While it's possible to purchase a property with as little as 5% down through an 'A' lender, 'B' lenders require a minimum down payment of 20% or greater. However, the requirements are not entirely straightforward.

Although 'B' lenders focus more on the property and its equity rather than the borrower's creditworthiness, they still consider the applicant's income and credit history. They will require some form of documented proof of income, regardless of the size of the down payment or the amount of equity in the property. This ensures that the borrower has a demonstrable ability to manage and repay the loan, therefore reducing the lender's risk.

The terms and approval of a mortgage from a 'B' lender, including the mortgage rate and the minimum down payment, can vary depending on any of the following three things:

- Type of property
- Credit
- Location

Type of Property

Is it a house or a condo? Condos are not quite as coveted as houses; therefore, condos may require a higher down payment in some situations.

Credit

While 'B' lenders are more lenient compared to 'A' lenders

when it comes to credit history, they still pay close attention to it. However, it's primarily used to determine the terms of the mortgage, such as the interest rate and the maximum loan-to-value (LTV), rather than as a requirement for qualification.

For instance, an applicant with a lower credit score, say 500, would typically be required to provide a higher down payment and would be offered a higher rate compared to someone with a score of 650. This is because a lower credit score indicates higher risk, which lenders offset with higher rates and additional equity. Every situation can be a bit different.

Location

Properties in urban areas are generally easier to finance compared to those in rural communities. The difference is often reflected in the required down payment and the interest rate offered by lenders. For instance, purchasing a property in a major urban centre like Toronto, Vancouver, or Calgary might require a minimum down payment of 20%. However, for a similar property in smaller communities such as Timmins, Penticton, or Medicine Hat, a larger down payment would generally be required, sometimes as much as 35%, depending on the location.

Furthermore, there are specific locations where 'B' lenders may not lend at all, regardless of the size of the down payment. This is due to the lender's assessment of the risk associated with certain geographical areas, which could be influenced by factors like market stability and property demand.

Cost of Using a 'B' Lender

Rates charged by 'B' lenders are typically around 0.50% to 2% higher than those offered by 'A' lenders. In addition to the higher interest rate, you'll also pay a lender fee equal to 1% of the loan amount, which is the standard fee charged by most 'B' lenders. For instance, if you are taking out a mortgage of $500,000, a 'B' lender would charge a fee of $5,000 (1%). This would be deducted from the mortgage proceeds, meaning you would receive $495,000 at closing. However, you would still be paying interest on the full $500,000 you're borrowing.

While 'B' lenders are much more flexible, they have their limits and there are many situations where an applicant still may not qualify. In such cases, the only option would be to apply with a private lender.

PRIVATE LENDERS

When a borrower is considered to be too risky, even for a 'B' lender, private lenders step in to fill this niche. As private lenders cater to the riskiest of mortgage loans, they also have the highest cost to offset the risk, which I'll be discussing shortly.

Private money typically comes from an individual as opposed to an institution. For example, instead of your lender being Scotiabank, it might be 'Joe Smith'. These are generally people who have accumulated wealth and are seeking investment opportunities. In this case, the opportunity is with alternative mortgage lending.

Private money can also come from what's known as a

Mortgage Investment Corporation, more commonly referred to as a MIC. A MIC operates by pooling money together from multiple investors to fund a portfolio of mortgages.

Private lenders vary in their qualification requirements, with different thresholds for how much they are willing to lend relative to the value of the property (loan to value). Some private lenders may cap their lending at 75% LTV, while others may consider lending up to 85%. A very select few might even consider as high as 90% in a strong real estate market. Even then, private lending options for 90% LTV are rare. With very little equity left in the home, the risk to the lender becomes significantly elevated. The higher the perceived risk, the higher the cost to the borrower.

Private First and Second Mortgages

The terms 'first' and 'second' mortgage refer to the order in which the loans were registered against the title of the property. For example, when you purchase a new home, the mortgage is considered a first mortgage as there are no other charges (mortgages) registered. It's the first one, hence the term first mortgage.

If you wanted to add another mortgage on the same property without discharging the first, then the new one would be considered a second mortgage. The position of a mortgage is determined solely by the date in which it was registered. If the initial mortgage is fully repaid and discharged, the second mortgage then shifts to the primary position, becoming the new first mortgage, as it's now the only loan registered on the property.

If you had two mortgages on the property and were to refinance the first, then it would be discharged and reregistered. This would move it to second place (second mortgage) and the current second would become the first mortgage since it was the first one to be registered. However, no lender currently holding a first mortgage would accept being behind another lender, meaning they wouldn't accept being in second position. In this case, the current second mortgage lender would need to 'postpone' their registration. This would allow the new mortgage being registered to take priority as the new first mortgage. The current second mortgage would then maintain its position in second place.

If the borrower were to default on the payments resulting in foreclosure or power of sale, the liens registered against the property would be paid out in order. This is why 2nd mortgages are not typically offered by 'A' and 'B' lenders. They are not willing to accept the added risk involved with being in the subordinate position. This is why most second mortgages are funded through private lenders.

Cost of Private Mortgages

As private lenders service the riskiest segment of the market, they are also the most costly. For first mortgages, rates can range from 3% to 5% higher than what a typical 'A' lender would charge. Rates are even higher on second mortgages, often reaching into double digits.

Fees

Unlike mortgages from 'A' lenders with no fees charged by the broker, there are always fees associated with private lenders. The fee can vary based on the size of the mortgage as well as the particulars of each individual situation. On a first mortgage, the fees might range from 1 to 3%. On a second mortgage, they could be in the 5 to 10% range. The larger the mortgage, the lower the broker fee. For instance, if you were borrowing $1 million on a first mortgage, the broker may only need to charge 1%. On $30,000, they may charge 10%.

In addition to broker fees, private mortgages usually carry an additional fee charged by the lender. This lender fee can range from 1 to 3%, depending on the situation. On second mortgages going up to 90% LTV, even higher fees can be expected. This is to reflect the elevated risk considering that there is minimal equity to protect the lender's investment should the borrower default on the payments.

Why would anyone want to pay such a high rate on their mortgage?

The quick answer is that they wouldn't. But private mortgages are reserved for worst case scenarios. If no one else is willing to lend the money, then there are no other alternatives.

Document Requirements for Private Mortgages

While some private lenders may ask for documentation similar to what's required by institutional 'A' and 'B' lenders, it's not unusual to find private lenders who require significantly less. The biggest question a private lender has in determining qualifying eligibility is whether the deal makes sense. They tend to focus more on the overall soundness and practicality of the situation, rather than adhering to standard documentation and qualification requirements.

Mortgage Qualification with a Private Lender

<u>Jim's Case</u>

Let's say Jim is looking for a second mortgage. He has a past double bankruptcy, a long list of current collections, and no current income source. He would like to borrow $100,000 on a second mortgage up to 85% LTV and is vague about what he will be using the money for.

Let's break down this deal bit by bit to illustrate how the lender will be reviewing it:

Double Bankruptcy

He has brutal credit with a double bankruptcy and a long list of collections. Some people never learn and it doesn't seem as though paying bills is, or ever will be a priority for him.

No Source of Income

Without any income, lenders would have serious concerns about his ability to make his payments on time... or at all.

High LTV

Going up to 85% of the home's value on such a risky applicant doesn't leave the lender much cushion in the likely event that she would have foreclose or initiate a power of sale.

The odds of this mortgage going into default are extremely strong, and for all these reasons, there isn't a single private lender who would consider lending Jim the money he's looking for. Not any sane one that is. The deal doesn't make any sense and would be a recipe for disaster for all parties involved... including Jim.

This is an extreme example to illustrate my point.

Now let's look at a situation that makes a bit more sense.

Joe's Case

Joe just finished going through a messy divorce and now finds himself in a difficult financial situation. He has accumulated substantial debt due to his legal proceedings with his former spouse and his credit score has suffered a significant blow. Joe is beyond eager to move past this turbulent chapter in his life and is now seeking a fresh start by rebuilding his credit and regaining financial stability. He comes to me looking for a second mortgage of $75,000, which will pay out all his creditors, leaving him with enough funds to pay for some small renovations. Joe is a dedicated government employee, having held a stable position for the past decade with an annual salary of $100,000. His home is located in a popular suburb of Toronto with a market value of $1.2 million with an outstanding mortgage of $250,000.

As I'm sure you can already tell, this situation sounds a lot more reasonable.

Here are the strong points of this deal:

Credible Explanation

There is a credible explanation for his current financial predicament which adds a level of understanding and context that is valuable for lenders.

Practical Use of Funds

The practicality and justification behind the purpose of the loan greatly strengthen his application. Debt consolidation can demonstrate a responsible approach to managing and streamlining finances, while renovations will add value to the property. This combination of factors makes Joe's request for a loan more compelling and will be viewed favourably by lenders.

Reasonable Loan Amount and LTV

With the combined total of Joe's existing first mortgage and the proposed second mortgage amounting to $325,000 on a $1.2 million home, the LTV is only 27.08%. As there is a substantial amount of equity remaining in the home, the lender has significant protection in the event of borrower default.

Desirable Location

As Joe's property is located in a desirable area, it further enhances the appeal of his application. Properties in sought-after locations typically have higher market demand, which can make them easier to sell. This assures the lender that the property can be liquidated efficiently, further reducing their risk associated with the mortgage.

Stable, Salaried Income

Given Joe's stable, salaried income and his long-standing job tenure, it is reasonable to assume that his income will remain stable in the foreseeable future. The fact that he is employed in a government position further strengthens this assumption, as such jobs typically provide more job security.

Just as Jim's situation was an extreme case of a deal that wouldn't make sense for a private lender, Joe's is an extreme example of one that would. Everything about it is logical, making it a compelling and sensible opportunity for private lenders.

THE IMPORTANCE OF HOME EQUITY

The most important component in the approval of a private mortgage is the amount of equity in the home. While Jim would have a better chance of finding a unicorn in his backyard than finding a lender to approve him, someone in a similar situation could potentially qualify if he had enough equity, and everything made sense.

What?

How could that situation possibly make any sense?

Jim's exact situation wouldn't. But if we change a few of the details, then it's possible that a private lender could consider approving the deal.

George is in the exact same financial situation as Jim, with a double past bankruptcy, a long list of collections and no source of income. He inherited the property from his parents and had been living there for the past 10 years. The home has a market value of $1.4 million and is owned free and clear. No money owing on it at all. He needs to borrow $100,000 to renovate the home, which will include a new kitchen, bathrooms, hardwood flooring and painting. As he doesn't have the money to make the payments, we can increase the loan amount to $120,000. This should more than cover the fees and the mortgage payments for the full one-year term. Plus, it leaves him some extra funds to use as a buffer in case the renovation runs over budget. Once the renovations have been completed, his plan is to sell the property.

This is what lenders will be looking at in this situation:

Low LTV

The loan to value stands at a mere 7.14%, given that he currently has no outstanding mortgage on the home.

Guaranteed Payments

Given that George has no source of income and has a track record of unpaid bills, we've proactively deducted the monthly payments from the mortgage proceeds up front. This eliminates the risk of the borrower defaulting on the payments as they are fully paid in advance for the full one year term. It also makes it easier on George since he no longer has to worry about making his payments on time.

Purpose of Loan

There is a clear and specific reason for needing the money. The complete renovation of the home will enhance the property's value, therefore increasing the already large equity position.

Exit Strategy

As his plan is to sell the home once the renovations are complete, the lender knows exactly how and when the loan will be repaid to her. As George has a clear exit strategy, it further reduces any doubt the lender may have had with approving the mortgage.

It's for these reasons that we would have no trouble getting George approved for the mortgage as everything about the deal makes sense.

EXIT STRATEGY

Since alternative lending has higher rates and fees, these types of mortgages are meant to be short-term solutions. This is why terms with 'B' and private lenders are generally limited to one or two years. Private lenders will want to see a realistic plan for how the funds will eventually be repaid to them. This is referred to as the exit strategy. It could involve selling the property or refinancing with a traditional lender after improving their financial circumstances, such as credit score or income stability.

In situations where clients require alternative lending due to poor credit, I'll take the time to coach them on rebuilding it over the term. This can significantly increase their chances of qualifying for a mortgage with more favourable terms at time of renewal, ideally with an 'A' lender. This puts the client on a path towards better financial health and more sustainable mortgage options in the future.

IS IT WORTH IT?

Securing a private mortgage can come with a hefty price tag, but whether this expense is justified comes down to the borrower's specific circumstances. There are some cases where people really need the money and have no other alternatives. It can help save their home from power of sale or can get them needed funds quickly. While expensive, private money can provide a much-needed bail out of a sticky situation. When you desperately need money and everyone you talk to slams the door, the availability of private money can be a breath of fresh air.

In some cases, the need for a private mortgage extends beyond emergency needs and might be purely for investment purposes, which was the case with Dave. He wanted to purchase a home that required considerable renovations. A fixer upper. His plan was to renovate the property to improve its value and then immediately flip it for a profit.

His problem was that no one would lend him the money.

I arranged a private first mortgage of $250,000 at an 8% interest rate. The legal, broker, and lender fees amounted to $10,000. Dave executed his renovation plan and, exactly one year after the purchase, he successfully sold the renovated home. After accounting for the costs of renovations, he was ahead by $100,000. His mortgage funding costs totaled $30,000 including interest and fees, giving him a profit of $70,000 on the flip. Considering no one else would lend him the money, the private mortgage allowed him to earn a significant return on an investment that he would have had to otherwise pass on.

In situations where traditional financing options are unavailable, a private mortgage can be a valuable tool, allowing investors to capitalize on opportunities that might otherwise be out of reach.

THE COST OF BAD CREDIT

Having bad credit can cost you thousands of dollars in the mortgage world. I've mentioned that mortgages with 'B' lenders can cost as much as 1.50% - 3% higher than that of an 'A' lender (including the 1% lender fee). On a $300,000 mortgage, this can translate into an additional cost of $4,500 - $12,000 per year. If you needed a private mortgage, then the additional cost would be significantly higher.

Bad credit is expensive. Period. Sure, there are many cases where there is a good explanation for the bad credit, such as an unforeseen and unfortunate event that life tossed your way. However, there are also many times when bad credit can be easily preventable. Consistently paying your bills on time is essential for maintaining a healthy credit report and avoiding the incremental damage of late payments.

Set up an automatic payment system if you need to. Many online banking platforms will allow you to do this, which can be an easy way to avoid significant hits to your credit score as a result of late payments.

NO CREDIT

There are some people who prefer not to have any credit at all. They may not want the burden of having to make credit card payments. Or in some cases, they may not trust themselves with having credit cards, so for that reason, they pay cash for everything.

The problem with this approach is that no credit is equivalent to bad credit in the lending world. Without a credit history, there's no track record for lenders to assess your reliability as a borrower. There is no evidence as to whether you'll make your payments on time... or at all.

No credit is equivalent to bad credit in the lending world.

Even the 'B' lenders put up their guard and become more stringent with their approval criteria for someone without a credit score. In fact, they would rather see bad credit than no credit in many cases. At least then they have an idea and can accurately assess their risk. When there has been no past demonstration of credit responsibility, 'B' lenders may still extend credit, but expect them to ask for a heftier down payment and to offer a higher interest rate than they would if there were a credit score on record.

HOW TO REPAIR AND/OR MAINTAIN YOUR CREDIT

Repairing bad credit is not a difficult process, it just takes some time and it's not going to happen overnight. With a bit of attention and consistent effort, your score will improve by focusing on the following points:

- Punctuality of payments
- Addressing arrears
- Managing credit utilization

- Keeping your accounts open

Punctuality of Payments

One of the simplest yet most effective ways to start repairing your credit is to make your payments on time. You may be thinking, "yes, thank you Captain Obvious!" But you would be surprised at how many people find it challenging to consistently meet payment deadlines. Maintaining punctuality in bill payments is a fundamental aspect of good credit management and is often the first and most important step in improving your credit score.

Addressing Arrears

If you have any loans or accounts in arrears, meaning payments are overdue, then you'll want to bring them up to date ASAP. As payment delinquencies will significantly impact your credit score, promptly resolving them will prevent further damage, allowing you to continue rebuilding your credit profile.

Any collections reporting on your credit bureau should be promptly addressed. If you don't agree with the collection, or think it's there in error, then you need to contact the creditor or collection agency to discuss the issue. The longer a collection remains unresolved on your credit report, the more challenging it can be to rectify.

Sometimes there might be a collection because of a charge that you disagreed with, or thought was unfair. For this reason, you may have refused to make the payment out of principle. However, it's still important to resolve the matter. Regardless of how right you think you may be, the presence of a collection on your credit report can significantly impact your score. This can in turn, impact your ability to qualify for a mortgage. Even if your score is still within qualifying limits, ALL 'A' and 'B' lenders will require the collection to be settled, even if you disagree with the charge.

Jane received a solicitation call from a phone company that offered her an amazing deal to switch providers. As there was a clear savings each month, she saw it as a no brainer, so she jumped on the opportunity. However, when Jane received her first bill, she noticed an unexpected $20 charge. She was certain this fee was waived as part of the deal. After a long conversation fighting with their customer service department, she was unsuccessful in getting them to remove the charge. Frustrated and feeling misled, Jane decided to stand her ground on principle. She paid everything on the bill, except for the $20 charge, then immediately switched back to her original provider. As she saw it, they made a false promise to get her business, so why should she have to pay? "I'll show them", she thought. It was only $20, but to Jane, it was the principal of the matter, not the money.

While her tenacity made her feel powerful, this collection plummeted her score to the point where she was not able to qualify for a mortgage through an 'A' lender. This left her with no choice but to proceed through a 'B' lender, increasing the cost of her mortgage by thousands.

When you refuse to pay a bill just to make a point, you're only hurting yourself. Right or wrong, suck it up, swallow your pride, and make the payment. It can mean the difference between getting approved or declined.

....

When you refuse to pay a bill just to make a point,
you're only hurting yourself.

....

Managing Credit Utilization

Going over your credit limit will negatively affect your score. Just because you have a $5,000 limit on your credit card doesn't necessarily mean that the creditor won't let you charge $6,000. While they may let the charges go through, exceeding your limit can have a significant negative impact on your score. To the credit reporting agency (Equifax and Transunion), you've exceeded your limit, which demonstrates irresponsibility with credit usage.

As discussed in Chapter Eight, you'll want to stay within 75% of your credit limit to maintain a healthy credit score. However, staying below 50% of the limit will give you even better results. This is even more important if you are in the process of rebuilding your credit.

If you find that your spending exceeds these percentages, then I suggest contacting your credit card company to request a higher limit. Having a higher credit limit won't negatively impact your credit score, but consistently maxing out or exceeding your limit will. For example, your credit score will be much stronger if you increase your limit to $10,000 and only charge $5,000 compared to spending the same amount on a card with a $6,000 limit. This is because a lower credit utilization ratio (the amount of credit you're using compared to your available credit) is generally viewed favourably by credit scoring models, reflecting responsible credit management.

Keeping Your Accounts Open

The worst thing you can do is close all your credit accounts. As I previously mentioned, having no credit can be viewed in the same way as having bad credit. It's important to maintain at least one, and ideally two, revolving credit accounts (such as credit cards or lines of credit) to build and maintain a sufficient credit history.

If you have an excessive amount of available credit, the temptation might be to close some accounts. However, it's not widely known that closing credit accounts can negatively impact your credit score, even though the effect might be minimal. If your credit score is strong to begin with, then closing a few accounts shouldn't have a noticeable impact on your score. But if you're going through credit recovery, then it's best to wait until you've sufficiently rebuilt your credit before closing the accounts. At that point, the impact shouldn't affect your ability to qualify for a mortgage. Rather than closing your accounts, you're better off just cutting up the cards you want to eliminate, while leaving the accounts open.

SECURED CREDIT CARDS

If you've experienced financial setbacks such as declaring bankruptcy, accepting a consumer proposal, or if you currently have no active credit, the first step on the path to credit recovery is to obtain new credit. In situations where your credit history makes it difficult to get approved for a standard credit card, a practical starting point is to apply for one that is secured.

A secured credit card requires a cash deposit which, in

turn, sets the credit limit. The deposit serves as collateral, eliminating the risk for the lender, allowing them to approve individuals with poor or no credit history. For instance, if you deposit $500, the issuer will provide you with a credit card that has a $500 limit. This deposit acts as security for the issuer, hence the term "secured" credit card.

You use it just like any other credit card. At the end of each billing cycle, you'll receive a statement detailing your balance and the minimum payment required. You have the option to pay off the entire balance or just make the minimum payment. If you decide to carry a balance, you'll pay interest on the outstanding amount... just like a regular credit card. Your activity on this card then gets reported on your credit bureau, and voila!

You now have active credit!

Just as I mentioned above, don't be even slightly late on any of the payments and ensure you don't go over your limit. This can be particularly detrimental when you are trying to rebuild your credit.

After using your secured credit card responsibly for around six months, you can approach the issuer to inquire about converting it into an unsecured card. This conversion would mean that you no longer need to have a cash deposit securing the credit limit, and it typically reflects an improvement in your credit standing.

If the issuer declines your request to convert the card to an unsecured one, don't be discouraged. Continue using the secured card responsibly for another six months before trying again. However, the exact timing of each request can vary depending on the severity of the credit issues.

Once your secured card is successfully converted to an unsecured card, consider applying for a second unsecured card. This can further enhance your credit profile by showing your ability to manage multiple credit cards responsibly.

Capital One and Home Trust are both institutions offering secured credit cards. Most major banks offer them as well; however, they may still decline you, despite the fact that it's secured. When applying, make sure it is in fact a secured credit card and not a Visa or Mastercard debit card, as they won't do anything for your credit.

As with any credit card, you want to ensure you're using it responsibly. Having new credit shouldn't give you an excuse to spend more money.

Use your credit wisely.

Having new credit shouldn't give you an excuse to spend more money.

Consistent application of these practices will demonstrate control of your finances and effective credit management, which will result in a gradually increasing credit score.

The rate at which your credit score improves can vary based on the nature and severity of the issues impacting your credit. For relatively minor infractions, such as exceeding the limit on a credit card, rectifying the situation can lead to a relatively quick improvement in your score. For instance, paying down your balance to below 50% of your credit limit.

On the other hand, recovering from a major financial setback such as a bankruptcy will be a much longer process. Bankruptcy has a profound and lasting impact on your credit score and remains on your credit report for six to seven years, depending on the province. This doesn't mean that it will take this long to rebuild the score, which could be done in as little as two years.

QUALIFYING FOR A MORTGAGE WITH REBUILT CREDIT

To qualify for a decent mortgage rate, you'll ideally want to have two active trade lines, preferably both revolving such as a credit card or a line of credit. Each revolving account should have a minimum credit limit of $1,000. Preferably higher.

A higher credit limit demonstrates stronger credit responsibility. If your cards have lower limits, then I would recommend asking the card issuer for an increase. For strong credit, each trade line should have a full one-year history, however, some lenders will require two.

Sometimes exceptions can be made if the amount of available credit falls a little short, but you may be somewhat limited in options. Some lenders can be real sticklers for borrowers to meet these minimum credit requirements.

CHAPTER TWELVE HIGHLIGHTS

- If you have damaged credit, you still may qualify for a mortgage through an alternative lender. A minimum down payment/equity position of 20% is typically required for it to even be considered.

- A private lender will approve a mortgage if the deal makes sense to them with the most important element being the amount of equity in the property.

- A private mortgage can be a valuable tool that can help real estate investors to capitalize on opportunities that might have been otherwise out of reach.

- As alternative lending can be expensive, it's intended to be a short-term solution.

- A second mortgage is usually offered at a higher rate than a first mortgage.

- Bad credit can get extremely expensive.

- Always ensure you pay all your bills on time and stay within 75% of your credit limit, however, keeping your balance to under 50% will give you even better results.

- When you refuse to pay a bill just to make a point, you're only hurting yourself by adversely affecting your credit.

- Try to maintain at least two credit cards, each with a minimum limit of $1,000 to ensure strong, healthy credit. A higher limit is even better.

- No credit is equal to bad credit.

- You can start to repair bad credit with a secured credit card.

- Having new credit shouldn't give you an excuse to spend more money. Use your credit wisely.

Life is full of ups and downs, and while we try to maintain solid credit, it can be tough when life decides to deal you a bad hand. While expensive, alternative lending can be a lifesaver for many. However, bad credit can often be avoided. Follow the credit management strategies I've outlined in this chapter, and ensure you've read and understood the information I've provided on credit back in Chapter Eight.

Believe me, life is a lot more fun when you don't have to worry about paying thousands of dollars in unnecessary expenses per year. Just think of all the possibilities for the money you are throwing away.

13

THE POWER OF REVERSE MORTGAGES

"Age is an issue of mind over matter. If you don't mind, it doesn't matter."
~Mark Twain

I'm sure you've seen all the TV commercials on reverse mortgages, which are receiving increasing attention and interest among homeowners in their retirement years. A reverse mortgage is a way for seniors to take equity out of their home without needing to qualify on credit or income, and without ever having to make a single mortgage payment.

They are generally available to those aged 55 or older with significant equity in their homes. Reverse mortgages can play a significant role in elevating the quality of life in your retirement years, while virtually eliminating financial worry, allowing you to enjoy a life of financial freedom.

They are primarily available to seniors, but what many are not aware of is there could be similar options available to you regardless of your age.

But is this a golden opportunity? Or are reverse mortgages just a subtle trap?

Let's take a deeper dive into how reverse mortgages work and explore the benefits they can offer. You'll then be able to determine if they are truly as good as they sound, or if they should be avoided.

UNDERSTANDING REVERSE MORTGAGES

A reverse mortgage allows you to tap into the equity in your property to support your financial needs, whether it's funding retirement, covering medical expenses, or fulfilling other goals. Unlike traditional mortgages which require monthly payments, a reverse mortgage will make payments to you. This is why it's called a *reverse* mortgage. You have the flexibility to choose how you receive the funds - whether as a lump sum, regular payments, or a combination of both.

BENEFITS OF REVERSE MORTGAGES

A reverse mortgage can provide much needed financial assistance for seniors looking to supplement their retirement income, giving them financial flexibility to enjoy a comfortable and worry-free retirement.

It can be a valuable source of funds that can help out in many ways:

- To eliminate financial pressure
- Debt consolidation
- Fund the purchase of real estate or other investment

- Settling outstanding taxes
- To provide financial assistance to children or grandkids
- Assist kids or grandkids with a down payment on their first home
- To allow for the provision of home care for a spouse
- Additional financial support after the loss of a spouse

In essence, a reverse mortgage transforms the equity in your home into a practical financial resource, enhancing your retirement years with greater financial freedom and peace of mind.

DISADVANTAGES TO A REVERSE MORTGAGE

A mortgage that you never have to worry about paying back, or even making payments can be a breath of fresh air to many. It really can help to significantly improve the lifestyle for those in their retirement years. But there are some disadvantages that need to be considered:

- Continual rising balance
- Higher rates
- Potential high penalty to return it early
- Decreased value of inheritance

Continual Rising Balance

As no payments are required, interest continues to build, and your outstanding balance continues to grow. The longer you're in the reverse mortgage, the higher the balance becomes.

High Rates

Rates on a reverse mortgage are generally around 1-2% higher than those of a traditional mortgage. The high rate means that a reverse mortgage may not be the ideal solution for everyone. However, for those who are unable to qualify for a traditional mortgage due to a fixed income, a reverse mortgage can be the perfect solution. It can be the difference between living your retirement years stressed out about money vs. living them without ever having to worry about money again.

Potential High Penalty to Return the Mortgage Early

If you choose to sell your home in the middle of the term, or refinance your reverse mortgage with another lender, then the penalty to return it could be steep. If you need to return it in the first year, it could be as be as much as 5%. But the further you get into the term, the lower the penalty becomes. Note that this can vary from one lender to the next.

Decreased Value of Inheritance

Taking out a reverse mortgage will affect the inheritance for your children, as the loan will need to be repaid from your estate, typically through the sale of the home. This means there would be less money available to leave to your kids.

You of course love your children and want to leave them as much as you can to help them out. But you also need to consider your own well-being. A reverse mortgage can significantly improve the quality of your life and happiness in your later years.

Should you choose to discuss the topic with your kids,

maybe kick off the conversation by highlighting how it would be a win for your happiness. After all, who wouldn't want their parents to be living their best life? Chances are, they will be on board, especially if they envision a future where you're too busy enjoying life to be crashing on their couch.

WHO IS ELIGIBLE FOR A REVERSE MORTGAGE?

When it comes to determining if you're a candidate for a reverse mortgage, there are three factors that come into play:

- Your age
- The equity in your home
- The location of the home

Age

This is the primary starting point. Reverse mortgages are available for homeowners aged 55 and above. The older you are, the higher the potential loan amount.

The Equity in Your Home

Equity refers to the portion of the home that you own outright and is equal to the value of the property, minus any outstanding mortgages or liens. For example, if you own a home valued at $1 million, and you owe $100,000, then you have 90% in equity.

A reverse mortgage will allow you to access as much as 55% of your home's value, however, this can vary based on your age. For example, if you're applying for a reverse mortgage at the minimum age of 55, then the total amount you're eligible to borrow would be reduced.

The Location of the Home

The geographical location of your property is another important factor. The real estate market varies greatly across different regions of Canada, and these variations can affect the terms of a reverse mortgage. For instance, homes in urban areas with higher property values might yield more favourable reverse mortgage conditions compared smaller regions. In other words, someone located in Toronto will generally be able to borrow a higher percentage of the home's value compared with someone living in Sudbury.

WHEN DOES A REVERSE MORTGAGE HAVE TO BE PAID BACK?

While you will never be required to make any payments on a reverse mortgage, it's still not a magical pot of money that never needs to be repaid. There are three instances where you would be required to repay the loan:

- When you say goodbye to the home
- When you pass on
- If you default on your obligations

When You Say Goodbye to the Home

If you decide to pack up and sell the home, the loan will need to be paid from the proceeds of the sale.

When You Pass On

We don't like to think about it, but it's a fact of life of course. When the last surviving borrower passes away, the reverse mortgage becomes payable in full. But don't worry, this doesn't mean that your heirs will be left scrambling. They have options such as selling the home or refinancing into a traditional mortgage. You generally have as much as 180 days to figure it out before the lender will expect to have the money returned to them.

If You Default on Your Obligations

This is a pretty easy one! As there are no payments that will need to be paid on a reverse mortgage, the lender does not expect much from you. As long as you keep up with the payments on your property taxes, insurance, and general home maintenance, then the lender is a happy camper and would have no reason to demand for the loan to be paid.

REVERSE MORTGAGE MYTHS

There are many common myths about reverse mortgages that leave some believing that they are a trap and should be avoided. This is a common occurrence whenever a topic isn't wholly grasped by individuals, resulting in the propagation of false information and misguided beliefs.

Let's tackle these common misconceptions head on.

MYTH 1: YOU LOSE OWNERSHIP OF YOUR HOME

At no point would you lose ownership of your home with a reverse mortgage. The title stays in your name, keeping the ownership with you. Even when you pass away, the heirs have full control of what they want to do with the property. However, it's important to note that the loan does need to be settled at that point. They can choose either to sell the property or to refinance it into a traditional mortgage.

Myth 2: You Will Owe More Than Your Home is Worth

This is also false. A reverse mortgage requires there to be a significant amount of equity left in the home at the time of funding. This ensures that the balance of the loan doesn't surpass the value of the home. In fact, there are some reverse mortgage providers who guarantee that you will never owe more than your home's market value.

Myth 3: You Have to Pay Taxes on the Money You Receive

Another popular myth is that you will be taxed on the funds received from a reverse mortgage. Remember, this is still a loan where interest is charged. Even though you'll be receiving a large sum of money, it's still borrowed funds, not income, therefore it's not taxable.

Myth 4: You Can be Evicted from Your Home

Providing that you comply with loan terms–namely, maintaining the home and paying your property taxes and insurance– you're good. You can live there as long as you want without having to worry about someone showing up at your door with a giant hook to yank you out.

WHERE TO GET A REVERSE MORTGAGE

There is only a small handful of reverse mortgage providers in Canada. As each one can have their own unique benefits or advantages, it's best to reach out to a mortgage broker who is knowledgeable on the subject. Not all of them will be, as reverse mortgages are a bit of a different animal altogether. It begins with a consultation where your mortgage professional will guide you through the entire application process.

CAN YOU GET A REVERSE MORTGAGE IF YOU ARE UNDER THE AGE OF 55?

If you contact any of the reverse mortgage providers in Canada, their answer will be a hard no. However, there may be alternatives that function similarly to reverse mortgages, even if they're not labelled as such. These options can be accessible to younger homeowners if there is sufficient equity in their property. A seasoned mortgage broker can assess your situation and guide you towards the most suitable financial solutions available for your age group.

CHAPTER THIRTEEN HIGHLIGHTS

- Reverse mortgages can provide financial flexibility to seniors enabling them to enjoy a comfortable and worry-free retirement.

- Reverse mortgages are a way for seniors aged 55 or older to take equity out of their homes, without any credit or income requirements.

- There is never a need to make a single mortgage payment.

- The lender can make monthly payments to you, you can take the funds in one lump sum payment, or a combination of both.

- The maximum loan amount can vary depending on your age, property location and the amount of equity in your home... to a maximum of 55% LTV.

- Disadvantages of reverse mortgages include higher rates, potentially high penalties, and decreased value of inheritance for loved ones.

- A reverse mortgage only needs to be paid back when you sell the home, pass on, or default on your obligations. This is as simple as ensuring your property taxes are paid and the property is maintained.

- There is a small number of reverse mortgage providers. It starts with a consultation with a knowledgeable mortgage broker who can determine the best fit for your situation.

Reverse mortgages can put seniors in a position of financial freedom and security when they may otherwise be struggling. With no income requirements, and limited qualifying criteria, a reverse mortgage can be the perfect solution for many who are looking to ease the financial pressure.

If you or your parents are over the age of 55 with equity in the home, then a reverse mortgage may be the ticket to ensuring a secure and comfortable future.

CONCLUSION

There is no doubt the mortgage world can be confusing. Really, you're at the mercy of the person you're dealing with, particularly if you don't take the time to shop around and talk to different banks and brokers. The biggest mistake one can make is to walk into a bank and give them your mortgage business without doing any research or questioning the advisor on their credentials. Just because someone is sitting behind a desk with a bright and shiny big bank logo on their business card, it doesn't necessarily make them a knowledgeable and trustworthy individual. The same applies when dealing with a licensed mortgage agent.

By having a much stronger sense of how mortgages work, you can contact your bank or broker armed with knowledge, giving you the upper hand in beating the bank at their own game.

Knowledge is power!

With the right knowledge, you can save thousands of dollars

over the term of your mortgage, but you must act on what you've learned in this book. Of course, this can be a lot to swallow. Mortgages are complex machines with many moving parts and unlimited combinations... with each situation being unique. A quality mortgage professional can put it all together for you, removing the overwhelm, while helping you strategize to keep as much of your hard-earned money in your pocket as possible.

Having advised well over 5,000 people on their mortgages over the past 17 years, I'm convinced that those obsessed with the lowest mortgage rate will end up with less money in their pocket by the time they're mortgage free. Getting a low mortgage rate is important, but if it becomes your primary focus, then you could be missing out on the valuable advice, guidance, and strategies that a true mortgage professional can provide... both before and after closing.

If you're fortunate enough to find someone who truly prioritizes your best interests and offers competitive mortgage rates, then you're well positioned for maximum savings over the life of your mortgage... even if there might be slightly lower rates available. There is a lot more to saving money on your mortgage than just the rate itself. I've provided many examples throughout this book.

You now have a game plan.

This information will give you a significant advantage when shopping for your next mortgage. If you read all the way through, you'll have a better understanding of mortgages then most Canadians.

The information in this book will also come in handy when

you come to the Paul Meredith Team looking for your next mortgage!

Stay in touch by subscribing to my weekly email newsletter with market updates and money saving tips:

www.easy123mortgage.ca/blog

I look forward to working with you on your mortgage in the near future.

ACKNOWLEDGEMENTS

Making the decision to write a book can be an overwhelming experience, let alone the process of actually writing it. The first edition of *Beat the Bank* released in 2017 had taken over two years to complete, with many interruptions and setbacks during the process. This fully updated third edition took more than 300 hours of painstaking effort, which I was able to complete in only three months... while maintaining my typical 60-hour workweek. Yes, that's correct, I had no life during this time. But with perseverance, dedication, and commitment, I was able to see it through to completion.

The first edition of *Beat the Bank* was originally slated for release in the fall of 2016, and the final draft was completed by late September of that year. Almost as if on cue, new mortgage regulations were announced days later that required me review, change and re-write content throughout the book. Everything needed to be accurate and fully up to date for its release. Just one more hurdle I needed to overcome. No problem at all!

There are several people I would like to thank who helped make *Beat the Bank* the fine piece of Canadian literature that it is. What? Too dramatic?

I would first like to thank my wonderful and amazing mom who was a huge help in editing the original version of *Beat the Bank*. Going through line by line and picking out every single word, letter and typo that were missed from previous edits is a chore. Just when I thought I had caught all the typos, she of course found more. Thank you so much for taking the time mom! You're the greatest mom in the world and I love you very much!

Next, I would like to thank my very close friend Dr. Peter Kelly, for the many hours spent going through every page of the first edition meticulously. This was a very busy and challenging time for him in his life, both personally and professionally. The fact that he took so much time out of his crazy schedule to proofread, edit and offer suggestions means a lot to me. His input has led to better and more polished final version.

And then there is Shayne Slinn. While I'm confident in my math, I'm very grateful to have Shayne's math wizardry at my fingertips to verify all my calculations and correct any mathematical typos. He played an important role and his input was very much appreciated.

I'd also like to thank Matt Imhoff, who is Canada's leading expert on mortgage penalties and someone who I'm proud to call my friend. Despite his own demanding schedule, he generously took the time to review the section on penalties to verify its accuracy.

Then there is Luisa Sanchez, my operations manager and team leader. Since 2015, Luisa has been at my side, equally committed to ensuring our clients receive the best possible experience. From day one, Luisa has treated my business as if it were her own and has played an integral role in bringing it to where it is today. Luisa is not just my right-hand person... she has become one of my best friends and one of the most important people in my life overall. Luisa, you're a true rockstar and I cannot thank you enough for all your effort and commitment over the years.

Lastly, but certainly not least, I extend my deepest gratitude to my incredible team for their relentless effort and commitment. Each member has shown an unwavering dedication to excellence, ensuring that every client receives the utmost care and attention. Their dedication ensures that our clients feel valued as if they were part of their own families. This remarkable level of service and personal attention is a testament to their professionalism and the core values that define our team. Their hard work not only upholds but elevates our reputation, making a significant difference in the lives of those we serve. For this, I am truly grateful and proud to work alongside such a dedicated group of professionals.

COMMON MORTGAGE TERMINOLOGY

AMORTIZATION

The amount of time it takes to pay a loan down to a zero balance over a fixed period based on equal periodic payments, including accrued interest on the outstanding balance.

ANNUAL PERCENTAGE RATE (A.P.R.)

The APR factors in the full cost of a loan including any associated fees expressed as a yearly percentage rate.

APPRAISAL

An estimate of the value of property, performed by an accredited appraiser.

APPRAISED VALUE

An opinion of a property's fair market value, based on an appraiser's knowledge, experience, and analysis of the property.

ASSUMABILITY

An assumable mortgage is one that can be transferred from the seller of the home to the new buyer. The new buyer would have to qualify in the same way they would for any other type of mortgage.

Assumption

The agreement between buyer and seller where the buyer takes over the rate and payments on an existing mortgage from the seller. Assuming a mortgage can potentially save the buyer money in an environment where rates have increased since the original arrangement of the mortgage.

Accelerated Biweekly

Dividing your monthly mortgage payment in half and then making that payment every two weeks. The result works out to making the equivalent of one additional monthly payment per year which goes directly to the principal, therefore accelerating the payoff of the mortgage. This will reduce a 25-year amortization down to roughly 22 years, saving the borrower a substantial amount of interest.

Basis Points

Basis points (abbreviated as BPS) are fractions of 1%. For example, 1 basis point is equivalent to 0.01%.

Blanket Mortgage

A mortgage registered over at least two pieces of real estate as security for the same mortgage.

Borrower (Mortgagor)

One who applies for and receives a loan in the form of a mortgage with the intention of repaying the loan in full.

Bridge Loan

A loan to cover a borrower for the portion of down payment coming from the sale of their current home where the closing date of the new home falls before the sale of the current home.

BROKER (MORTGAGE)

A licensed professional who brings a borrower and a lender together, but doesn't lend out their own money, nor do they work for the lending institution. A broker represents multiple mortgage lenders and can give the borrower more options over going to the mortgage lender directly.

CASH FLOW

The amount of cash left over from rent payments after all expenses have been paid on an income-producing property.

CLOSING DATE

The date in which the real estate transaction is finalized and the property and funds legally change hands.

CLOSED MORTGAGE

Any mortgage with restrictions on additional payments made before its maturity. Most mortgages in Canada are closed. This is the opposite of an open mortgage.

CMHC (CANADIAN MORTGAGE AND HOUSING CORPORATION)

One of three organizations in Canada offering mortgage default insurance on high-ratio mortgages.

CLOSING COSTS

Costs such as legal fees, title insurance, land transfer tax, etc, that are incurred when purchasing property and are paid by the borrower on closing date.

Conventional Mortgage

Any mortgage with a loan to value (LTV) ratio of 80% or less (A mortgage with a down payment of 20% or more).

Credit Bureau

A report documenting the credit history and current status of a borrower's credit standing.

Credit Score

A credit score used to determine a borrower's credit worthiness and is comprised of past credit utilization. There are two credit reporting agencies in Canada, Equifax and Transunion.

Debt Service Ratio

A ratio expressed as a percentage demonstrating your monthly debt obligation in relation to your gross monthly income. There are two debt service ratios used in Canada: the GDS and TDS, described below.

Default

Failure to make the scheduled payments on a mortgage.

Delinquency

Failure to make payments on time, which can be either your mortgage payment or any other monthly debt obligation reporting on your credit bureau.

Down Payment

A percentage of the purchase price required for a borrower to pay on or before closing date when purchasing real estate.

The minimum down payment required is 5% on a purchase up to $500,000 and 10% on any borrowed amount over $500,000.

EQUITY

The difference between the fair market value and current debt secured against the property.

FIRST MORTGAGE

The primary lien against a property.

FIXED RATE MORTGAGE

The mortgage interest rate is locked in throughout the term of the mortgage.

GDS

(see Gross Debt Service Ratio)

GENWORTH FINANCIAL

One of three organizations in Canada offering mortgage default insurance on high-ratio mortgages.

GROSS DEBT SERVICE RATIO (GDS)

The annual charges for principal, interest, taxes and heat divided by the annual gross household income. This can also be determined on a monthly basis. The maximum GDS ratio for mortgage qualification is 39%. The GDS ratio along with the TDS ratio (total debt service ratio) are used together to determine mortgage qualification on income.

HARD MONEY

A term more commonly used in the United States which is

another name for private money, which is the term typically used in Canada.

HELOC

A Home Equity Line of Credit is exactly as the name implies. It's a line of credit secured against the equity in your home.

HIGH RATIO MORTGAGE

Any mortgage in Canada with a loan to value (LTV) higher than 80% requiring mortgage default insurance. For example, a mortgage with less than 20% down payment. The opposite of this would be a conventional mortgage, which would have 20% or greater down payment.

INTEREST ONLY MORTGAGE

A loan where the payments cover only the interest and therefore there is no principal being paid down. These mortgages are typically one-year terms. As there is no principal being paid back, there is no amortization period. Interest only mortgages are primarily given through private mortgage lenders.

INSTALLMENT

The scheduled mortgage payment that a borrower agrees to make to a lender.

INTEREST

The main cost associated with borrowing money.

LIABILITIES

A person's financial obligations, which include both long term and short-term debt.

LIEN

A claim against a piece of property for the payment or satisfaction of a debt.

LOAN-TO-VALUE RATIO (LTV)

The relationship between the amount of the mortgage loan and the appraised value of the property expressed as a percentage.

MARKET VALUE

The highest price that a buyer would pay and the lowest price a seller would accept on a property.

MATURITY DATE

The date in which the principal balance of a mortgage becomes due and payable. The mortgage could then be paid off in full, renewed, or switched to a different lender.

MONTHLY FIXED INSTALLMENT

The principal and interest portion of a mortgage payment.

MORTGAGE

A legal document that offers a property to the lender as security for payment of a debt.

MORTGAGE BROKER

An individual or a company who arranges mortgages with multiple lenders. This is a free service for qualified borrowers.

The mortgage specialist at the bank is not a broker as they

only arrange mortgages through the bank they work for.

Mortgage Term

The length of time for which the money is borrowed. The most common mortgage term is 5 years, but can also be 6 months, 1, 2, 3, 4, 5, 6, 7 or 10 years. Not to be confused with amortization.

Mortgagee

The lender.

Mortgage Default Insurance

Insurance that protects the lender should the borrower default on the mortgage loan. This is what allows a borrower to purchase a home with less than 20% down payment.

Mortgage Life Insurance

A type of term life insurance. In the event that the borrower passes away while the policy is in force, the debt is paid from the insurance proceeds.

Mortgagor

The borrower or homeowner.

Negative Amortization

When the fixed payment on a variable rate mortgage no covers all the interest when rates have increased. The mortgage balance therefore increases instead of decreasing.

Negative Cash Flow

When operating expenses on a rental property are greater than the rental income.

NET OPERATING INCOME (NOI)

Income produced by a property after deducting all operating expenses (not including mortgage payments) from the gross rental income produced by the property. Cash flow is determined by subtracting mortgage payments from the NOI.

OPEN MORTGAGE

This allows the borrower to make additional payments of any amount or pay off the entire mortgage at any time without penalty.

POWER OF SALE

When the lender forces the sale where they have been unsuccessful in collecting on defaulted payments by the borrower.

PRIVATE MONEY

Money lent by private individuals to borrowers who don't qualify through traditional lending sources.

RATE HOLD PERIOD

A lender's guarantee that the mortgage rate quoted will be good for a specific number of days from date of application.

TRADE LINE

A credit card, line of credit, or any type of loan that appears on your credit bureau.

ABOUT THE AUTHOR

After having multiple bad experiences going through the mortgage application process, Paul figured there had to be a better way. People deserved to have better treatment, better service, and more overall respect from professionals arranging their mortgage. He decided to take things into his own hands by entering the mortgage business in 2007, and since then, he has never looked back. He strives to ensure client's needs are attended to promptly with strong communication through the entire process. Over the years, he has built a solid reputation as Canada's leading mortgage expert.

He can be seen as the exclusive mortgage broker on seasons 2, 5, 6 and 7 of the popular real estate reality television show *Top Million Dollar Agent*, which has aired on Global, Rogers, Slice TV, Amazon Prime, Tubi, etc.

Paul currently resides downtown Toronto where spending quality time with his friends and family is something that is extremely important to him. In his spare time, whenever he can find it, he enjoys reading, writing, downhill skiing and snowmobiling, however his biggest passion is boating.

CONTACT INFO

Get in touch for all of your mortgage needs!

www.easy123mortgage.ca
pmteam@citycan.com
647-368-5009

twitter.com/paulmeredith
facebook.com/mortgagebrokertoronto
Instagram.com/paulmeredithteam
linkedin.com/in/paul-meredith-ontario-
mortgages-317578a

Paul Meredith
Mortgage Broker
CityCan Financial Corporation
LIC 10532

Manufactured by Amazon.ca
Bolton, ON

41339638R00247